Derek Maybury '09

WHERE SWIFT AND BERKELEY LEARNT

Lesley Whiteside
with Andrew Whiteside

Where Swift and Berkeley Learnt

A History of Kilkenny College

*with illustrations
by Rachel Clarke*

the columba press

First published in 2009 by
the columba press
55a Spruce Avenue, Stillorgan Industrial Park, Blackrock, Co. Dublin

Cover by Bill Bolger
The cover pictures are, *left:* Jonathan Swift (detail), by Francis Bindon, Photo ©
National Gallery of Ireland, *right:* George Berkeley, attrib. Francis Bindon, repro-
duced by kind permission of the Board of Trinity College, Dublin.
Origination by The Columba Press
Printed in Ireland by ColourBooks Ltd, Dublin

ISBN 978-1-85607-647-0

Table of Contents

Foreword

Many who commend the study of history like to quote the maxim 'Those who neglect history will be condemned to repeat it.' While there are aspects of Kilkenny College's past which might make these words worth pondering, by and large this is a much more encouraging story of achievement and progress. If it is true that history is the queen of the sciences, it is particularly so in the context of the history of a place of education and learning – after all the history of such a place opens windows for us on every other subject, every other aspect of evolving human endeavour. So this is not simply an anecdotal account of people, places and events. It is in a deeper way the story of changing educational philosophy and how that was implemented in a specific institution through the centuries. It is an account of curricular change, of the coming and going of particular subjects and fashions, of the ways in which developing understandings of how to engage with and open young minds have textured the activities of every classroom.

From time to time a great and historic institution does well to stand back, to reflect and to write anew its own story. In the case of Kilkenny College, such an opportunity has been grasped in the most timely way through the vision of Philip Gray and the scholarship of the co-authors Lesley and Andrew Whiteside. On behalf of the Board of the College and the wider diocesan community we salute them all and trust that this work will have a wide and grateful readership. And it will remind us too that, although education like society changes a great deal over the years, human nature itself, as the sages of ancient Israel ever remind us, does not alter all that much. So it is that the principles and values of the founding fathers of ancient places of learning actually remain ever contemporary. The Chair of the Board or the Bishop of Ossory can visit the school precincts in 2009 and find people young and not so young living, laughing, arguing and longing in much the same way as our predecessors might have done several centuries ago.

When this book is first published it will be eagerly sought out both by those of an historical bent and those who have particular *pietas* in relation to the college as their place of education or work, or the school to which they have sent their children. However, long after we have all left this world the day will come when a reader in some future century will take this volume from a library shelf (and come what may, we believe there will always be books and libraries), open it curiously and wonder whether the college she or he knows can truly be the successor of the very different place whose story up to the early 21st century is described in these pages. For that reader names like Gray and Whiteside will seem as distant in the annals of the college as Berkeley and Swift may seem to us. As we with smiling countenances greet that putative collegian and reader of this work across the centuries, all we can do is to express our confidence that between us and her will lie a now mysterious yet linear trajectory of continuing college development and of commitment to the enrichment of Irish society. Kilkenny College, and indeed the other worthy foundations that over the years joined forces with it, have stood the tests of time with distinction, adaptability and principle and there is little doubt that the story you are about to read will continue purposefully. In that sense a volume such as this, written from the perspective of one particular moment, can be no more than an interim report (to use a great school word), but few interim reports could rival the learning and depth of this one. Please enjoy its pages gratefully.

Don Brown, Chair of the Board of Kilkenny College
Michael Cashel and Ossory

Preface

We want to thank Dr Kenneth Milne and Mrs Jennifer Strevens for reading the manuscript critically; Mrs Rosemary Day and Mrs Rebecca Campion for proof-reading; Rachel Clarke, the daughter of past-pupil, David Clarke, for maps and drawings which enhance the publication; Rodney Cromer for photography; Dr Raymond Refaussé of the Representative Church Body Library for helpful advice and assistance with records; Brenda Collins, of the Irish Linen Centre in Lisburn, who helped us to interpret details on the working of the Lintown factory school and the weaving of the girls in the Celbridge school; to Mrs Violet Shattock for making available the material which she collected from Celbridge girls some years ago.

We are appreciative of the co-operation of members of staff of the Bodleian Library, the Church of Ireland College of Education, Hampshire Record Office, the Irish Architectural Archive, Kilkenny County Library Service, the National Archives, the National Library and Trinity College library.

We are grateful to the large number of past pupils and former members of staff who provided us with insights into their experience of school life. These recollections will be preserved in the newly-established college archives.

List of illustrations

The illustrations are taken from the Kilkenny College Archives, with the exception of those indicated below. It is regretted that efforts to contact the copyright owners have been unsuccessful in some cases. Omissions will, if possible, be put right in subsequent editions. The recent team photographs were taken by Oliver's of Kilkenny. Some items have been skilfully copied by professional photographer, Seán Magee, of Mullingar.

Given its close historic connections with Kilkenny College, a large number of illustrations has been sourced in Trinity College, Dublin. The following items (marked * in the list) are reproduced by kind permission of the Board of Trinity College, Dublin: George Berkeley, attrib. Francis Bindon; James Butler, 1st Duke of Ormond, studio of Peter Lely; Jonathan Swift as a student, unknown artist; George Berkeley by James Latham; memorial to Richard Baldwin by Christopher Hewetson; bust of William Magee by Joseph Watkins. In addition, the Keeper of Manuscripts has provided the petition against Booth (MS 5777 413).

Introduction

This history celebrates the legacy of three benefactors who recognised the importance of education for the individual and society. James Butler, first Duke of Ormond, Bishop Richard Pococke and William 'Speaker' Conolly were pioneers, establishing schools which fulfilled a unique role in developing education in Ireland.

It also celebrates the unique history of Kilkenny College in its first phase, when it far excelled all other Irish schools in producing men who were not only the intellectual leaders of their time but whose fame has lasted to the 21st century. Virtually everyone in Ireland knows something about Jonathan Swift and can tell the basic story of *Gulliver's Travels*. Many visitors from overseas prioritise a visit in his honour to St Patrick's Cathedral, while St Patrick's Hospital, the psychiatric hospital which he founded by his will, is another famous Dublin landmark. It is extraordinary that the name of George Berkeley, an Irish philosopher bishop, is commemorated in two modern American university foundations, Berkeley College in Yale University and Berkeley College in California. Similarly, three centuries after he was a student there, Trinity College, Dublin honoured him when naming the new library.

In its first phase Kilkenny College educated the sons of many of the most important families across the country. These included the earls of Cork and the earls of Tyrone. Men of such families typically held high-ranking positions in the church, judiciary, legislature, the government or the military, and their sons were expected to follow suit. Kilkenny College was chosen to prepare those boys for a high-class university education and the careers assigned for them. Thus among its past pupils were countless members of parliament, one lord chancellor and one chief justice of Ireland and numerous other influential officials. Several past pupils, including George Beresford, Marquis of Waterford, John Stafford, Earl of Aldborough, and William Willoughby Cole, Earl of Enniskillen, became peers in their own right. Kilkenny College past pupils wielded a great deal of power in Ireland. Their influence was not restricted to Ireland, for some became governors or senior judicial figures in the colonies.

Kilkenny College, as a classical school catering for boys from the highest echelons of society, had little in common with Pococke's school in Kilkenny and Conolly's school at Celbridge, which were intended to train poor children for a trade in the linen industry or, in Celbridge's case, for farming. By the beginning of the 20th century, however, the three schools offered much the same education to children from the same type of family. The merger in 1903 of Kilkenny College and the Pococke School on the college site secured the immediate future of a Protestant secondary school in Kilkenny. Such were the difficulties of the next 70 years that the amalgamation of Kilkenny College and Celbridge Collegiate in 1973 seemed the only way to save either school. That move enabled the development of a vibrant co-educational boarding and day school for the southeast, operating on a new site with modern facilities.

It is impossible to understand the evolution of Kilkenny College without knowing something of the history of the Anglican Protestant community in Ireland. After the terrors and traumas of Cromwellian rule, the restoration of the monarchy under Charles II was greeted with immense relief. Restoration optimism was expressed in many constructive ways, as in the establishment of Kilkenny College by James, Duke of Ormond about 1666. The whole Protestant community lived in fear under King James II, as his Lord Deputy, the Earl of Tyrconnell, pursued a policy of Catholicisation. As Anglicans were replaced in government, the law and the army, Tyrconnell moved against other Protestant institutions. Kilkenny College was closed and the building confiscated by the authorities in 1688. The headmaster, like many other Protestants, was forced into exile. He returned after the Williamite victory and reopened the college, which flourished under the Protestant ascendancy. In the first half of the 18th century Anglican leaders of society, many of them past pupils of Kilkenny College, behaved as if it was their right to govern and control the country. By the end of the century, there was a growing awareness of the rights of the Roman Catholic majority. As the Penal Laws were repealed, the universal right to education became increasingly obvious and the Protestant endowed schools came under scrutiny. In the 19th century, in the face of Catholic emancipation, growing nationalism and frequent governmental inquiries, Kilkenny College fared badly. Even when inquiry led to reform, the government's scheme for Kilkenny College was ineffectual.

Only when it was taken over by the Incorporated Society in 1903 did the college begin to recover.[1] From 1907 to 1917, under two outstanding headmasters, numbers, results and confidence soared, even in the war years, but another decline was inevitable. In the 20th century the Protestant community was severely depleted by the losses of the First World War and then experienced a crisis of confidence in the decades after Irish independence. The whole country suffered from a lack of educational provision, employment opportunities and economic growth. Progress in the 1950s and 1960s did not greatly increase optimism for the future in the Protestant community and so it was that few could believe in the 1970s that Kilkenny College and Celbridge Collegiate could continue separately as viable schools. Major economic, educational and ecumenical changes since the merger in 1973 have led to the Protestant community playing its full part in Irish society and have enabled Kilkenny College to assume a new role, offering a broad curriculum and many opportunities for self-development to all its pupils, Protestant and Catholic.

In reading this history, it is also important to understand the changing role of the Incorporated Society, for it was involved in the Pococke School from the beginning and in Celbridge from 1809; in 1903 it assumed control of the amalgamated school in Kilkenny; in 1973 it effected the merger of Kilkenny College and Celbridge Collegiate. The origins of the Society lay in the desire of early 18th century philanthropists to establish charity schools which would train poor children for useful employment, so that they would not be a financial burden on the parishes. While this was the sole reason for setting up charity schools in England, in Ireland there was the further purpose of winning over 'popish' children to Protestant and English ways, in the hope that rebellions would cease. The Society was founded by royal charter in 1734 and in the first century of its existence received over a million pounds of government funding for the establishment and running of charter schools throughout the country.[2] Sadly, these primary schools failed utterly in their objective, leaving a legacy of resentment of their proselytising and suspicion as to the role of the Protestant establishment in education. The first commissioners of Irish education, appointed in 1788, expressed serious concerns about the charter schools but it was nearly 40 years before action was taken. The Royal Commission of Irish Education Inquiry, established in 1824, visited charter schools and deplored their state. In advance of their first report, one commissioner, John Leslie Foster, wrote to the home secretary:

> It will be impossible for the state to continue its connection with the Incorporated Society. Cruelty, plunder and neglect in the masters, corruption in the officers, ignorance and vice in the children and a studied concealment of the untoward results ... on the part of the Committee of Fifteen, are the features of the system.[3]

While a small number of the Society's schools, such as the girls' school in
Celbridge, were in good order, as Kenneth Milne writes, 'the charter schools
were dealt a mortal blow by the *First Report*'.[4] The government cut financial
support for the charter schools, so the Society was obliged to close schools
and cut the numbers of pupils. Even those schools which were allowed to
continue were affected: for instance, the numbers in Celbridge were reduced
by a third and in 1840 the Pococke School changed from an industrial school
for Roman Catholic boys to a conventional school for Protestants.

By retrenchment and reform, a gradual transformation enabled the
Society to find a new and useful role, that of providing secondary education
for the children of Protestant parents. Another vital development followed
the creation in 1885 of a commission to manage educational endowments.[5] It
took nine years for the Society to win approval of its scheme but changes
followed as soon as it was sanctioned in 1894. A new boarding and day
school, Mountjoy School, was built in the north of Dublin city and it soon
became the Society's leading school for boys. All the Society's other eight
schools were outside Dublin. Of these, Celbridge emerged as the Society's
leading school for girls, while others had to amalgamate. In 1903, as we have
seen, the Incorporated Society took over Kilkenny College and merged it
with the Pococke on the college site.

The fortunes of the Society in the 20th century reflected those of the
Protestant community at large. Rationalisation and closures culminated in
the 1970s when the Society merged its Kilkenny and Celbridge schools and
relinquished control of those in Dublin and Cork. As the latter schools
became Mount Temple and Ashton comprehensive schools, the Society
devolved direct management of its remaining schools, in Bandon, Dundalk,
Kilkenny and Sligo, to local boards of governors. Those schools continue to
receive building grants and financial aid for pupils in need and can now
nominate members to the Incorporated Society, which maintains an
overview of developments.

This history is intended to be an academic account of the schools, written in such a style that it will be read by current pupils and their families. It
cannot be a definitive history, as there is a serious lack of internal records,
particularly in relation to Kilkenny College, for which even 20th century
records are few and far between. There is one overriding reason for the paucity of
records in all three schools: that none of them was constituted with its own
board of governors. In such a school the headmaster and bursar were answerable
to a board which met regularly on site. The bursar had to produce minutes of
each meeting, which were scrutinised and signed at the next meeting. He also

had to produce annual accounts. In due course this organisation gave rise to written headmasters' reports, correspondence and a variety of other records, which are a rich source of information beyond the formal record. For much of their existence, the Pococke and Celbridge schools had principals who were at least subject to review by the Incorporated Society. Although the statutes of Kilkenny College provided for governors and official 'visitors', there was no bursar and the headmaster was obliged only to keep a register of pupils and an inventory of property. Not all headmasters did even that: the registers are incomplete and there are no extant inventories. If they kept other records, they would have regarded them as their own possessions and would have felt free to take them away or to destroy them on their retirement.

Readers may find it unsatisfactory that there are so many gaps and un-certainties in this history but it is important not to airbrush them out. On the other hand, by bringing these grey areas to light, this publication might well lead others to uncover new information to explain the fluctuating history of Kilkenny College.

CHAPTER ONE

Origins

Looking back from the 21st century, in which everyone in the developed world has a right to an education, it is difficult to envisage a world in which it was the privilege of a tiny minority. In the predominantly agricultural society of the Middle Ages, there seemed to be little need to educate the ordinary people. Even with those constraints, in England there are great schools of medieval foundation, such as Winchester College and Westminster School, but, because of its unsettled history, there are no parallels in Ireland. Most education took place in small, short-lived schools, often operated by a local clergyman, and the only school in the country which can claim continuous existence since the 16th century is St Patrick's Cathedral choir school, Dublin, established by Edward VI in 1547.

From the beginning of the Reformation in Ireland there was great stress on the importance of education. To put it bluntly, it was hoped that, if the Irish learned to speak and write in English, they would become loyal and hard-working Protestant citizens. The limited success of this aspiration can be seen from the 18th century writings of two former Kilkenny College pupils, Jonathan Swift and Walter Harris. Writing on 'the causes of the wretched condition of Ireland', Swift reiterated the need for such a school in every parish, in the belief that the native Irish could only be helped by persuading them to accept 'our customs and ways'.[1] Similarly, Harris, in his history of Dublin, noted that the boys in The King's Hospital were 'carefully instructed in the necessary principles of religion', which 'gives the fairest prospect of their becoming virtuous and useful members of the community'.[2]

It is against this background that Piers Butler, 8th Earl of Ormond, founded a grammar school in Kilkenny in 1538. Adrian Empey attributed his initiative to 'a genuine interest in letters and in promoting Renaissance civility like aristocratic patrons elsewhere in Europe'.[3] This foundation marked the beginning of the Butler family's commitment to secondary education in Kilkenny, a commitment which was to last for the best part of five centuries. Piers Butler died in 1539 but his wife Margaret, daughter of the Earl of Kildare, continued his interest in the school, which was situated at the west end of the churchyard of St Canice's Cathedral. There is very little inform

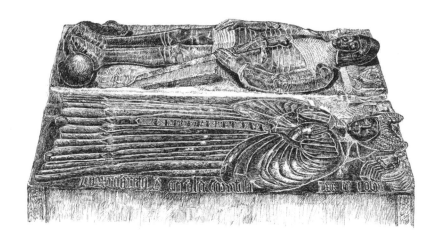

ation on the early years of the school but it is likely that William Johnson, a graduate of Cambridge, was schoolmaster in Kilkenny for several years.[4] A biographical dictionary of Cambridge graduates includes an entry for him and definitively associates him with the Ormond school: 'He went to Ireland and became master of the grammar school founded by Piers, Earl of Ormond, and his lady in the precinct of the cathedral of St Canice, Kilkenny. It is uncertain how long he held this situation but he seems to have been ordained about 1551 and is termed the Earl of Ormond's schoolmaster in 1552.'[5] Johnson later became dean of Ossory and in that capacity perhaps had some role in the oversight of the school.[6]

Ironically, while parliament in 1538 passed legislation to establish a school in every parish to foster the English language and adoption of Protestantism, there was more enthusiasm for education among Roman Catholic teachers than their Protestant counterparts.[7] It also must be remembered that there had been only one Christian church until the Reformation and that, for decades afterwards, there was a very thin line distinguishing those who conformed to the Anglican church and those who did not. This helps to explain the conflicting loyalties of the next master, the Revd Peter White. Born in Waterford, he had been a fellow of Oriel College, Oxford and was highly regarded for his learning and his teaching. His patron was Thomas, Earl of Ormond, who had returned to Ireland from England in 1554 as head of the Butler family. It is likely that he recruited Peter White as part of a broader cultural initiative.

One famous pupil of White's was Richard Stanihurst, who is reported to have been in the school from 1557 to 1563. Born in 1547, he was the son of

Peter Lombard

James Stanihurst, the speaker of the Irish House of Commons. The fact that he was sent to the Ormond school is probably a good indication of the class of pupils attending during that period. Among the families whom Stanihurst mentioned as sending their sons to Kilkenny were the Archers, Butlers, Comerfords, Dormers, Garveys, Lombards, Shees, Strongs, Waddings, Walshes and Whites. From them came three important churchmen: Peter Lombard, who became Roman Catholic Archbishop of Armagh in 1601; Thomas White, a Jesuit, who founded the Irish College at Salamanca in 1592; and Nicholas Comerford, a Jesuit priest at Madrid. All three were sons of important families in the commerce of Waterford.

Stanihurst wrote about his school as a place out of which 'have sprouted such proper imps, through the painful diligence and laboursome industry of that famous lettered man, Mr Peter White, as generally the whole weale public of Ireland, and especially the southern parts of that island, are greatly thereby furthered'. Stanihurst delighted in his own experience of White: 'It was my happy hap … to have been one of his crew … and I will acknowledge myself so much bound, and beholden to him and his, as for his sake, I reverence the meanest stone cemented in the walls of that famous school.' Stanihurst provided a lively description of White's approach to educational discipline:

> This gentleman's method in training up youth was rare and singular, framing the education according to the scholar's vein. If he found him free, he would bridle him, like a wise Isocrates, from his book; if he perceived him to be dull, he would spur him forward; if he understood that he were the worse for beating, he would win him with rewards; finally by interlacing study with recreation, sorrow with mirth, pain with pleasure, sourness with sweetness, roughness with mildness, he had so good success in schooling his pupils … that in the realm of Ireland was no grammar school so good.[8]

Writing about the teaching of classics in Ireland, W. B. Stanford concluded that few schools covered such a wide range of literature as that which the boys in Kilkenny read: Aesop's fables, Cato, Terence, Ovid, the Greek New Testament, Isocrates, Horace, Seneca's tragedies, Hesiod, Juvenal, Persius, Homer, a 'comical author' and some Hebrew, and that Kilkenny in this respect resembled schools in England.[9]

In June 1566 White was appointed dean of Waterford. He was recommended by his predecessor, Patrick Walshe, who had remained as dean since his promotion as Bishop of Waterford in 1551. Walshe described White as 'a man very well learned' and 'of virtuous sober conversation, by whose industry and travail a great part of the youth ... have greatly profited in learning and virtuous education'.[10] In 1570, however, he was deemed unsuitable because he was one of the clergy who had not conformed to the Church of Ireland.[11]

Colm Lennon has summarised White's achievements in glowing terms: 'White's role was extremely significant in bringing on a generation of talented scholars who made their way to universities in England and on the continent ... All were responsible for contributing in some way to an Irish intellectual flowering in the later Renaissance period. White was the midwife of that movement.'[12] White's legacy continued in society for generations for, as Stanihurst put it, 'From this man's school, as from the horse of Troy, men of the highest learning came to light in the state'.[13] It seems, however, that the school fell into terminal decay after White's time.

If the Ormond school had ceased to function by the beginning of the 17th century, Kilkenny was in the same position as most other large towns and cities in Ireland, as far as educational provision was concerned. Diocesan free schools initiated by Elizabeth I in 1570 did not prosper[14] and the diocesan

St Canice's Cathedral, Kilkenny

school for Ossory does not appear to have been more successful than the average, as is shown by the report of the regal visitation of 1615. It stated that there was 'a public schoolmaster … whose name is Penyngton, a minister and preacher. He keeps the public school at Kilkenny but few students resort to this school, by reason of their backwardness in religion.'[15] When James Butler became 12th Earl of Ormond in 1633, he 'threw his full weight behind the Church of Ireland, becoming the most publicly committed Protestant among the native nobility'.[16] In Kilkenny he responded to the advances in local Catholic education by becoming the patron of the free school under the headmastership of John Wyttar.[17] His financial support for the Protestant school allowed it to grow and by 1641 there were two additional teachers.[18]

During the 17th century other networks of schools began to emerge in the Irish provinces, some of which produced leaders of Irish society. In Dublin, the grammar school at St Patrick's Cathedral was flourishing academically by the second quarter of the 17th century. According to its historian: 'Between 1637 and 1644, the period covered by the earliest surviving TCD register, two pupils out of every three educated in Dublin matriculating into the university were from the school' and the school's past pupils made up 'at least a fifth of the total entry'. Some of the older, brighter pupils studied Greek but 'all others occupied the whole of their time learning Latin'.[19]

The plantation of Ulster led to two waves of establishing schools in that province. The first phase comprised royal schools and originated in James I's 1608 decree 'that there shall be one free school at least appointed in every county, for the education of youth in learning and religion'. This gradually led to the opening of schools at Armagh, Cavan, Dungannon, Enniskillen and Raphoe.[20] Several of the schools were severely disrupted by the violence of 1641 and Cavan, for example, does not appear to have functioned from then until 1661, after the Restoration. The second phase in Ulster involved similar free schools. The Free School of Londonderry was founded in 1617 by Mathias Springham, of the Merchant Taylors' Company. Nearby, at Lifford, a free school was founded by the will of Englishman Richard Hansard, who died in 1619. Hansard's intention was for a classical school but there is no evidence that it was ever realised.

Ulster was much better provided for than the rest of the country. In Munster, the Earl of Cork founded schools at Bandon, Charleville, Lismore and Youghal in the first quarter of the 17th century. During his life he gave financial aid and left money in his will for building schoolhouses and for salaries.[21] In Leinster, the only early 17th century initiative occurred in 1629, when corporations were founded by Charles I in Banagher and Carysfort, near Rathdrum, and the charters of incorporation granted land to support free schools in the towns. In the Restoration period, there were significant initiatives. In 1669 Charles II granted a charter to schools founded by Erasmus Smith, an Englishman who had secured valuable property in Ireland through the Act of Settlement. The governors, drawn from the highest echelons of church and society, set about the establishment of grammar schools at Drogheda, Galway and Tipperary. Erasmus Smith's schools were intended for the provision of free education to all of his tenants' children and also 20 poor children in the vicinity of each school. Schoolmasters were appointed on the basis of being 'of the Protestant religion and well known for their ability, industry and good conversation'.[22] The children were to be taught Greek, Hebrew and Latin as a preparation for university. Alongside that classical education, less academic pupils were taught writing and arithmetic 'to fit them for trade and employment'.[23] There was also a requirement that the children be regularly catechised.

In the same year the Corporation of Dublin founded a charity school and obtained a royal charter for it in 1671. The Hospital and Free School of King Charles II, Dublin was generally referred to as the Blue Coat School and, more recently, The King's Hospital. Unlike the royal schools in Ulster, it did not receive assistance from the state but was endowed by the Corporation and depended also on private donors. The first pupils were admitted in 1675, with an intake of 60 children, including three girls. Most of the boys came from a poor city background and 'were destined for a life of obscurity'. The pupils, who were all children or grandchildren of freemen of the city, were taught reading, writing and arithmetic to prepare them for trades and Latin was only to be taught if a boy's 'scholastic aptitude and prospects seemed to justify it'. By charter the headmaster had to be an Anglican priest and his primary role was 'to read the divine service, and preach and teach the word of God' and catechise the children.[24]

Classical grammar schools were founded in provincial towns by influential landowners in the latter part of the century. In the southeast, Richard Moore founded a school in Clonmel in 1685 for the free education of children of Protestant freemen of Clonmel.[25] There also appears to have been a similar school in Waterford supported by the corporation.[26] In 1696, Elizabeth, Countess of Orkney, provided a large endowment of lands for a grammar school at Midleton but the school did not open till 1717. In the 17th century there are occasional references to masters in Kilkenny but it is not clear how they performed their roles, if at all. By 1650 the school buildings were long in disuse as, in that year apparently, Captain John Joiner removed timber from the school house and used it in building a house near Kilkenny.[27]

In March 1661 James Butler was made Duke of Ormond and restored as Lord Lieutenant of Ireland, a position which he had held as far back as 1644. Commander of the Royalist troops in Ireland during the Irish Confederate Wars, his lands had been confiscated by Cromwell and he had devoted his energies and wealth to supporting Charles II in exile. In gratitude, upon the Restoration, Charles gave him an Irish dukedom, restored him to the lord lieutenancy and made large grants to compensate him for the fortune he had spent in royal service. As Ormond regained possession of his family's estates, he set about re-establishing the fabric of society. Imbued with the optimism of the time, he encouraged rebuilding after the traumas of the Cromwellian period and played a leading role in infrastructural improvements in Dublin. These included the initial development of the Phoenix Park and the building of four new bridges over the Liffey. An indication of the financial commitment that Ormond was willing to make to charitable establishments was his funding of the construction of the Royal Hospital in Kilmainham. The first of Dublin's great classical buildings, Ormond modelled this rest home for invalid soldiers and army pensioners on Les Invalides in Paris.

Like Piers and Margaret Butler, Ormond had a genuine interest in education; he also saw its development as an integral aspect of the Restoration. His involvement extended beyond his school at Kilkenny, for he later made a generous donation to The King's Hospital[28] and was one of the original trustees of the school at Clonmel. According to Thomas Carte, Ormond 'loved to encourage learning and lost no opportunity of doing service to learned men, particularly to such as were bred in the College of Dublin and he considered all knowledge as useful to a country'.[29]

After some years of preparation, Ormond's new school opened in Kilkenny around 1667 and, within a few decades, earned a reputation as the country's leading academic school. It was some time before it took the grand title of 'Kilkenny College'. As late as 1900 it was sometimes called 'Kilkenny Grammar School', chiefly in official papers, or 'St John's College', a reference to the local parish. For the sake of clarity, this history refers to it throughout as Kilkenny College.

CHAPTER TWO

New beginnings, 1666-1683

Ormond not only faced a huge task as Lord Lieutenant in restoring peace and prosperity in Ireland; he also had to cope with personal financial difficulties and the intrigues of his political enemies. It is, therefore, remarkable that he devoted time and money to founding a grammar school in Kilkenny.[1] His biographer gives the following account of the foundation: 'The duke had expelled [from Kilkenny] all the popish instructors of youth, and founded a Protestant school at

James Butler, first Duke of Ormond

his own charge... providing it with eminent and orthodox men of the Church of England'.[2]

It took some years to get the school going and, in the meantime, Ormond licensed the Revd Hugh Drysdale to 'teach the free school' in Kilkenny.[3] Drysdale had been ordained in the previous year and was the son of the Revd John Drysdale, a Scottish priest in the Church of Ireland. It is interesting to note that the reference is not to teaching 'at' or 'in' the school but simply teaching the school. This perhaps indicates that there was no designated building for the free school. In a similar way, Edward Wetenhall had been brought to Ireland in May 1672 to be master of the city free school in Dublin but had no schoolhouse and had to hire a room for classes at his own expense.[4] While the population of Kilkenny was sufficient to support a free school, there is no record of how many boys Drysdale taught.[5]

It was not until 1666 that the Duke of Ormond was able to secure for his foundation a large house in John Street, in the possession of one of his tenants. A survey was undertaken of the house in November 1666 to decide what alterations would be necessary and how much it would cost. The report of this survey provides a detailed account of the original building and indicates some of Ormond's intentions for the operation of the school:[6]

> The house is built three storeys high besides the garrets, but not all portioned nor well contained, and the garrets lie all open without portions but are boarded. And if it be designed for a school, that is … rooms for a master and his family and usher[7] or two and other servants and also … 30 small rooms … that is for lodgings for 60 scholars … for two in a bed … I consider it may be had there … as follows:
> 1st storey – the lower storey lies a foot higher than the level of the street
> kitchen 22 ft x 26 ft and two or three rooms as larders
> and an eating hall 22 ft x 60 ft
> 2nd storey – a very fair room towards the street 22 ft x 60 ft (I suppose big enough for the school) and at each end of this room may be several rooms designed for the conveniences of the master and the servants and the boys and his ushers of the schools and some lodging beside for 10 of the principal scholars if that is thought convenient
> 3rd storey – this storey I suppose will be most convenient for so many scholars' chambers as it is capable of; also one of the ushers ought to be on this storey to regulate those scholars from disorder as may happen
> 4th storey – the garrets – room … to make more conveniences and lodgings.

The overall dimensions of the building were given as 60 feet towards the street and 80 feet towards the garden. In the middle of the building was a small courtyard measuring 20 feet by 16 feet. The garden measured 60 feet by 80 feet. The survey estimated the cost of the alterations at £180. The work was overseen by John Morton, an army captain stationed in Kilkenny, who had been employed by Ormond for several years in the rebuilding of Dunmore House and Kilkenny Castle.[8]

We do not know exactly when the first headmaster, the Revd Edward Jones, was appointed and when he took in the first pupils but, as he was owed a half year's salary at Easter 1668,[9] we can surmise that the school opened late in 1667 or early in 1668. It is probable that Ormond waited until the school was ready before he appointed the master. Jones was born in Montgomeryshire in east Wales. He was the eldest son of Richard ap John, of Llwyn Rhirid, and an English mother, Sarah Pyttes. Presumably Welsh speaking, he was educated at Westminster School and Trinity College, Cambridge. While in university he was a friend of Isaac Newton. Having graduated in 1664, he was elected a fellow of the college in 1667.

A letter of 25 August 1668 emphasised the importance of the school to Ormond: 'I desire you would take very particular care that the schoolmaster at Kilkenny, Mr Jones, may be punctually paid his salary at the day and make it your work to give him all other assistance.'[10] Ormond considered education a vital element in the success of the Restoration. As Lord Lieutenant, his priorities were the preservation of the crown and of the Protestant interest and this consideration influenced his foundation. Writing in 1679, he recalled:

> Ten years since at least, finding that all the English and Protestants [in Kilkenny] and thereabouts were fain to send their children to popish schoolmasters, I set up a school-house there, that, valuing the rent and charge of the building, cost me £2,000 at least, and that I have ever since and do now give £150 a year to the master and usher.[11]

Not only was Ormond determined that his grammar school would succeed but, when he heard that the Jesuits were running a school in Kilkenny, he moved to suppress it.[12] It should not be thought, however, that Ormond was anti-Catholic. An Anglican, brought up in the household of the Archbishop of Canterbury, he was the odd one out in his family, for nearly all the Butlers were Roman Catholic. It was for this reason and because of his relatively liberal views that some of his enemies accused him of being a papist.[13]

Although the school in Kilkenny made some provision for the education of poorer pupils, its overall intention as an educational establishment was concerned with higher achievement. The first of Jones's pupils to enter Trinity College, Dublin was Thomas Ledisham, son of the dean of Waterford, who entered on 2 July 1668. Thereafter on average half a dozen of Jones's pupils went each year to Trinity. Such consistent performance at an early stage in his career illustrates both the quality of Jones's teaching and the standard and class of the boys attending the school. Several of Jones's early pupils[14] later became senior churchmen. They included John Hartstonge, Bishop of Ossory (1693-1714), and of Derry (1714-17), Samuel Foley, Bishop of Down and Connor from 1694 until his death the following year, and Michael Jephson, Dean of St Patrick's Cathedral (1691-94). Jephson's name is written inside a Latin textbook printed about 1676 for use in Kilkenny College. *Sacri Lusus in usum Scholae Kilkenniensis*, a little book of scriptural poetry, is a rare gem, for very few Irish school textbooks survive from the 17th century.[15]

By far the most influential of these churchmen was another dean of St Patrick's, Jonathan Swift. Within these pages it is only possible to give a brief view of important figures like him; there is a wealth of writings for the interested reader to consult.[16] Brought up by his uncle at Swiftsheath near

Textbook, c. 1676, for
use in Kilkenny
College

Kilkenny, Swift and his cousins were sent to Kilkenny College. Disappointingly, however, among his vast and diverse writings there is little surviving that sheds light on his experience of school. What he did write indicates that he was reasonably happy:

> I formerly used to envy my own happiness when I was a schoolboy, the delicious holidays, the Saturday afternoon and the charming custards in a blind alley; I never considered the confinement ten hours a day, to nouns and verbs, the terrors of the rod, the bloody noses and broken shins.[17]

The only other anecdote includes even less information about the school:

> When I was a schoolboy at Kilkenny, and in the lower form, I longed very much to have a horse of my own to ride on. One day I saw a poor man leading a very mangy lean horse out of the town to kill him for the skin. I asked the man if he would sell him, which he readily consented to upon my offering him somewhat more than the price of the hide, which was all the money I had in the world. I immediately got on him, to the great envy of some of my school fellows, and to the ridicule of others, and rode him about town.[18]

Swift may not have written much about his schooldays but there is no doubt that they had a great influence on him, for some of his former schoolmates

were in his inner circle. These included John Hartstonge and Richard Helsham, his personal physician, whom Swift viewed as 'an ingenious and good humoured physician, a fine gentleman, an excellent scholar'.[19] Helsham was Professor of Natural Philosophy in Trinity College from 1724 and Regius Professor of Physic from 1730.[20]

Swift was renowned as a satirist even before he became Dean of St Patrick's in 1713. Until that time he had spent considerable periods in England and viewed his move to Dublin as exile. In the following years, however, he consciously developed an Irish identity and a caustic style. A 1720 pamphlet attacking economic policy in Ireland outraged the British government and a few years later his *Drapier's Letters* frustrated the government's plans for solving a shortage of coins in Ireland.[21] Swift continued his satirical attacks on the establishment for the rest of his life and even the universal children's favourite, *Gulliver's Travels*, was intended as a broadside against official hypocrisy.[22] His writings and his public profile made him one of the most significant and best known figures in Ireland.

Swift was a school contemporary of Richard Baldwin, Provost of Trinity College from 1717 until his death in 1758. They do not seem to have been friends in school and their opposing political views did not encourage friendship in later life. While Swift was a Tory, Baldwin's trials in the Jacobite period made him a Whig. When Jacobite forces took over Trinity in 1689, he fled to England but returned after the Williamite victory and spent the rest of his life as fellow, vice-Provost and Provost. Severely autocratic and frequently engaged in disputes with his political opponents, Baldwin carried out an extensive building programme in Trinity, including the library with its famous long room, and left his large estate to the college on his death.[23] He has been described as 'a forerunner of the more severe type of Victorian head-

Richard Helsham

master, with sound but unimaginative scholarship and an insistence on hard work and the observance of a strict disciplinary code'.[24] Although Swift had left Kilkenny College before that other eminent pupil, George Berkeley, was born, the two names are inextricably linked as leading political thinkers of the Anglo-Irish ascendancy of the 18th century, as we shall see in the next chapter.

Another notable past pupil of Jones was Nathaniel Hooke. The son of a nonconformist clergyman, he entered Trinity College in 1679 but did not stay long. He studied at Sidney Sussex College, Cambridge, where he became involved in radical politics. He was one of the leaders of an unsuccessful rebellion against James II in 1685 but, after years in exile, swore allegiance to him and converted to Catholicism. He fought at the Battle of Boyne in 1690, after which he fled to France, where he continued a military career that ended at the rank of *maréchal de camp* (the equivalent of major-general).[25] Hooke was not the only past pupil who had a military career. Robert Parker, who served in Marlborough's military campaigns, left a memoir in which he explained the circumstances of his enlisting in 1683:

> My father, who lived on a concern of his near Kilkenny, kept me at school in that town, till I was fifteen. The old Duke of Ormond was then Lord Lieutenant of Ireland, and here it was that he resided for the most part, and had with him … his grandson. He, being a youth of a military disposition, had enlisted a company of the Protestant schoolboys, among them I was one; these he armed with wooden guns, and took great delight in marching and exercising them before the duke and duchess. From this trifling circumstance, I was induced to entertain a high opinion of a military life, and was determined to take the first opportunity of entering into the service in any shape.

Parker was not alone in being induced: 'above thirty of those young gentlemen … bore commissions in the army and some of them became colonels and general officers'.[26]

Jones was appointed Dean of Lismore in 1678. From there he was appointed Bishop of Cloyne in 1683, where he served until his translation in 1692 to a diocese in his native Wales. There, as Bishop of St Asaph, he fell into disfavour and in 1701 was suspended from office. He was reinstated a year later but died in 1703. Jones was succeeded in Kilkenny by the Revd Henry Ryder. Like Jones, he was educated at Westminster School and Trinity College, Cambridge, graduating in 1663. Born in France and educated in England, Ryder did, however, have Irish connections: his English grandfather, John Ryder, had been a dean and bishop in the Church of Ireland and had been held in high regard for his learning. Henry Ryder had been headmaster of St Patrick's Cathedral Grammar School in Dublin since 1672.[27]

There is no register of pupils for this period, so it is impossible to compile a list but occasional references in his papers show that some of the boys were sons of Ormond's employees and that they expected to benefit from his patronage after they had left school. For instance, in 1683 Lodowick Jackson, who had come to Ireland with the duke (presumably at the Restoration), called on Ormond to appoint his son, who had been educated in Kilkenny College, 'to wait on his grace or his lady duchess as page, or to attend on Lord Ossory in his travels.'[28] Likewise, Giles Clarke, a nephew of James Clarke, the controller of Ormond's household, enjoyed three stages of patronage from Ormond: he was educated in Kilkenny College, took his degrees at Oxford, where Ormond was chancellor and probably paid his fees, and was then appointed chaplain to one of Ormond's regiments.[29] The career of John Hartstonge is a prime example of the effect of Ormond patronage: from being chaplain to the first duke, he was appointed by his influence to the archdeaconry of Limerick in 1684, was chaplain to the second duke during the Flanders campaign and finally became bishop in 1693.

In the early years of the college's operation, Ormond was never free from political difficulties, national and personal.[30] He must have found it impossible to maintain a close interest in his grammar school. His wife, formerly Lady Elizabeth Preston, clearly did and she probably reflected his opinion. In 1682, concerned that Ryder was not sufficiently well paid, she wrote to their son, the Earl of Arran:

> If upon Dean Jones's preferment there be any sinecure held by him that is in your gift, I desire you will bestow it on Mr Ryder, the schoolmaster at Kilkenny, for his greater encouragement to continue still there; otherwise I fear without some such help he will quit that place, and then that school will break, which has hitherto had great credit and been an advantage unto the town.[31]

Her fears were allayed for, a month later, she wrote to Arran:

> I thank you for your good intendment unto Mr Ryder which if it may be by giving him a sinecure, it can no ways hinder his present undertaking, but encourage him

to continue it, as I find he is resolved and never to look for further preferment, if he may obtain some additional help to what he has, who is a hospitable man, and much valued in the place where he lives.[32]

Ryder remained as headmaster until he was appointed Bishop of Killaloe in 1683.[33]

It is significant that the first two headmasters were both at Westminster School and Trinity College, Cambridge. If they were at all like their headmaster, the renowned Richard Busby, they were fine classics teachers and stern disciplinarians. Busby was a noted royalist, who would have been known to Ormond. It is likely that he was consulted about Jones's appointment, perhaps also about Ryder's appointment, although, of course, Jones may have suggested his successor to Ormond.[34] The careful choice of headmasters with this background suggests that Ormond understood what was needed to establish his grammar school on a firm footing. Under Jones and Ryder it developed as one of Ireland's leading schools, drawing boys from prominent Anglo-Irish families all over the country, some of whom went on to Oxford or Cambridge.

CHAPTER THREE

Survival, 1684-1702

The Kilkenny career of Edward Hinton, headmaster from 1684 to 1702, mirrors the drama of Irish political events. Appointed in the peaceful Restoration period, his position, his school and even his life were endangered by Jacobite rule in Ireland. The Williamite victory enabled him to continue building up Kilkenny College as a school of the highest repute. Hinton had been educated at Merton College, Oxford and prior to his arrival in Ireland he had been master of the free school at Witney in Oxfordshire. A classicist like his predecessors, while he was at Witney he also worked on an edition and translation of Plutarch's *Morals*.[1] It is not hard to understand how Ormond found his new headmaster, for the duke had been chancellor of the University of Oxford since 1669 and had numerous contacts there. He may also have consulted Robert Huntington, Provost of Trinity College, who knew Hinton from Merton College.[2]

One of the first developments of Hinton's time was the issue by the Duke of Ormond of 'statutes, orders and constitutions … for the due government and managery and improvement' of the school.[3] A comparison with the statutes of Witney Grammar School reveals Hinton's influence in drawing them up.[4] The statutes comprised 25 sections prescribing how the school should operate. The first statute explained the necessary attributes of the master: 'at least … a Master of Arts either here in Ireland or one of the universities of England, a person of good life and reputation, well skilled in humanity and grammar learning, loyal and orthodox, who shall take the oaths of allegiance and supremacy and conform to the doctrine of the Church of Ireland'. The Christian ethos of the college was further promoted in Statute 15, requiring daily prayers in the master's household. The duke's concerns in this regard were not simply political, for several of his own personal prayers are recorded and reveal a profound personal faith.[5] Another statute appointed the Bishop of Ossory, the Bishop of Ferns and Leighlin and the Provost of Trinity College as visitors of the school, to 'examine the proficiency of the scholars' and the performance of the master and usher, and investigate any breaches of the statutes. They were specifically empowered to order any changes which they thought necessary, in which case the master had to implement them at once.

The third statute outlined the academic duties of the master: 'to instruct the scholars in religion, virtue and learning in the Latin, Greek and Hebrew languages, as also in oratory and poetry according to the best method which he and the visitors shall judge most effectual to promote knowledge and learning'. The master was responsible for discipline and there were rules for suspension and expulsion for misbehaviour, with automatic expulsion for any boy involved in a barring out of the master or usher. Until the 20th century, when a school was in a bad state, rebellions were common. These usually took the form of a 'barring out', when the pupils barricaded themselves in and kept the masters out. There were, for instance, two barrings out in The King's Hospital within a short period, the first in 1838, the second in 1842.[6] While many rebellions erupted spontaneously, some were carefully planned and involved a lot of violence, with boys bringing in guns and gunpowder, and occasionally the authorities had to bring in soldiers to quell the revolt.[7] It is not, therefore, surprising that this offence carried automatic expulsion.

At a less serious level, the master was to 'make diligent inquiry after such as shall break, cut or deface or any ways abuse the desks, forms, walls or windows of the school or any parts of the house or trees in the meadow and shall always inflict open and exemplary punishment on all such offenders'. It is interesting that specific mention is made of the trees, for over the centuries the Irish showed little concern for them. A drawing of the city in 1698 by Francis Place shows the college park covered in row after row of deciduous trees.[8] Statute 17 ordered the master to make sure that the trees 'be carefully preserved and improved'. That did not stop boys of successive generations carving their names on them. The statutes were not unduly negative towards the boys, for two afternoons a week were set aside for recreation, when the boys had the use of the meadow.

Statute 20 placed the responsibility for the upkeep on the master. Statute 22 instructed the visitors to inspect all buildings and the grounds (including the trees) and order the master to undertake any maintenance, in default of which Ormond would have it done and deduct the cost from the master's salary. This statute placed a considerable burden on the master and caused endless trouble until the responsibility was given to a board of governors in the late 19th century.

If it is true that schoolboys believe that rules are there for breaking, it is equally true that the school statutes were little honoured by those in authority. It was for fear of this that they were 'to be read audibly and distinctly by one of the scholars' at each visitation. That may have been done but the effect was small. If the statutes had been followed, Kilkenny College would have been spared many of the problems it suffered over the centuries.

In compliance with the statutes, Hinton was the first master to maintain a register of pupils. This source reveals much about the calibre of the boys attending the school and makes it easier to trace their careers in later life. Hinton was, however, only settling in to his job when a threat arose to the survival of the school. As soon as James II succeeded to the throne in 1685, his ardent Catholicism endangered the peace and prosperity of the Restoration. Protestant institutions, such as Ormond's school in Kilkenny, had every reason to be fearful and there was a growing sense of foreboding. In August 1686 the Bishop of Ossory, Thomas Otway, reported on a visitation:

> On the last Thursday in July the visitors were at his Grace's school, where they found all things well, considering the great discouragement all things are under here, in which the very schoolboys have their share, who would be more humorous if the times were more serene. The master is certainly a very industrious man. There are in the school fifty-one.[9]

Three months later, Ormond wrote to Bishop Otway, implying that one challenge had been staved off:

> so … that I presume you will hear no more of that matter, nor if it is in my power to prevent it of any other that may hinder or divert you from continuing the successful care you have had to govern and improve that college. My intention in erecting and endowing the school at Kilkenny was good, and if it shall be frustrated, I shall be very sorry for it, but not ashamed of my attempt.[10]

Ormond was by then an old man and his influence was severely reduced under James II. From the moment he was appointed Lord Deputy in 1687, the Earl of Tyrconnell began to remove Protestants from significant posts in Ireland and replace them with Catholics. In England in June 1688 James was deposed and his Protestant son-in-law, William of Orange, and his daughter, Anne, became king and queen. Although James fled to France, Tyrconnell continued to rule Ireland in his name rather than that of William III and so the situation for men like Hinton was even more dangerous. In July 1688 Ormond died and Hinton fled to England, where, like so many others, he was attainted. William King, later Archbishop of Dublin, gave this explanation:

> Great care was taken to discourage such Protestant schoolmasters as remained, and to set up popish schools in opposition to them. Thus they dealt with the school of Kilkenny, founded and endowed by the charitable piety of the late

Duke of Ormond; they set up a Jesuit school in the town and procured them a charter for a college there; they drove away the Protestant schoolmaster, Dr Hinton, who had officiated in it with great industry and success, and seized on the schoolhouse, commonly called the college and converted it to an hospital for their soldiers.[11]

In March 1689 James sailed from France to Ireland in the hope of regaining his kingdom. Having marched to Dublin, he was welcomed by the Irish Catholics, who hoped that he would succeed and restore them to their former lands. While he was spending the winter in Kilkenny, Dr William Daton, parish priest of St Mary's and Dean of Ossory, lobbied for his support for the Roman Catholic college which he was operating in the city. As Kilkenny College was now vacant, with its endowments confiscated, Daton acquired it for his college.[12] In February 1690 a royal charter was granted, which stated that: 'William Daton … and other pious and learned men [had] for some years now, with great efforts on their part, and with great benefit on the part of many of our subjects, been sedulously educating the souls of the young in the true faith of Christ, in good moral virtues and in doctrine.'[13] What was termed the Royal College of St Canice operated there for a few months before the defeat of the Jacobites in July and the return of Protestant rule in Ireland.[14]

The school register implies that Hinton returned to Kilkenny and resumed his office at the end of 1691. Soon after the resumption of the school, proposals were submitted to Ormond for the creation of a foundation of scholars as 'the surest way to raise funds and to perpetuate the credit and eminence of [the] school'.[15] The submission envisaged the fitting out of the house adjoining the school to accommodate 30 scholars:

> That the major part [i.e. 16] of them be maintained by your Grace and the rest filled up by benefactors, all of which are to go by the general name of Ormond scholars. That their allowance be according to that given the scholars in Dublin College …
>
> That the rules of election and government of this society be taken from the statutes and practice of Westminster School. That £100 per annum be settled on the College of Dublin as an additional exhibition to their scholarships, the Provost and his assistant to come every year as they do to Westminster to elect 4 or 5 constantly out of the foundation.

There is no indication that these proposals were adopted but the document contains useful details about the expenses involved in the running of the school. It is interesting that, apart from the headmaster, the only 'officers' mentioned were a cook, butler and bed maker.

Some of Hinton's pupils had also fled to England in 1688, while others went home. One of them, Toby Caulfeild, the grandson of Lord Charlemont, entered Trinity College in July 1690, aged 19. It is safe to presume that he must have had some kind of tuition between 1688 and 1690 or else he would have been admitted in 1688. Caulfeild duly graduated and was ordained. Two years later he went to serve in a remote part of the diocese of Killala, a move which he viewed as 'a prelude to better livings'.[16] He was one of several pupils who later benefited from the patronage of the second duke of Ormond. Caulfeild associated himself with Ormond in the hope of being favoured and, soon after the duke was appointed Lord Lieutenant in 1703, he appointed Caulfeild as one of his domestic chaplains.[17] In correspondence Caulfeild described his 'week's attendance at the castle where I shall say grace every day, for I hear the duke will have some of the Commons at dinner in public'.[18] Likewise, it was Ormond's patronage which secured the appointment of Hinton's son, John, as vicar of Carrick-on-Suir in 1705.

Early in 1692 there was an interesting correspondence involving Hinton, Huntington, the Provost of Trinity College, and Bartholomew Vigors, Bishop of Ossory, about the potential threat from a proposed new rival school at Abbeyleix. Bishop Vigors explained: 'I am not fond of too many schools but our constitution does allow and suppose one in every county, however I am highly sensible of the necessity of a good maintenance to make them useful in any degree and will encourage that part by all the fair ways I can by God's help.'[19]

Hinton became Archdeacon of Cashel in October 1693 but remained headmaster till his death in late 1702 or early 1703. It is disappointing if he thus contravened the instructions of the statutes that the master should 'constantly inhabit and reside at the house ... and in person attend the duties of his place', as he had been involved in their framing. On the other hand, his church appointment may have been given to compensate him for heavy losses between 1688 and 1691.

Hinton educated some of Kilkenny College's most illustrious pupils. Preeminent among them was the famous philosopher, George Berkeley. Although George Berkeley was a little younger than Thomas Prior, they became close friends and may have forged that friendship at school. Contemporaries at Trinity College, they both achieved distinction, Berkeley as an eminent philosopher and bishop, and Prior as founder of what became known as the Royal Dublin Society.[20] When he was a student at Trinity College, Berkeley read a paper on the cave of Dunmore, a well-known natural curiosity in Co Kilkenny. In it he referred to recollections 'at a distance

Memorial to
Thomas Prior

of almost seven years. The material for the paper, a vivid and well-written
account, which shows the accuracy of a proficient pupil, must have been
gathered during an expedition of his schooldays.'[21]

In many ways Berkeley epitomised the Anglo-Irish of the 18th century in
his efforts to define Irishness, as has been noted by Roy Foster: 'As a Trinity
student of eighteen [he] referred to the Irish people as "natives"; a few years
later he had come to think in terms of "we Irish". Those who in the 1690s
called themselves "the Protestants of Ireland" or even "the English of this
kingdom" could see themselves as "Irish gentlemen" by the 1720s.'[22] From his
Principles of Human Knowledge in 1710, through a series of Irish tracts, he
established himself as a distinctively Irish writer. The very title of his 1760
tract, *The Querist*, highlights his questioning approach to issues. While he
did not adopt Swift's acerbic tone, his writings were, nevertheless, challenging, for there was rarely an answer to his questions. Berkeley's concern for a
distinctive Irishness was cultural as well as political, as is exemplified by his
advice to William Conolly to use nothing but native Irish materials when
building Castletown, his great house at Celbridge.[23]

It was an extraordinary decision for this Irish philosopher priest to buy and live
on an American plantation. From 1728 to 1731 Berkeley lived in Rhode Island,
where he had a plantation worked by slaves. In this, his stance contrasted with that
of another past pupil, Hugh Drysdale, who, as lieutenant-governor of Virginia

from 1722 to 1726, sought to control the slave trade. Berkeley's American odyssey occurred in the pursuit of a scheme which he had devised for establishing in Bermuda a college to train clergy for the colonies. He raised a large sum and persuaded a number of his colleagues that they would, in principle, join the staff. He also obtained the promise of a parliamentary grant but it was not forthcoming. In 1728, in the hope of forcing the issue and finding an alternative location for his college, he gave up his position as Dean of Derry, bought a plantation and moved to it. In the few years while he was in America, Berkeley had considerable influence, for he was the first noted philosopher and literary figure to live in America and the only senior Anglican priest. By 1731, however, it was obvious that the parliamentary grant was not going to come and he returned to London. On his departure, he donated his house and farm to Yale University and used the Bermuda funds to buy books for the Yale and Harvard libraries. While the Bermuda project came to nothing, Berkeley's reputation as a churchman was enhanced and within three years he was appointed Bishop of Cloyne.

Although Berkeley was very much a figure of the Protestant ascendancy, as bishop he was generous and tolerant, believing, on one hand, that he must work for the conversion of Roman Catholics, on the other, that he had a duty of care for those in his diocese. One of his concerns was education, the importance of which he stressed in words that probably recall his own experience at Kilkenny College:

> The hopes of the future age depend on nothing so much as the education of the present. Early habits of hardiness and industry introduced into young children render their whole lives easy and happy to themselves, and useful to their country.[24]

Another lifelong friendship between Hinton boys was that of the dramatist William Congreve and Joseph Keally.[25] Although Congreve is still regarded by some as the greatest master of English comedy, his plays are no longer staged. They are the source of many familiar quotations, such as 'Heaven has no rage like love to hatred turned, nor hell a fury like a woman scorned.'[26] If, as Voltaire

William Congreve

suggested, Congreve 'spoke of his works as trifles that were beneath him,'[27] he may have felt that he had not fully used his education under Hinton. He worked on Latin translations and, according to one source, his knowledge of the Greek poets was 'not ... common even in a college'[28] but Hinton might have hoped that such a gifted pupil would make his career as an academic classicist. That Congreve may have been a challenging pupil is suggested by lines from one of his plays:

To find a young fellow that is neither a wit in his own eye,
Nor a fool in the eye of the world, is a very hard task.[29]

It has been suggested that, as a schoolboy, Congreve may have seen productions by the Smock Alley Players, a Dublin-based professional theatre company. This suggestion arises from the fact that Ormond was the company's leading patron and that there was 'a long tradition of performing plays' in Kilkenny College.[30] Some of Congreve's letters to Keally reveal his interest in Ormond's patronage and suggest a close relationship between Congreve and the duke. For instance, in 1707 Congreve wrote: 'My lord, Duke of Ormond, whom I waited on yesterday, talks of going for Ireland on Monday next. I would not miss such an opportunity if it were not thought absolutely necessary for me to stay here.'[31]

Hinton's headmastership was significant in maintaining and, more importantly, restoring high standards despite the enormous upheaval. It is remarkable that this English academic was prepared to return to Ireland after the Williamite war and was, within a short time, able to turn out scholars of the highest calibre.

Swift's Walk, 1960s

CHAPTER FOUR

In high reputation, 1702-1781

There was a significant change in the identity and status of Kilkenny College in the 18th century. The catalyst for this was the impeachment of James Butler, the second Duke of Ormond, in 1715. One of the most powerful men of his time, a favourite of William III and Queen Anne, he was Lord Lieutenant of Ireland from 1703 to 1711, then commander-in-chief of the armed forces. When George I became king, Ormond lost his influence and his many enemies soon had him impeached for high treason. He forfeited his lands and wealth and fled abroad.

His right to appoint headmasters in Kilkenny College passed to the Provost and fellows of Trinity College.[1] This was a logical interpretation of the statutes, which had made provision for the lack of a male heir but had not envisaged the possibility of the duke's impeachment! As it turned out, he had no male heir and the Ormonds never recovered the right of appointment. While they had appointed Oxford or Cambridge graduates, the board of Trinity College invariably appointed one of their own alumni, whose standing they usually confirmed with the award of an honorary doctorate. It was primarily this development which led to a changed identity and reduced status of Kilkenny College. The leaders of Irish society had obviously been impressed with the calibre and credentials of the headmasters whom the Ormonds had appointed. Products of prominent schools and the foremost universities, no-one could have asked for more suitable men. The next generations of prominent Irishmen were less inclined to send their sons to the college once it had an Irish headmaster, a graduate of Trinity. A growing provincialism was evident in several ways: loss of a breadth of vision, which English headmasters had brought; an inability to recruit boys from the best families all over Ireland; and fewer boys proceeding to university in Oxford or Cambridge.

Although the college lost impetus and status as it became a more local school, demographic records show the potential for a Protestant boarding school in the southeast. About 1732, when David Dickson maintains that it was 'drawing a cross-section of gentry children from the four provinces' and was 'not exclusively Anglican',[2] estimated percentages of Protestants for the

Co. Kilkenny, showing
Kilkenny College
families

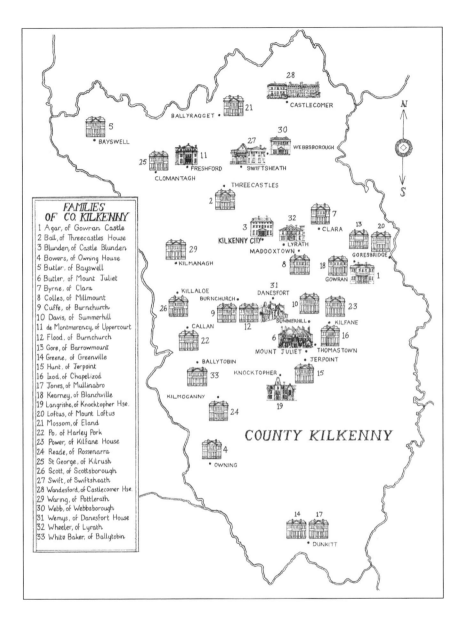

FAMILIES
OF CO. KILKENNY
1 Agar, of Gowran Castle
2 Ball, of Threecastles House
3 Blunden, of Castle Blunden
4 Bowers, of Owning House
5 Butler, of Bayswell
6 Butler, of Mount Juliet
7 Byrne, of Clara
8 Colles, of Millmount
9 Cuffe, of Burnchurch
10 Davis, of Summerhill
11 de Montmorency, of Uppercourt
12 Flood, of Burnchurch
13 Gore, of Barrowmount
14 Greene, of Greenville
15 Hunt, of Jerpoint
16 Izod, of Chapelizod
17 Jones, of Mullinabro
18 Kearney, of Blanchville
19 Langrishe, of Knocktopher Hse.
20 Loftus, of Mount Loftus
21 Mossom, of Eland
22 Po, of Harley Park
23 Power, of Kilfane House
24 Reade, of Rossenarra
25 St George, of Kilrush
26 Scott, of Scottsborough
27 Swift, of Swiftsheath
28 Wandesford, of Castlecomer Hse.
29 Waring, of Pottlerath
30 Webb, of Webbsborough
31 Wemys, of Danesfort House
32 Wheeler, of Lyrath
33 White Baker, of Ballytobin

south midlands and southeast were: Carlow 20, Kilkenny 9, Queen's Co (Laois) 16, Tipperary 9, Waterford 8, Wexford 17 and Wicklow 33 per cent.[3] The small number of Roman Catholics who attended may have done so because Kilkenny College offered higher educational standards than local Catholic schools could provide.[4]

The last two headmasters appointed by the Duke of Ormond were William Andrews (1702) and Edward Lewis (1713).[5] Both were Oxford graduates and do not appear to have had any Irish connections. When Andrews became Archdeacon of Ossory in 1713, he was succeeded by Lewis, who, like Jones and Ryder, had been educated at Westminster School. Sadly, there is no information about the operation of the college during their time, the only indications being the successes of their past pupils in various fields. Among Andrews's pupils, Walter Harris made his name as an historian, his works including his *History and antiquities of the City of Dublin*.[6] Michael Cox, son of Sir Richard Cox, Lord Chancellor of Ireland, was later Archbishop of Cashel.[7] Caleb Cartwright, who left Kilkenny College for Trinity College in 1716, became a lecturer there and was made professor of natural philosophy in 1738. Some of the boys whom Andrews taught became educators themselves. William Markham, for example, having served in the War of the Spanish Succession, worked in Kinsale as a Latin schoolmaster.[8] During his time as headmaster Lewis neglected to enter his pupils' names in the register. They are consequently lost, with the exception of boys who matriculated to Trinity College directly from Kilkenny. Among them were high-ranking members of society, including local politicians, such as James Agar, and Trinity College academics, such as William Andrews.

Thomas Hewetson's appointment in 1743 was the first made by the board of Trinity College. Thomas's parents, Thomas Hewetson, of Co. Carlow, and Ellen Rothe, of Butler's Grove, Co. Kilkenny, both came from important local families. The Hewetsons were 'a well-established Protestant family, stalwart representatives of the rural landowning gentry, tracing their ancestry back to an Elizabethan clergyman who settled in Ireland'.[9]

For much of Hewetson's time it was not obvious that the tide was ebbing away from Kilkenny College. According to William Colles, a local alderman, it was 'in high reputation. They have now between 50 and 60 boarders, most of them the sons of men of distinction'.[10] Among Hewetson's most distinguished past pupils were two Chief Justices of the Court of Common Pleas, Hugh Carleton and John Toler. Carleton was Solicitor General for Ireland from 1779 until his appointment as Chief Justice in 1787. Created Baron Carleton in 1789, he became Viscount Carleton some years later. The ultra

conservative John Toler, as attorney general, became notorious for his severe prosecution of those involved in the 1798 rebellion. Promoted chief justice of the Common Pleas, he presided at the trial of Robert Emmet. He held that position until 1827, when his long-term adversary, Daniel O'Connell, forced his resignation. Then aged 82, he was raised to the peerage as the Earl of Norbury. Toler's brother, Daniel, was one of many members of parliament who were at school under Hewetson.

Another of Hewetson's distinguished past pupils was his nephew, Christopher Hewetson, long considered Ireland's greatest sculptor. The son of Christopher Hewetson, JP, of Thomastown, and Elizabeth (née Hewetson), sister of the headmaster, he entered Kilkenny College in September 1745. It is suggested that he studied under John van Nost the Younger, the leading monumental sculptor in Dublin at the time. In his late twenties he left for Rome to pursue a career in sculpture. His greatest work in Ireland is the monument to another Kilkenny past pupil, Provost Richard Baldwin, for the examination hall in Trinity College. Among other notable former pupils, the Hon. William Beresford, son of the first Earl of Tyrone, was Bishop of Ossory and later Archbishop of Tuam (1795-1819). It is also possible that Pierce Butler, one of the original members of the Senate of the United States, was educated by Hewetson: Pierce's brother, Thomas, who was an Irish parliamentarian, was certainly taught by him.

It was probably also Thomas Hewetson who educated Andrew Fitzgerald, later the co-rector of the Academy in Kilkenny, the forerunner of St Kieran's College.[11] He returned to Kilkenny in 1791 from academic life in Lisbon and, along with Patrick McGrath, ran the school until 1800. Another past pupil who followed Hewetson's example as an educator was John Moore. Highly regarded as master of a school in Donnybrook, he was appointed headmaster of the Royal School, Cavan in 1806. He settled the school on a permanent site and remained there till he was well into his eighties, before resigning in favour of his son.[12]

An account of the school in Hewetson's time came indirectly from one of his pupils, Edward Denroche, who lived nearby on John Street. He described 'the old college as bearing a general resemblance to the ancient mansion of

Christopher
Hewetson's
memorial to
Richard Baldwin

the Rothe family still standing in High Street'. Denroche's description provides a useful source to compare with the survey of 1666 as:

> a quadrangular building with a central court. In the street front were two arch-
> ways, still remaining in the wall at each side of the present entrance gate. These
> archways gave entrance to the central quadrangle, and between them, projecting
> into the street, was a high double flight of steps, which gave admittance to the
> first floor. The school-room was a lofty and very large apartment and was situate
> on the east side of the quadrangle; the windows of which, large and of massive
> framed timber, looked out on the mill-race. The domestic buildings were two stories
> high and occupied the west side of the quadrangle, where the stables and out-
> offices of the present college stand.[13]

In October 1772 Hewetson became rector of Freshford and was also vicar of
Kilbrin, Co. Cork and a canon of Cloyne Cathedral.[14] He was succeeded by

Richard Pack, the second son of Thomas Pack, of Ballinakill, Co. Laois. Pack was the first past pupil to be appointed headmaster and 20 years later his son, Anthony, became the only other past pupil to hold the position. In 1775 Pack received instructions from the Provost, John Hely-Hutchinson, who was, of course, one of the visitors, to modify the course of instruction in Kilkenny College so as to prepare the boys for examination in Latin and English prose composition. Hely-Hutchinson also tried to persuade the masters of the royal schools and Erasmus Smith schools to do the same.[15] At the time, boys were trained only to translate from the classics into English and did little composition. This new emphasis was designed to raise standards but it does not appear that Pack implemented it.

Pack died in office in March 1781. It is an indication of the changed identity and decline in status of Kilkenny College that fewer past pupils of his time distinguished themselves. Paul Helsham was typical of the more successful pupil, in that he came from an important local family and the pinnacle of his career was his appointment as Archdeacon of Ossory. It is impossible to say whether the leading Irish families stopped sending their sons due to a crisis of confidence or because standards fell under the Irish headmasters but, by 1781, the decline was so serious that the school was 'nearly ruinous'.[16] This was the view of the first educational commissioners, who reported that the school, 'formerly of great credit', had 'fallen in its character in the time of the last master'. It proved a major challenge for Pack's successor to restore Kilkenny College to its former position.

CHAPTER FIVE

Turning its back, 1781-1820

View of Kilkenny
from the southeast

There is no record of neglect or mismanagement by any of the headmasters described in the previous chapter but it must be presumed that at least one of them allowed the school to decay both physically and in its standing as a place of education. In the next 40 years, new premises had to be built and the college was subject to the first two government reviews.

John Ellison, who was appointed to Kilkenny College in 1781, was another headmaster with local connections. He was the second son of the Revd Thomas Ellison and Mildred Cooper, of Oldgrange, Co. Kilkenny.[1] As the schoolhouse was in severe disrepair, he faced an uphill struggle and immediately started negotiating parliamentary grants for the construction of a new building. After several applications to the Irish House of Commons, he was successful in securing funding of £5,064. This was a remarkable achievement, for almost all parliamentary grants at the time were for infrastructure and Kilkenny College was the only school to obtain one.[2]

By the end of 1781, Ellison had rented a large house on Patrick Street, which he used as a temporary home for the school.[3] He advertised in a local newspaper that it was 'a large roomy house, with an extensive playground behind it   where he will be able to accommodate a much greater number of boys and much better than in the old college'.[4] Within a few months, the visitors had approved the architect's plans and Ellison advertised for tenders from craftsmen. The architect was Charles Vierpyl, a son of Simon Vierpyl, the famous stonecutter.[5] Understandably, the new building was designed to face Kilkenny Castle, across the river. The first stone of the new building was laid on 30 July 1782 by the 12-year-old Walter Butler, later first Marquis of Ormond. Contemporary reports that the new building on John Street had the capacity to accommodate as many as 80 boarders in single beds suggest that previously boys had often to share a bed.[6]

In March 1787 Ellison petitioned the Irish parliament for compensation for an additional £1,064-9-4½ spent on the new building. According to him, the project was 'universally allowed to be one of the best and cheapest public works ever executed in this kingdom'. Apparently the new school building had been seen by many members of parliament, some of whom were no doubt past pupils, and Ellison was careful to tell them that he had 'paid the strictest attention to economy in every part of the work' but 'had the mortification to find that it could not possibly be completed without exceeding very consid-erably the sums granted by parliament for that purpose'. He attributed the excess cost to 'several unforeseen difficulties' but chiefly to having received false estimates. He had been 'reduced to the unfortunate alternative of either leaving the work unfinished, or completing it at his own risk, and throwing himself on the bounty of parliament'. He trusted 'the House [of Commons] would not suffer him to be a loser … in completing a public work of national importance'.[7] The success of his petition says a lot about Ellison's powers of persuasion and his reputation in the highest ranks of Irish society.

The first commission on Irish education conducted its inquiry during Ellison's headmastership. By the 1780s there was widespread concern about the state of education in Ireland and Thomas Orde, who was appointed chief secretary in 1784, was determined on reform. In 1787 he introduced propos-als to parliament for a new system of education from primary to university level.[8] It is a striking illustration of Kilkenny College's diminished status before Ellison's arrival that Orde made no mention of it in his original pro-posals for expanding classical education in Ireland.[9] Although he did not get his proposals through parliament, in 1788 a commission was established 'to examine and enquire into the state and condition of all schools and school-houses, the number of scholars in each, the mode of instruction … and the conduct of all masters and ushers …'[10]

Ellison received wholehearted praise in the commissioners' report, issued in 1791. Commenting on his rebuilding that 'the money has been usefully expended' and 'an excellent house' provided, they judged that 'the credit of his school … has been revived by Dr Ellison, of whose conduct and care of his scholars, as well as of his course of instruction, we think it necessary to express an entire approbation.'[11] This was in stark contrast to the bulk of the commissioners' report, which condemned the Incorporated Society's charter schools and found many other schools shamefully neglected. Of the royal schools, only Armagh gained their approval and they recommended that the masters at Cavan and Raphoe should be dismissed for dereliction of duty. Although there was supposed to be a free school in each diocese, they found that 12 of the schools had no master and six of these were not operating at all. Of the 24 grammar schools of private foundation, Kilkenny College with 36 boarders and 29 day pupils had the largest numbers, while many were in a disgraceful state.

The commissioners reflected many of Orde's proposals in their report. Deploring 'the want of good schools' for the more academic pupils and the lack of training in composition in Latin or English, the commissioners thought that the remedy lay in the establishment of a collegiate school in connection with Trinity College and with existing 'great schools', named as Kilkenny College and Drogheda. Their idea was that headmasters and assistants would be recruited from Eton, Harrow, Westminster or Winchester and that the system of education adopted in the collegiate school would depend on which English school provided the recruits. The expectation was that the great schools would introduce the same system.[12] This idea came to nothing as the report was effectively suppressed. Ironically, its sharp criticism of Irish education may have made the necessary reforms seem too daunting. While the report was not even printed until the 1850s, the commission itself set a useful precedent for government reviews of education. Headmasters from then had to be aware that their school might be open to official inspection. While such a prospect was not threatening for a headmaster like Ellison, it was uncomfortable for the less able and less hard-working. Of course, the headmasters of Kilkenny College were subject to annual review by the visitors (the bishops of Ferns and Leighlin, Ossory and the Provost) but that may not have happened in practice. If it did happen, it clearly was not as searching as the educational commissions proved to be.

As might be expected, a number of Ellison's past pupils distinguished themselves in later life. Probably the most important was Abraham Colles, the foremost surgeon of his day in Dublin, serving as resident surgeon at Dr Steevens's Hospital and Professor of Anatomy, Surgery and Physiology at the Royal College of Surgeons. Richard Ponsonby, son of William, Lord

Ponsonby, was another prominent former pupil. He was for several years up to 1806 headmaster of Banagher School. He was Dean of St Patrick's Cathedral from 1818 to 1828 before being appointed Bishop of Killaloe and Kilfenora. A few years later he became Bishop of Derry and Raphoe. As a governor of the Erasmus Smith schools and president of the Church Education Society, he took an active role in the promotion of education. There are strong indications that his brothers, who rose to fame outside Ireland, were also past pupils. William was a military officer and John an eminent ambassador with numerous postings. William's death at the Battle of Waterloo in 1815 was commemorated by an impressive monument in St Paul's Cathedral, London. The Duke of Wellington spoke of his personal grief 'for the fate of an officer who had always rendered very brilliant and important services and was an ornament to his profession'.[13] A Kilkenny contemporary also at Waterloo was Major-General Sir Denis Pack, a nephew of the former headmaster.

Ellison resigned in 1793, on being presented by Trinity College to the rectory of Conwal.[14] His successor, Anthony Pack, was the son of the previous headmaster, Richard Pack, and had been educated at Kilkenny College.[15] Pack faced the second government review of the school but before that he had to cope with the negative effect of the 1798 rebellion, which featured sectarian conflict in the southeast. Prior to that year, there had been 43 boarders, of whom 10 were from Roman Catholic families but the divisiveness of the rebellion led to the

withdrawal of the Roman Catholics from the school.[16] Perhaps some of the pupils who were withdrawn moved to the Academy (later known as St Kieran's College) for educating boys prior to training for the priesthood.

Anxiety about the state of education, particularly of the charter schools, led to the establishment in 1809 of a new commission, which came to be called the Board of Education.[17] The 12th report was devoted to classical schools, including Kilkenny College. The commissioners praised Pack for maintaining the progress of his predecessor: 'The plan of instruction varies little at Kilkenny School from those adopted in the other great classical schools in Ireland; and it appears to us that Dr Pack has regularly and carefully attended to the duties of his situation.'[18]

The reports, based on a detailed examination of headmasters, give a fair picture of the internal arrangements of each school. Pack provided the commissioners with an account of the course of instruction for each of the six forms in the school.[19] The overriding focus was on Greek and Latin but there was some attention to English oration as well as to history and geography. He explained that the extra masters did not 'interrupt the classical business' but attended after school hours, the writing master and French master from 5 p.m. to 7 p.m. every day and the drawing master on half days. The typical school day opened with prayers at 6.30 a.m. in the summer and 7 a.m. in winter and the scripture readings of the day were read after breakfast by boys of the head class. On Saturdays after breakfast the boys delivered speeches in English, in prose or in verse, and were afterwards examined in the church catechism and instructed in sacred history. Breakfast was typically bread and milk, gruel or stirabout;[20] dinner was half a pound of meat and broth, with bread or potatoes but little or no vegetables; supper was bread and milk. Weak beer was often given at dinner, as the water was not fit to drink. This diet was very similar to that in other schools.[21]

When Pack was examined in 1809, he stated that he had 20 boarders and 24 day pupils, and a teaching staff of two resident assistants. The annual fees were 30 guineas for boarders and 4 guineas for day pupils. (In addition there were entrance fees of 6 guineas for boarders and a guinea for day pupils.) Pack resigned that year[22] and Andrew O'Callaghan, from Cork, was appointed headmaster at the beginning of the following year. As the commissioners did not complete their report until 1812, they included figures for that year in their report. By then O'Callaghan had 46 boarders and 39 day scholars, including a small number of Roman Catholics (two boarders and five day pupils). His staff had expanded to a head usher, two other ushers and an English assistant, and the boarding fees had increased to 34 guineas per annum.[23]

While Kilkenny College did well under Pack and flourished for a time under O'Callaghan, it is noteworthy that their salary, fixed at £140, compared badly with that of similar headmasters. For instance, the headmaster of Galway Grammar School had a salary of £100 as well as annual income from property of more than £200, while at Cavan, one of the smaller royal schools, the headmaster had a salary of £400. As the 19th century progressed and headmasters faced the growing cost of repairs to the school, that salary became a big issue.

Abraham Brewster

In his early years O'Callaghan produced some famous pupils, one of whom was Abraham Brewster, who rose through the ranks to be Lord Chancellor, the highest ranking legal position in Ireland. Another was local boy, John Banim. While at school, Banim's chief interest was in literature and art. He preferred a 'flowing and spirited metrical version' to O'Callaghan's 'strict, grammatical translation' of Latin prose. He showed 'a very remarkable talent for drawing and painting' while at school. One of his drawings from his schooldays survives in the college archives: a caricature of O'Callaghan with his trademark weapon of punishment.[24] Writing about the drawing in 1877, Robert Fishbourne described himself as one of 'the last remaining specimens of the class brought up under the rod of Andrew O'Callaghan'.[25] Banim left Kilkenny in 1813 to attend the academy of the Royal Dublin Society. He pursued a career first as an artist and then as a writer, chiefly of historical fiction. In his novel *The Fetches* he writes at length about his *alma mater*: 'Turning its back, in suitable abstraction, upon the hum and bustle of the small though populous city, it faces towards the green country, an extensive lawn spreading before it, and the placid river running hard-by, and is altogether appropriately and beautifully situated.'[26]

It is rare to have a first-hand memoir of what the school looked like so long ago:

The entrance to the school-room was immediately from the street, through huge oak folding doors, arching at [the] top, to suit the arched stone doorway, and gained by two grand flights of steps at each side, that formed a spacious platform before the entrance, and allowed under them a passage by which visitors approached the college. To the left was another gateway, where carriages had egress. The whole front of the building was of cut stone, with Gothic windows composed of numerous small panes of glass, separately leaded, and each of diamond form, giving the appearance of a side or back rather than of a front, on account of its grotesque gables, chimneys and spouts, the last of which jetted into the street, to the no small annoyance, in rainy weather, of the neighbours and the passengers; while, from the platform before the school-room entrance, the lads of the college contrived, in all weather, further annoyances of every description.[27]

This recollection makes it clear that boys have not changed much in the two centuries since Banim was a schoolboy! According to him:

John Banim

Neither the broad Nore, nor the mill-stream, nor yet the high front wall that ran from the side of the college to the brink of the latter, completely succeeded in keeping within proper bounds, at improper hours, the mettlesome race of young students.

Stories are whispered on the spot of stolen orgies at midnight, in confidential taverns through the town; of ardent breathings at the windows of not the ugliest lasses in the suburbs; of desperate wars between the native youth and the fiery sojourners; and all the *et ceteras* that spring from proximity to a small town of such an establishment.[28]

Another of O'Callaghan's pupils, writing anonymously, recalled his 'classical education … at … one of the first schools in the United Kingdom'. He remembered walking by the river: 'whilst wading through some Greek or Latin author, ever and anon stopping to try a cast, sometimes rewarded with success'. He had bought a fishing rod from the shop in John Street run by John Banim's father and admitted to having been distracted by fishing while at school:

Years, the freest from care I ever enjoyed, passed. I grew up to be a man. The passion for angling remained deep rooted as ever. During my school days I have been punished for absenting myself, and in after years suffered some loss on account of it; however, it still remains, and even now, although in 'the sear and yellow leaf', when opportunity offers, my wife and I sally forth intent on the destruction of the finny tribe, and return sometimes with a full basket.[29]

The poet Thomas Bibby, another outstanding pupil, was said to have spoken of his headmaster 'with profound respect'.[30] Having entered Trinity College at a young age, he obtained a gold medal in science there when only 13. He was also reported to be one of the finest Greek scholars of his day but extreme eccentricity prevented him from pursuing a public career. Benjamin Cronyn's education under O'Callaghan led him to Trinity College and ordination. Having served his curacy in Co. Longford, he emigrated with his young family to Canada and served as a pioneer priest in London, Ontario. Given his powerful ministry there and the fact that 'of the 42 clergy voting, nine were Trinity College, Dublin, men, and at least another six had been born in Ireland or had an Irish background',[31] it is not surprising that he was elected the first bishop of the diocese of Huron in 1857.

It has been suggested that O'Callaghan resigned in 1820 because 'he immersed himself in the great religious controversies of the day'.[32] Numbers certainly declined sharply after O'Callaghan publicly opposed the work of the Bible Society but it is unlikely that this was the only reason for his unpopularity. A letter in 1816 from the father of a pupil sheds light on the nature of O'Callaghan's administration and probably points to factors in the decline.[33] At issue was the boy's extra tuition from the classical usher at the school. O'Callaghan vehemently opposed it and told the boy he was 'at liberty to quit'. The boy went home to explain the situation to his father, who urged him to return to school the next morning. The father's account, though partially second-hand, is presumably accurate:

> In the course of that day Mr O'Callaghan called my son from his seat and asked him why he went home the day before. His reply was to inform his father of the treatment he met with, on which he gave him sixteen slaps and told him to quit as soon as he pleased, naming others in town fit enough to instruct him. His hand was in such a state Surgeon Pack was resorted to and he was obliged for some days to use a sling.

Next day, when the father sent his son to school, O'Callaghan prevented him from entering. This triggered the immediate resignation of the assistant usher, who declared to the father that he 'could not remain with so morose a character no more than the numerous set of ushers that left him within a short period'. O'Callaghan now had only one usher to assist him. The father, however, suggested that this was 'perhaps sufficient', for the declining school numbers, describing 13 boarders and 12 day boys as 'a wretched remnant of the children of the freemen and gentlemen of Kilkenny and its vicinity, all of whom at one period [O'Callaghan] had but were removed for various causes, which I suppose the parents will have no hesitation in declaring on a proper investigation'.

O'Callaghan's successor, reporting to the Board of Education in 1824, outlined the decline. There had been 16 admissions in 1815 but only three in 1817. He had heard O'Callaghan say 'that in the year 1810 … there were more than 100 boys at school … of whom 67 were boarders'. Ten years later at the end of O'Callaghan's time, there were only five boarders and perhaps just seven day pupils.[34]

If we review pupil numbers during this period, we can trace the restoration of Kilkenny College under Ellison, fluctuating fortunes in Pack's time and, after early success, deterioration under O'Callaghan's headmastership. This illustrates the importance of the headmaster to the reputation of a school. While a headmaster like Ellison attracted pupils, one like O'Callaghan in his later days had the opposite effect. Standards inevitably fell if there was an unhappy atmosphere and word soon spread about fits of temper and errors of judgement. Yet again, the incoming headmaster of Kilkenny College had to rebuild its reputation.

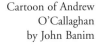

Cartoon of Andrew
O'Callaghan
by John Banim

CHAPTER SIX

Under examination, 1820-1864

William Baillie, from Co. Tipperary, who had graduated from Trinity College in 1816, was appointed headmaster of Kilkenny College in 1820 and steered it for over 20 years. Under Baillie the school soon recovered from the severe decline under O'Callaghan and, by 1821, the numbers were comparable with most of the other classical schools in Ireland.

Classical school	County	Number of pupils
Armagh Royal School	Armagh	82
Banagher School	Offaly	37
Bandon Grammar School	Cork	20
Cavan Royal School	Cavan	22
Charleville School	Cork	20
Clonmel School	Tipperary	18
Dundalk School	Louth	49
Dungannon Royal School	Tyrone	32
Enniskillen Royal School	Fermanagh	70
Eyrecourt School	Galway	0 *
Kilkenny School	Kilkenny	37
Lismore School	Waterford	40
Midleton School	Cork	0*
New Ross School	Wexford	26
Preston School, Ballyroan	Laois	33
Preston School, Navan	Meath	2
Raphoe Royal School	Donegal	22
Wicklow School	Wicklow	6
Youghal School	Cork	30

Number of pupils in classical schools in Ireland in 1821[1]

* The schools at Eyrecourt and Midleton did not have pupils at the time due to the extensive disrepair of their school buildings.

The next educational commission, which examined the state of the school in Baillie's early years, made little comment but James Glassford, one of the commissioners, reported on his visit in October 1824. There were 22 boarders and 41 day pupils; the instruction was 'the usual classical course' and included Hebrew and logic. Baillie had 'established a circulating library for the boys', containing 'religious … historical and miscellaneous works, moral and didactic'.[2]

It appears that Baillie initiated a system of annual examinations with premiums, certificates and medals. He certainly formalised these as a scheme not only for the monitoring of academic progress but also for motivating the pupils with rewards. Baillie advertised the results at length in the local newspaper, the greatest award being a silver medal.[3] It is likely that prospective parents were attracted to the college by this scheme, which was probably Baillie's intention. As he established himself, he could point to the success of his past pupils as evidence that he ran a good school.

Baillie was remembered in the biography of an illustrious former pupil as 'not only a good classical and Hebrew scholar but a man of earnest piety' who 'must have made his influence felt as such'.[4] The pupil was William Magee, later Archbishop of York, the second most senior position in the Church of

William Magee

England. A pupil in Kilkenny from 1833, aged 11, to 1835, Magee's biographer explained that 'in the short time he was there he mastered the long classical course which was then required for entrance into Trinity College'. This achievement presumably indicates not only Magee's ability but also the quality of the teaching. An early incident in the rough boarding environment of Kilkenny was recounted many years later by the archbishop:

A big boy came up to little Magee who was very low and grieved at his first severance from home, and holding in his hand a fruit tart he said, 'New boy, do you like tart?'

'Oh very much,' said little Magee, looking wistfully at the tart.

'Then,' said the other, 'look at me eating one!'

Apparently Magee 'never forgot the stab to his feelings which this gave him'. Recollections by his contemporaries at Kilkenny College are interesting not just because of Magee's later fame but because they enable the reader to understand what school was like at the time for an exceptionally intelligent boy. One account was glowing in his praise of Magee's ability:

He did not take part in any of our school sports. As a young man he learned to fish and was fond of the rod and line. During play hours and intervals from study he was rarely without a book in his hands, some history, biography, or novel, in English or in French, which he could translate fluently. Indeed he generally had several books stowed away in his pockets. He mastered his school business thoroughly, and was always at the head of his class, which was the class above me, although he was my junior, and junior to all my class fellows by over two years. In Greek and Latin he knew not only the text thoroughly, but the notes. We read the Delphin editions of Horace and Virgil, and the notes, being in Latin, were as difficult to beginners as the text. He was a boy of very precocious intellect, and as he had a splendid memory, and read much, he had a very extensive vocabulary for a boy …

Before we broke up for the summer vacation, it was usual to have a debate, to which the public were admitted. One year the subject was 'The relative merits of history, oratory, and poetry.' Magee spoke with such earnestness and eloquence that he was applauded to the echo. He seemed to me then, as he often seemed to me afterwards in the pulpit, or on the platform, to grow in stature, as he warmed and enlarged on the subject of the three Sisters. He was then barely thirteen years of age.

Another account confirmed Magee's bookish nature, remembering him:

generally reading French books (with which his father supplied him), especially Molière's comedies. To them he paid devoted attention, and on a wet day repeated hundreds of lines to me and others; always supporting the characters with as much individuality as a regular stage expert …

He was a great chess-player for so young a boy. One of the day boys used to bring a chess-board and men. This was left in Magee's desk until the play-hours and, if the weather was fine, the two boys adjourned to the lower seat in the dark walk, and fought out their battle without much interruption.[5]

The one great drawback in his school life was, there was no boy in the school who was capable of discussing general literature with him in a conversational manner. This want forced him in a great measure into solitary reading, and so left the majority of his school-fellows quite in the dark as to his great mental capacities.[6]

According to the same account, Magee was 'a favourite pupil' of Professor William Spalding, a famous Scottish elocutionist, 'who came over from Edinburgh six weeks before the summer vacation, to prepare us all for our great … exhibition on speech day, just before the holidays', and it was felt that Magee's 'great success as a public speaker arose in no small degree from the excellent tuition he received from this great master of elocution'.

The more academic boys like Magee benefited from Baillie's ability as a classics teacher, as testified by another past pupil, Nathaniel Alcock. Alcock dedicated his book on cholera to Baillie's successor, John Browne, 'a sincere and kind friend', but registered that he had 'imbibed' from Baillie 'any taste for the classics I possess … which I am not ashamed to say, I still cultivate'.[7]

Brunel's viaduct at
Goitre Coed,
Glamorgan, on
which Samuel
Downing worked

Arthur Gore Ryder, an enthusiastic classicist at Trinity College, where he won
the Berkeley Gold Medal,[8] was headmaster of Carrickmacross Grammar
School (1850-57) and of Tipperary Grammar School (1857-67). Samuel
Downing, having worked in England as a civil engineer with the famous
Isambard Kingdom Brunel, was Professor of Engineering at Trinity College
from 1852 to 1882. During those years 'some 400 students passed through the
school of engineering, many of them attaining eminent positions in the profession, a testament of his skill as a teacher'.[9]

Baillie's guidance was acknowledged by another of his clever pupils,
Henry William Mathew, who was the plaintiff in an extraordinary trial in
1851. (Mathew entered Kilkenny College in 1836 and left in 1842 at the age of
15. In his junior freshman year at Trinity College, he achieved two firsts.) In the
course of his evidence, Mathew spoke of his schooling: 'In the first year I
obtained the annual medal: I fell off in attention after that; Dr Baillie persuaded
me to read for sizarship, but when ready to enter I entered as a pensioner;
during the latter years of my stay at school I was not so attentive as I was at
first.'[10] As the issue of the trial was the validity of his confinement in a psychiatric hospital, it was vital for him to call witnesses who would testify to his
sanity, both as schoolboy and adult. Several of his contemporaries at
Kilkenny College were called, including Thomas D. Hargrave, who had
become a surgeon. His evidence was that Mathew was intelligent and normal.
At one time he and Mathew 'were left together when illness broke out among
the pupils; his conversation was that of a rational person; he was studious and
was distinguished for his ability; he was always head of his class; I recollect he

was fond of music, and used to devote the time other boys devoted to play to his books.'[11] It was such evidence that enabled Mathew to win his case.

George Bernard Shaw's uncle, Walter J. Gurly, was educated by Baillie. The famous writer told about his uncle's schooldays in much less complimentary terms. There was perhaps a degree of artistic licence but, if we are to believe him, we must conclude that Baillie was over-trusting of his boys:

> He had been educated at Kilkenny College, the Eton of Ireland; and when he was the smallest boy there, and the only one who could squeeze himself out under a certain gate, he was habitually sent by the older boys at night into the town to make assignations for them with prostitutes, his reward being whisky enough to make him insensibly drunk.

Shaw regretted this influence on his uncle's character, believing that 'if he had been cultivated artistically in his childhood he would have been a man of refined pleasures and might have done something in literature' rather than '"a gluttonous man and a winebibber", a scoffer and a rake, because no other pleasures had ever been revealed to him and denied to him'.[12]

After 22 years as headmaster, Baillie resigned in 1842, having being presented by Trinity College to the rectory of Clondevaddock, Co Donegal.[13] John Browne, believed to be from a humble background in Elphin, Co Roscommon, came to Kilkenny, having been successful as headmaster of a similar school in Bandon since 1826.[14] Having brought some pupils with him from Bandon, Browne advertised in the Cork press to attract further boys to Kilkenny. Listing the academic successes of his pupils, he 'confidently' hoped 'that these will be considered satisfactory proofs that sound principles of general knowledge and well-established habits of industry are successfully cultivated under his care'.[15] His marketing piece continued in similar vein:

> In every branch of education, none but the ablest masters shall be engaged; and … to obviate a complaint too often made against classical schools, there will be two masters, one an English gentleman of great ability and experience, the other a mathematician of the highest attainments. The domestic arrangements shall be such in every respect as will best secure the personal comfort and health of the pupils. The situation of the school-house is proverbial for its healthfulness: it is very beautiful and well adapted for study and retirement.

We know very little about Browne's administration until he was examined by the endowed schools commissioners in 1855. As the previous commission in the 1820s had been followed by the establishment of a national system of primary education, these were the first commissioners who could concentrate on secondary schools. Their inquiry was more thorough than before and they

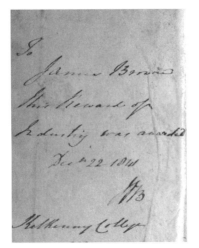

Inscription initialled
by the headmaster,
William Baillie, and
title page of a prize
book awarded to
James Browne, 1841

interviewed not only headmasters but also other officials and governors of
schools. They were not easily satisfied and prised open the lid on many a can
of worms in the endowed schools. Although the immediate response to the
commission report was disappointing, it ultimately paved the way for
government involvement in secondary education.

When Browne was questioned by the commissioners, he said that there
were between 60 and 70 pupils in Kilkenny College. Typically, they did not
accept this figure and, when pressed, he had to concede that the number was
closer to 40. His explanation for his vagueness was: 'There is always a good
many coming and going, some leaving for the university.'[16] Asked to expand,
he said that four boys entered Trinity in the previous July, taking 2nd, 4th,
7th and 10th places. Seeking to regain ground he continued: 'One got double
honours in classics and science in January. Five gentlemen who were pupils
of mine are junior fellows of the university. Three got professorships in succession … In England, at Woolwich and at the East India College, not one
of my pupils has ever been rejected.'

He also stated that he had a very small number of Roman Catholic pupils
from time to time and that he entrusted their religious education to a long-
serving Roman Catholic master, Denis McCarthy. McCarthy was described
as fourth master, after two other assistants.[17] Browne was certainly put on the
defensive, as can be seen from his remark: 'I do not find here the same desire
for classical education that I found in Cork. I consider that strange in this
large and wealthy community. I do not find that any of the gentry send their
sons to the learned professions.'

Under questioning, Browne conceded that the visitors did not visit. He waved this aside, on the basis that the Provost knew the success of the school from the honours attained by its former pupils in Trinity, while 'the bishop knows the working of the school perfectly. I see him often at his house'. Such an answer was not likely to impress the commissioners. Browne also stated that the building was 'in perfect repair' and that he had spent 'a great deal of money on it out of my private purse. Trinity College gave me £300 and gave me a claim on my successor for one third of the expenditure.' According to him, the school had been in a bad state of repair when he was appointed and he had spent £1,900 on a new roof, new slating and offices. The commissioner who compiled the report concluded that, given the length of time since they were written, the statutes were open to a certain degree of latitude but that 'total abandonment' could not be condoned. Their abandonment led to damning criticism from him:

> The statutes relating to the visitation of the school have been completely disregarded, no visitation having taken place for perhaps a century … An illustration of the wisdom of [Statute 21] and of one of the mischiefs it was intended to guard against, is furnished by the evidence of Dr Browne … who stated to me that upon his appointment he found the school house a mere wreck.
>
> I cannot imagine a more serious misprision of duty on the part of a public body than is involved in the neglect with which this school has been treated by the governors and visitors. The master has received no directions whatever as to the government of the school and has made acquaintance with the statutes simply a matter of curious research.

The commissioner's view of the education of the boys was less stern:

> I examined a class in … Euripides. The pupils translated the passage correctly; and making some allowance for the suddenness and surprise of the examination, I was satisfied with the knowledge of parsing shown by individuals, so far as syntax merely is concerned. They were, however, extremely deficient in the knowledge of derivations, comparative philology, or any thing implying a little reading. I examined a class in Horace but the history of the poet was completely unknown. The pupils of the Virgil class made several false quantities and had never learned prosody … and generally the pupils seemed to have learned nothing more than to construe and to parse. They are not exercised in English composition or general history … Their pronunciation of French was bad but I found no reason to complain of the translation and three or four pupils learning German answered rather satisfactorily. I was far better pleased with the result of my examination in Euclid and Algebra, both of which appeared to be well and radically understood; but altogether, the school did not strike me as equal to its resources, although I do not believe that on the part of the master there is any want

of zeal or ability, as far as there is room for their exercise in the course of education he has adopted for his pupils.[18]

The commission's painstaking investigation into the operation of the endowed schools revealed the urgency of reform but it was many years before the government acted. In the meantime, schools like Kilkenny College were left to their own devices. Despite the commission's unenthusiastic report, one historian maintained that 'the school flourished under [Browne's] management and seven of his pupils became fellows of Trinity College'.[19] Certainly, many did well in university and served the church with some distinction but they were not prominent figures like their predecessors in Kilkenny College.

Arthur Gore, who won a classical scholarship in Trinity in 1850, was awarded a senior moderatorship in mathematics and science in 1852 and a first class Divinity Testimonium in 1853. Ordained in 1855, he served in England, rising not to the highest ranks but to be Archdeacon of Macclesfield from 1884 to 1893 and canon residentiary of Chester Cathedral from then until his retirement in 1911. W. H. S. Monck was Professor of Moral Philosophy (1878-1882) in Trinity College and was a pioneering astronomer, making the first ever electrical measurement of starlight in 1892. George J. Watson was untypical of Kilkenny boys in that he became an outstanding amateur jockey and successful racehorse owner in Australia. Another boy who emigrated to Australia was Wellesley Bailey but he quickly moved on. Invited to India by his soldier brother, Christopher, he obtained work with the American Presbyterian Mission in 1869. So affected was he by the plight of leprosy sufferers that he founded what is now called the Leprosy Mission, a charity whose work is still vital in many countries. According to his biographer, Bailey did not have happy memories of school and remembered many years later 'the college suppers which consisted of bread and water seasoned with pepper and salt to disguise the inadequacy'. He 'admitted that he was a poor scholar and that school gave him no pleasure'. He was in Kilkenny College with his three brothers and they protected one another against the 'banter and ragging'. He did, however, recall that the two Swifte brothers 'came in for a lot of persecution from the other boys because their father showed an interest in the possibility of air travel'.[20] The boys may have been scornful but there was huge excitement for those who visited Swiftsheath in 1857 to see the aerial chariot, a flying machine designed by Lord Carlingford.[21] Gabriel Stokes had a distinguished career in India, serving as Chief Secretary of the Madras government (1898-1903). Appointed Governor of Madras in 1908, he was awarded a knighthood in the following year.

Left: George Watson
Right: Wellesley Bailey

At that time there must have been a music teacher of some sort, as a college band gave weekly performances for the entertainment of the public.[22] Browne's career at Kilkenny ended in 1864 with his appointment by the Marquis of Ormond to the parish of Carrick-on-Suir.[23] As there is no internal information, it is impossible to know how well the college was operating by the time of his retirement but the educational commission's report would suggest that decline had set in. The rest of the century saw a severe decline and a serious challenge to the future of the college.

CHAPTER SEVEN

Decline, 1864-1890

The records for the period from 1864, when John H. Martin was appointed headmaster, to 1890, when his successor, James M. Weir died, are very thin but it was clearly a time of almost unremitting decline. Martin, from New Ross, had been headmaster of the diocesan school in Sligo from 1862 to 1864 and might have been expected to build on the positive legacy of Baillie and Browne. On the contrary, by 1871 numbers had fallen to 37 and by 1887 there were no pupils at all.[1]

Two outbreaks of scarlet fever, one in 1873, the other in 1879, played a major role in this decline.[2] Scarlet fever, formerly called scarlatina, is a contagious disease caused by an infection of the throat with streptococcal bacteria. Today it is treatable with antibiotics but at that time it was very serious. The chief danger was that the patient would develop pneumonia or rheumatic fever, which could prove fatal. There was at least one death in the 1879 outbreak.[3] An epidemic might begin when a boy complained of a sore throat and a fever. The school authorities would hope against hope that he had only a bad cold but would be anxious next day if he vomited and had muscle aches and abdominal pain. A day later, if a rash appeared on his throat and chest, it was likely to be a case of scarlet fever. The school had to be closed at once and would inevitably remain closed for some time. It was doubtful how many of the boys would return. In Martin's case, the closure of the school in 1873 proved to be the end of his headmastership.[4] Weir's headship survived the outbreak of 1879 but numbers never recovered. There were, however, other causes of the decline, the chief of which was the lack of interest and supervision by the visitors. In addition, both headmasters suffered because they were responsible for repairs, while the value of the endowment had shrunk over the years until it was woefully inadequate. Although the 'dilapidations' system operated in some other schools, it was burdensome for a master who had such a small income to have to pay for repairs. Both Martin and Weir fought many battles with Trinity College over their liabilities but achieved no solution. These combined factors made the job unattractive and it is therefore surprising that Weir passed up a salary of £250 as classics master at Portora, for the dubious honour of becoming headmaster of Kilkenny College on a much smaller income.

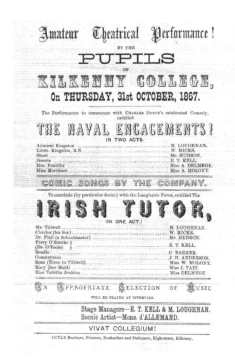

Notice of a theatrical performance, 1867

In Martin's early years, the situation looked promising. Even before he took over, Martin placed a positive advertisement in the press. As he was a classicist, he gave priority to teaching Greek, Hebrew and Latin for university entrance. With R. J. Macnamara, 'First Honorman in Science, TCD', and 'masters of high attainments' in 'mathematical studies', he promised that 'special attention will always be given to the preparation of pupils for the military colleges and for military and civil appointments generally.' He also committed himself to providing French for all and German at an extra charge 'when desired'. The premises were reported to be in good condition and the playground as 'well suited for cricket and other healthful and manly amusements'.[5] If sporting activity in the college is any indication of stability, all may have been stable in the early years. College teams played cricket matches, most frequently against the local army regiment but sometimes against Dublin teams. Home matches took place on the college lawn and it is probable that, with such small numbers in the college, masters were the backbone of the team.[6]

As has been seen, Martin's headmastership foundered with the outbreak of scarlet fever. When the college reopened with six or seven pupils in 1874, the new headmaster, James Weir, brought a number of pupils with him from the Limerick Collegiate Academy, the school which he had established at

School group, 1873
Back row L to R: Waring (sen.), —, Mr T. Ryan, —, Mr Ryan, Monsieur Gibori, Dr J. H.
Martin, Mr Frost, A. M. Archer, —, Mr Archer, R. Lett, R. Constable, H. Cooper.
Middle row: D. Doxey, H. J. Watters, Harpur, —, P. Acheson, —, J. A. James, D. Deane,
Whitcroft, C. L. S. Hungerford, P. Fitzgibbon, —.
Front row: —, H. Acheson, —, Waring (jun.), J. Harpur, B. Acheson, —, —, —, Whitcroft,
W. Bradshaw, W. Gorman, W. Stephens, W. H. Cooper

Pery Square.[7] A clergy son from the Dingle peninsula, and former Scholar of
Trinity College, Weir was the first lay headmaster of Kilkenny College.[8] By
1875 he had an experienced senior assistant in Frank A. Potterton, former
master of the Collegiate School, Newry, and the brother of an inspector of
education.[9] It is interesting that in the same year Weir was looking for a
native teacher from France or Germany to teach both languages 'convers-
ationally and theoretically'.[10] There was, however, no stability in his teaching
staff. Among the many teachers who stayed for a short time was a man who
would later become famous for his role in the revival of Gaelic games.
Michael Cusack had taught commercial subjects at Blackrock College in the
previous academic year, during which time he took an active interest in
schoolboy cricket. He taught in Kilkenny College from January to April 1876
but returned to Dublin on getting married.[11] Not only was Weir constantly
looking for teaching staff; it seems that he was open to a better appointment
for himself. A 'local news' item in *The Irish Times* in 1875 stated that he 'is a
candidate for the professorship of Greek and the vice-presidentship of the
Queen's College, Cork'.[12]

Within a few years there was serious concern at the state of the school.

The educational commission visited in October 1879 and found it 'in a melancholy state', although 'the house and gardens [were] there to testify that there was once a flourishing school'. In its report in 1881 it concluded that 'the present master is … unfit to raise a school' and 'the appointment of a good and young headmaster, with some connections, would probably raise it again to a condition of usefulness'.[13] In the interim the prospect of a damning report galvanised the visitors into action. Lord Arthur Butler and Professor J. P. Mahaffy inspected it and found only seven boys attending, the only assistant being Weir's undergraduate son. They identified necessary improvements to the building and the education, one of which was 'an assistant with a high reputation'. They thought Weir 'competent to instruct' but concluded 'the failure of the school is due … to the age and want of energy of the master, who seems to have taken the office rather as a place of retirement than for the purpose of working a great and honourable foundation.'[14]

In June 1880, the Provost wrote to the Bishop of Ossory, William Pakenham Walsh: 'I have come to the conclusion that nothing can be done to benefit the college unless either by removing the present headmaster or by obliging him to provide a qualified assistant.'[15] Weir defended himself doggedly, asserting that, when he took over, the school had been closed for nine months after the 1873 outbreak of scarlet fever and was 'in the condition of a dilapidated barrack, scarcely an unbroken window or door in the whole establishment'. He had multiple excuses for the fall in numbers, including the recent outbreak of scarlet fever, 'the mania for sending boys to England and to schools that can hold out the inducement of exhibitions and prizes', and interference by priests, leading to Roman Catholic boys being withdrawn. To cap it all, the parents of a boy who had died during the outbreak of scarlet fever had publicised his death and this created such alarm that only one boarder returned and no new boarders came.[16] Weir claimed that he had formerly employed graduate assistants 'of high standing' but that to engage assistants in the current situation 'would look like appointing officers without soldiers'.[17]

The visitors, despite their own findings and the commission report of 1881, did nothing more. While Kilkenny College was declining, the first tentative steps were being taken towards government involvement in secondary education and the reform of the endowed schools. Although the Intermediate Education Act[18] of 1878 did not herald a national policy for secondary education in Ireland, it created a board and an examination system which had a profound effect on schools. Government funding came through prizes to pupils and fees to schools, on the basis of results in the examinations held by

the Intermediate Board. The curriculum was modelled on the English grammar school system and so the emphasis was literary and academic. Latin, Greek
and English earned by far the most marks and, therefore, most generous fees,
while maths, history, geography and modern languages were less valued and
science came a poor third.

The system had certain negative effects, in that schools, knowing that
finances and reputation were dependent on success in the Intermediate
examinations, were inclined to devote all their efforts in that direction, to the
exclusion of a broader education. It also discouraged teachers from a more
stimulating approach and led them to concentrate on 'exam techniques', a
complaint which is still common today. Few teachers understood that pupils
should be taught to think for themselves and the Intermediate system made
that even less of a prospect, yet it should have been obvious that a child cannot become a scientist without learning to work out things for himself, nor,
as was then much desired, a classicist without developing an ability in prose
composition. The Intermediate Board did produce improvements over the years
in which it operated. By the beginning of the 20th century, it was fostering the
development of science teaching and was establishing the principle that fees
to a school should depend on factors additional to results. Before the First
World War it had managed to set up an inspectorate, in the hope of raising
standards but, by the time of Irish independence in 1921, the system was in
need of radical reform.

The Educational Endowments Act of 1885, in establishing a permanent
commission to reorganise endowments and draft new schemes of management,
marked the beginning of the reform of endowed schools.[19] The commission
began its work by investigating the state of schools under its remit. On 29
October 1887 the commissioners, with Lord Justice Fitzgibbon in the chair,
toured the Kilkenny schools, after which they held their inquiry. It established that the Provost and Bishop Walsh had visited the school in the previous December, had only found three pupils there and had reported to
Ormond on desirable developments. A subsequent visit by the bishop
showed that some of these improvements had been made but there were no
pupils.[20] When Fitzgibbon asked the reason for the fall in numbers, the bishop's
explanation was that when Weir was appointed, 'he was the only candidate,
because the endowment is very small; he had previously conducted a well-
known school and had turned out a tolerably large number of well-educated
pupils but now, on account of his advanced age … he is not able to give the
energy that is required for the work.' The commissioners spent some time

discussing ways of making the endowment more useful, until Fitzgibbon interjected: 'Bear in mind that there is actually no school at present.'[21]

While the Roman Catholic bishop, Dr Abraham Brownrigg, openly called Kilkenny College a failure and made a bid for a share of its endowment for local Roman Catholic pupils, all the other witnesses believed there was a need for it, if it were operating properly.[22] What emerged was that the school which David Creighton founded in 1880 in Parliament Street, at that time known as Kilkenny Civil Service Institute, was effectively fulfilling the role which Kilkenny College should have been performing.[23]

At interview, Weir adopted the same defence as in 1880. He reiterated his excuses for the failure of the school but was pulled up on his complaint about competition from other schools. As one of the commissioners pointed out, competition was nothing new and was not, therefore, a valid explanation. Further, Dr Thomas Hare, Dean of Ossory, stated that many of the boys who were sent away from Kilkenny to school did not go to England but to schools in Tipperary or Drogheda and, more damning still, that some of them had started in Kilkenny College but had been removed by their parents. While Weir made a bad impression, he scored some points in contradicting the bishop's evidence. One has to question the bishop's grasp of the facts: pressed as to Weir's age, Walsh had suggested that he was about 70, whereas he was 62. Weir, moreover, had not been the only candidate at the time of his appointment but had been selected through competition.[24] More seriously, the bishop was not aware that there was provision to dismiss a headmaster due to age or inefficiency, which shows that he had not read the statutes properly! It can fairly be said that, if all parties had followed the statutes, Kilkenny College would not have been in such a bad state.

The commission, believing that the way forward was for Kilkenny College to become a local school under local management, produced a scheme[25] for a new governing body, consisting of the Marquis of Ormond, three *ex-officio* governors (the Bishop and Dean of Ossory and the Provost) and five representative governors (one to be nominated by Ormond, a second by the Provost and senior fellows, three to be elected by the diocesan council). Under the 1885 Act, the inspector appointed by the Lord Lieutenant was to visit once a year at least. The governors, who were to meet at least twice yearly, were given general supervision and control, with power to determine what was taught and to appoint a headmaster qualified to give instruction in Intermediate subjects.[26] They were also made responsible for the mainten-ance of the buildings, a much-needed reform which was intended to relieve

View of
Kilkenny College

the headmaster of the dreaded dilapidations. Sadly the problem of headmasters paying for repairs continued. It may have played a part in the departure of the first headmaster under the new scheme and was a prominent feature of the downfall of the second.

There were detailed regulations for admissions. Ormond could nominate five day pupils free of charge[27] and the governors could nominate ten day pupils at half fees.[28] While Kilkenny College was not strictly a denominational school, both these categories of pupil were to be Protestant, local, needy, attending a school in the city or county, and of good character. In addition, the school was open to fee-paying pupils either as boarders or day pupils. It is interesting that, although the college was to continue for the moment as a school for boys, provision was made for female pupils to be admitted in the future. Despite Weir's continued protestations, the commissioners decided that he should be pensioned off. Weir, rather dismissively, said that 'the general opinion is that [Kilkenny College] will ultimately fall into the hands of the Roman Catholics'.[29] In any case, when the scheme came into operation, it did so under a new headmaster, T. Brian MacDermot.

It is no surprise that there were few distinguished past pupils from this period. One of them, Charles Burtchaell, had an illustrious career in the army. When, as major-general, he was appointed director general of medical services of the British forces in France in 1918, he credited his success in no small degree to his education in Kilkenny College. His brother, George, was an

Left: Thomas Westropp
Bennett (see pp 93-94)
Right: Daniel Wilson

important genealogist.[30] Another past pupil was Daniel Wilson, chancery, land registry, bankruptcy and land judge of the supreme court of Northern Ireland from 1921 to 1932.[31] Having served as an officer in the First World War, he was MP for West Down from 1918 to 1921, Solicitor General for Ireland from 1919 to 1921 and Recorder of Belfast from then until his death in 1932. Although he received his formative education elsewhere, as a young boy David Beatty was at Kilkenny before a highly distinguished career in the Royal Navy, serving as admiral from 1919 to 1927. William Micks was a highly-respected civil servant, most notably as secretary of the Congested Districts Board and chairman of the Viceregal Poor Law Reform Commission. J. W. Joynt was principal of Nelson College, a boys' school in New Zealand, from 1889 to 1898, and subsequently registrar of the national university.

Until the scheme produced by the commissioners under the Educational Endowments Act, it looked as if Kilkenny College was in terminal decline. It remained to be seen if the scheme provided the framework for a resurgence, the most basic question being its ability to attract pupils.

CHAPTER EIGHT

New schemes, 1890-1907

Not much is known about Kilkenny College under the succession of head-masters from 1890 to 1903 but it is clear that none of them established him-self firmly enough to make a major impact. The new scheme introduced by the educational endowment commissioners could only have worked under a dynamic headmaster, a man who could attract enough pupils to make the college viable for the foreseeable future. By 1901 the governors realised that their only hope was an amalgamation with the Pococke School.

In 1891 the first headmaster appointed by the newly-formed board of governors was Dr Brian MacDermot. A history teacher and joint author of a number of textbooks, he had been headmaster of the prestigious Portarlington School prior to his appointment to Kilkenny.[1] Like his predecessor, he was a layman. A few months later it was reported that the college, which had been 'reopened since October last' was 'showing signs of regaining its former position already'. The piece went on to claim that it was 'a most suitable institution for sons of the clergy going on for the clerical profession on account of the constant supervision exercised by ... clerical dignitaries'.[2]

Within a year MacDermot was advertising 'special attention' to foreign languages and 'a class for candidates for Woolwich and army literary examin-ations'.[3] In addition to a mathematical and English master, he had a 'foreign master', Bergmeister, who was a graduate of the University of Innsbruck and taught German as well as French. In June 1892 MacDermot reported to the governors that he had expended a large amount in restoring the college from 'a very dilapidated condition' but that they needed to overhaul the sanitary and sewage arrangements as a matter of 'extreme urgency'. The picture he paints, which was probably accurate, is horrific.

> The water closets are defective and have had to be quite closed up, the drains and pipes connecting them with the principal sewer are in a wretched condition and the principal sewer itself, which discharges into the millrace in times of high water, becomes flooded, with a result which is most dangerous to health, that the sewage becomes locked in and emits at times an offensive odour ... Should any outbreak of illness occur through defective sanitation, the result would be disas-trous to the prosperity of the college.[4]

Kilkenny city

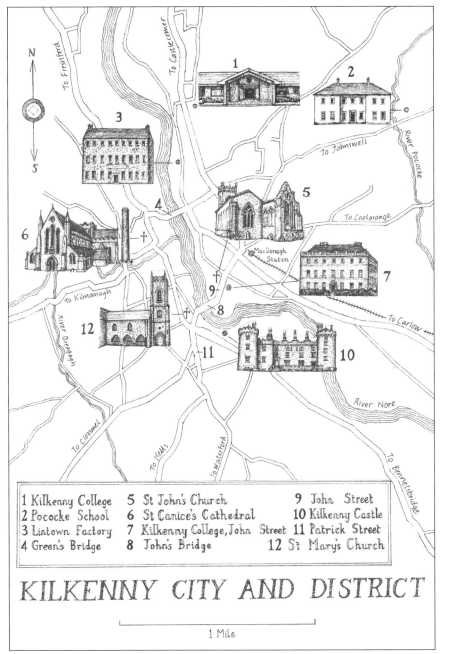

KILKENNY CITY AND DISTRICT

1 Kilkenny College	5 St John's Church	9 John Street
2 Pococke School	6 St Canice's Cathedral	10 Kilkenny Castle
3 Lintown Factory	7 Kilkenny College, John Street	11 Patrick Street
4 Green's Bridge	8 John's Bridge	12 St Mary's Church

1 Mile

The spectre of another period of closure, like those during the headships of Martin and Weir, faced the board. Until the advent of main drains and modern sanitation, all residential institutions struggled to avoid outbreaks of the life-threatening diseases caused by bad drains. The fear of diphtheria, typhus, typhoid fever and the like was ever present. In the case of Kilkenny College, not only the staff and pupils were at risk but the people of the city, who could be affected by sewage going into the Nore. It has not been possible to establish what remedial action, if any, was taken by the board.

In October 1893 MacDermot left suddenly and the parents were asked to remove their boys until a new headmaster was appointed. A piece was submitted to a local newspaper urging the board to keep the school open under an experienced member of staff but this was ignored.[5] Considering this cavalier attitude, it would not have been surprising if few returned in February 1894 under the Revd George W. Baile. He had been educated at Ranelagh School, Athlone, where his father, Robert, was headmaster. Having acted as an assistant master there in the early 1880s, he was ordained soon after graduating from Trinity College. Prior to his appointment to Kilkenny, he had been deputy secretary of the Sunday School Society. His interest in education and the reputation of his family may have been factors in his appointment but he was seriously lacking in experience.

We know little about his time as headmaster but the number of pupils grew quickly. He undertook improvements to the building in 1896, which he described as 'extensive alterations and additions to afford more accommodation'.[6] He advertised the college as preparing the boys 'for the universities, army and navy, the civil service, the banks, intermediate examinations, etc.' and offered as an enticement eight house scholarships, four of which were reserved for clergy sons.[7] He encouraged participation in sport and the local newspapers record matches in cricket and rugby as well as hockey, the college being one of the first schools in the country to take up the game, joining the Irish Hockey Union in 1894.[8]

In December 1898 the governors professed their 'entire satisfaction' with Baile.[9] Perhaps, however, the 'little fortune'[10] which he had spent on the premises proved his undoing, for a year later he was in serious financial trouble. He was declared bankrupt and, although the governors threatened dismissal, he was allowed to resign. It was embarrassing enough to the college that his name appeared frequently in the papers in relation to legal proceedings but worse was to come. The governors had to take him to court in 1901, as he would not give up possession of the college and the new headmaster and his assistant masters could not get in. He was then disputing his forced resignation and was counterclaiming for £1,500 'alleged to have been expended on the grounds and in repairing the college'. Although the governors pointed out that 'under his appointment there was no obligation imposed on the defendant to expend money on repairs,'[11] the whole business showed that the problem of dilapidations lingered under the new scheme. Baile went first to England, then, in 1903, he moved to Brazil, where he served as chaplain of the consulate at Pernambuco till 1917. He died in France in January 1918, serving as an army chaplain.

It was a difficult start for Thomas Pettipice, who took office as headmaster in January 1901 but could not operate the college until the law suit was settled. From Co. Sligo, he had been headmaster of the Blue Coat School, Drogheda, since 1896 and was previously headmaster of the cathedral school in Derry, where he was held in high regard.[12] He was an inspector of endowed schools and had written textbooks on geography and English grammar.

In 1901 there were 16 pupils of whom one was a girl and 13 were boarders.[13] Pettipice's prospectus of that year was carefully crafted to convince prospective parents that Kilkenny College could fulfil the educational needs of any pupil, aged nine and upwards, irrespective of ability. The scope of each of the four departments (preparatory, commercial and civil service, intermediate and university) was presented in the most positive terms. In the case of the preparatory department, for instance, there was implied assurance that juniors would be protected from bullying seniors.

> The preparatory department is intended for children under 11 years of age. These have a separate dormitory, a separate study and such modification of dietary as suits their tender years. The headmaster recommends that boys should enter this department as soon after the completion of their eighth year as possible. The high class elementary instruction imparted is of very great importance to the subsequent career of the boys.

Pettipice was obviously striving for early recruitment, knowing that, if pupils came before the age of 11, they would be likely to stay in the secondary school. His teaching staff consisted of a classical master, a mathematical master, a teacher of music and modern languages and an extern teacher for shorthand and typing. The intermediate department taught physics, chemistry and drawing and in 1902, in common with other schools, Kilkenny College sought funds for a laboratory, in order to fulfil the new requirements of the Intermediate Board. Pettipice expanded:

> The headmaster's varied experiences enable him to adapt the several college courses to the needs of all classes. The assistant masters are selected with due

regard to high qualifications as scholars, ability as teachers and general fitness for the training of the intellectual and moral faculties of children.

The greatest care is bestowed on those pupils who for various reasons do not intend to compete in any public examination. The system of cramming is discouraged; individuality of treatment is a feature; the permanent interests of each pupil are kept constantly in view, and the charge of any boy, who in the opinion of the headmaster, is not making satisfactory progress, will be at once resigned.

Pettipice was imaginative in introducing Gouin's method of language teaching.[14] Although Gouin is almost forgotten, much of his 'direct method' has been absorbed into modern teaching. Instead of the accepted 'grammar translation method', which was based on the traditional way of teaching the classics – drumming in grammatical rules and long lists of vocabulary, and translating into English – Gouin held that all classroom activity should be conducted in the target language, that everyday words and sentences should be taught first, with an emphasis on question and answer exchanges between teachers and on correct pronunciation. Grammar, if taught at all, should be taught inductively. The method suited small classes such as Kilkenny College had at the time. A report of a concert in April 1902 drew attention to the progress since it was introduced: 'The items given in French, consisting of songs, recitations, dialogues, etc., deserve special mention, and show the excellence of the Gouin system of teaching ... which was introduced in the college more than a year ago.'[15] It is not clear how long Kilkenny College continued to follow it.

From time to time Pettipice organised concerts in Kilkenny College, 'to demonstrate the progress of the pupils in elocution, music and other refined and refining studies connected with their school training.'[16] The programme included physical drill with arms by a group termed the College Volunteers. A piece in the *Kilkenny Moderator* of 3 January 1903 reads like a press release:

> The success of the school, as tested by public examination, has been highly creditable during the last two years. Boys and girls have gone forward to almost every department of the public service, and the records of the school show that there is not a single instance of failure since the appointment of the present headmaster. These results could only be secured in a school where individuality of treatment is a special feature, and where both the headmaster and his assistants possess high qualifications as scholars, and special aptitude for developing the intellectual and moral faculties of children.

While all of this reads well, it does not reflect the reality that Kilkenny could no longer support two secondary schools for boys.[17] From 1901 the Bishop

of Ossory played a pivotal role in negotia-
tions for the amalgamation of Kilkenny
College with the Pococke School, run under
the Incorporated Society. The amalgamation resulted in the closure of the Pococke
in the summer of 1903, after which its boys
transferred to Kilkenny College.[18] The college
became one of the foundation schools of the
Society and was governed by its central committee, the former board of governors being
downgraded to the status of the local committee. After this, entrants sat the Society
entrance examinations, which were held
throughout the country. The better national

D. A. Chart

schools took them seriously and prepared their pupils thoroughly. Entrants
to the Society's schools might be awarded full or partial scholarships (known
as foundation or assisted scholarships), depending on their results and on
financial circumstances. The college was reduced to a four-year cycle, after
which those boys who wanted to continue had to transfer, mostly to
Mountjoy School in Dublin. The chief aim of the more ambitious boys was
to win the Society senior scholarship, which would pave their way to
Mountjoy. There began a tendency for a boy to go to Kilkenny College and
his sister to Celbridge Collegiate, a trend which found its conclusion 70 years
later, when the two were merged.[19]

The amalgamation with the Pococke School was effected in the summer
of 1903 and most of the Pococke boys transferred to Kilkenny College in
September. Pettipice's services were no longer required and he was pensioned
off. He was ordained soon after leaving Kilkenny and served as a rector in Co.
Carlow from 1905 till his death in 1922. W. A. Shekleton, an Ulsterman who
since 1875 had been headmaster of Primrose Grange School, Sligo, was
appointed to the headmastership of Kilkenny College in June 1903. Aware of
the imminent closure of Primrose Grange, some boys came with Shekleton
and briefly formed a strong northwestern contingent in a very southeastern
school. Shekleton's background was firmly in the Incorporated Society: not
only had he been headmaster of one of the Society's provincial schools, he
had been educated at the Society's schools in Dundalk and Santry.
Remarkably he was the first and only headmaster of Kilkenny College not to
have a university degree – all but one of his predecessors had at least a master's degree.

Norman and Eleanor
Bor on a botanical
expedition in India

During Shekleton's headmastership, Kilkenny was included in the itinerary of a visit to Ireland by King Edward VII. One local newspaper reported:

Outside the entrance to St John's College in John Street, a stand was erected from which the students and several friends were enabled to have an excellent view of the royal procession. The entrance was magnificently decorated. Over the gate was a massive crown, and banners, streamers and bunting of all descriptions added to the effectiveness of the picture. On the right hand side was the motto in white on a red background 'God save the King and bless the Queen'.[20]

There is little information on the careers of past pupils of the 1890-1907 period. David Chart, having worked in the Public Records Office in Dublin, moved to Belfast after independence, where he was appointed head of the new records office for Northern Ireland in 1924, a post which he held for 24 years. An authority on Irish history, his works include *An Economic History of Ireland* and *A History of Northern Ireland*.[21] Norman Bor worked as a botanist in India for many years before becoming assistant director at the Royal Botanic Gardens in Kew.[22] John Hobson transferred from the Pococke School to Kilkenny College in 1901 and went on to Mountjoy School in 1902. He was later headmaster of the Collegiate School, Nenagh and of Cork Grammar School (1922-47).

Without the amalgamation with the Pococke, it is doubtful if Kilkenny College could have survived for long. The new arrangement offered a greater supply of entrants and access to better funding but Shekleton was not enough of an academic to restore the college to its former position in Irish education. His 'brief but successful career' in Kilkenny ended with his death in 1907 and he was succeeded by the Revd John Mason Harden, under whom, according to one noted authority, 'the school did much to revive its ancient fame'.[23]

CHAPTER NINE

A golden era, 1907-1917

From 1907 to 1917 Kilkenny College had two distinguished headmasters under whom its reputation soared. John Mason Harden was an academic in the best tradition of Kilkenny College. A double gold medallist of Trinity College, he read for an LL.B and LL.D. while headmaster at Kilkenny College, later took a doctorate of divinity and was elected a member of the Royal Irish Academy in 1923. An expert on Ethiopic Christian literature, his range of scholarship was extremely wide.[1] Before his appointment to Kilkenny he was principal of a theological college in Portugal. When he left Kilkenny in 1914, it was to become principal of the London College of Divinity. Headmaster of The King's Hospital from 1922 to 1927, he was elected Bishop of Tuam in 1927. Harden was a polymath, who knew at least nine languages. No matter how academic he was, the school could not fully 'revive its ancient fame', as the boys had to finish their school career in Mountjoy. Kilkenny's former fame rested on attracting boys from the best families in Ireland and preparing them for university in Dublin, Oxford or Cambridge, from which many went on to distinguish themselves in public life. The 20th century Kilkenny College was not in that league, even under such an illustrious headmaster as Harden. He was, however, a cultured, enlightened and inspiring influence in the school.

After the difficult years at the end of the 19th century, it was vitally important that Harden raised the profile of the school and gave the boys reasons to be proud of it. The annual prize giving, for instance, was a grand affair, with the large schoolroom decorated with flags and evergreens and the school colours draped behind the platform. The programme included numerous musical items, accompanied on the piano by Mrs Harden. In his speeches, Harden revealed a thorough grasp of developments in the educational field, realising, for instance, the importance of success in the new experimental science course. Under his guidance, Kilkenny College achieved very favourable reports from the Intermediate Board. His own teaching of Greek (which he reintroduced) and Latin won high praise, while the teaching of English, geography, history and general knowledge impressed. Excellent progress was reported in the new science course and in drawing, while maths was taught in a thought-stimulating fashion.

A mild-mannered man, he was unusual among his fellow headmasters in that he hated caning. Described by one of his pupils as:

> Not a man who inspired fear in his pupils, rather respect. He was not a great believer in the rod as a sovereign remedy for all juvenile offences as many pedagogues are. He was the only master I ever knew who could truly say on caning a boy that the infliction hurt himself more than the victim. When he caned a boy, which was a rare occurrence, it was far more painful for the victim to watch his agitation as he administered a 'slog' which wouldn't crack an egg, than to take the blow.[2]

This description of Harden was written by Mark Wilson, last Chief Justice of the supreme court of the Gold Coast before Ghanaian independence.[3] A memoir which he wrote in 1915 gives an unusually detailed picture of Kilkenny College. He vividly recalled his first night, in 1909, in a dormitory littered with trunks:

> I can well remember a big fellow named E. V. Twiss getting up on one of the trunks ... and declaring that he was a noble headset ... and possessed a sjambok-like instrument (which he here produced) specially made during the holidays to smarten up the grabbers. The excellent effect he was producing on us ... was almost destroyed by the owner of the box on which he was standing rushing in and pushing him off with undignified haste and violence.

There was a hierarchy, in which third year boys were 'headsets', who expected to be fagged by the first year 'grabbers'. In between were the 'secondsets', who were no longer fagged. The grabbers 'polished boots; fetched drinks; ran errands; "scouted" for cricket balls, rolled the crease, made beds in the morning, did in fact everything that the headsets were too lazy to do themselves'. As part of the fagging system, Wilson in his first term won a bogus reading competition, the prize being 'the great honour of reading *The Keys to the Classics*, of which the learned headsets availed themselves in their explorations of Virgil, Livy, Horace, etc.' At 7 a.m. he was expected to 'take up a perch on the end of some headset's bed in the big dormitory and for a solid half-hour recite' the translation. Another unpleasant job was 'worm fagging', grubbing up worms for headsets to use as bait when fishing in the Nore.

There were four ordeals which new boys had to endure. The first was the secondsets versus grabbers fight on 'the Bog' (school lawn), which invariably led to bloody noses, black eyes and torn shirts. The second was 'the telephone':

> In the upper lavatory (washroom) there were two parallel hollow tubes with a slight bend in the middle, which were used for towel rails. It was the custom to fill these with soapy water, the bend in the middle enabling the pipes to hold a good quantity. Then each unsuspecting grabber was in turn hauled in and ordered to speak through the 'telephone' to one of the old hands at the other end. After a few sentences had been exchanged and when either the ear or the mouth of the victim was pressed to the other end of the tube, the other fellow blew hard into his end, when the filthy water squirted forth over the face of the unfortunate grabber, who scrambled down to cleanse himself amid the hearty laughter of the unsympathetic bystanders.

The third ordeal was the grabbers' 'Christening', at which new boys were given a nickname:

> A basin of water was 'prepared', that is to say, a handful of salt was put into it, likewise some pepper and ginger and mustard. The whole was thickened by the addition of some soapsuds … Into this 'witch's soup' the grabber was 'helped' to put his face and head, while a previously selected nickname was bestowed on him by the 'clergyman'.

A nickname like 'Pudden' suggested that the boy was plump; 'Scaly' was used when he had a skin disease; a boy who got ink over his face might be called 'Smudger'; 'Foxy Nob' had a long nose; a boy who looked like a girl or was effeminate would be given a girl's name; one boy, who used to sing songs of dubious merit was nicknamed 'Bood the Lewd'! The fourth ordeal, to sing or recite in front of the pupils, could be seen as a harmless amusement but Wilson regarded it as the worst. Worse than any of this, some of the headsets amused themselves by sending a grabber to another headset with a message such as 'You're a dirty, scaly fool.' If the grabber refused to go, he would get 'belted' by his torturer and if he went to deliver the message, he would get belted by the recipient.

As a secondset, Wilson and another boy were in a dormitory where they fagged the four or five grabbers. That stopped when the headsets found out and three of them came and 'gave us a most unmerciful scragging'. The authorities had also heard of the goings-on and transferred Wilson and his mate to another dormitory, where a group of secondsets was lording it over the grabbers. A couple of days later

> there filed into the room the whole Company of Headsets, armed to the teeth with twisted towels, knotted ropes, canes and other schoolboy instruments of torture. They proceeded to hold a court martial on the offending three, who had dared to arrogate to themselves the privileges of their betters and, of course, the finding of the court was a foregone conclusion. Forthwith the three culprits were tied back-upwards on their beds and soundly flogged.

At the top of the hierarchy were the prefects. Usually three in number, they were chosen from the fourth-year boys and wore a silver Kilkenny College badge as a sign of office. They were expected to maintain discipline but were not allowed to administer corporal punishment, which was reserved exclusively to the headmaster. From the boys' point of view, their most important job was to ask for a holiday on all possible occasions. Prefects were allowed 'town-leave' every afternoon, while the other boys were never permitted to go out of the gates without special leave. Theory and practice did not accord, however, and boys might 'bunker' (break bounds) many times a day. Wilson admits to doing this constantly in his first two years but was caught by the staff on only one occasion.

The boys had a variety of amusements, ranging from the harmless to the dangerous and obnoxious. A great favourite was pillow-fighting, the only brake on their enthusiasm being the sixpence fine for a torn bolster. 'We didn't in the least mind them hitting our hands but when it came to hitting our pockets, that was a different story.' On autumn Sunday afternoon walks, many boys amused themselves by raiding private orchards for apples. Another pastime, acceptable in those days, was collecting birds' eggs. Wilson recalls that the well-wooded lawn and the river banks were 'a veritable paradise' for birds, many of which lost their eggs to schoolboy raids. The boys likewise persec-uted the bats which roosted in the stump of an old tree at the end of Swift's Walk. While some boys were proper line fishermen, others went in for eel-fishing.

> A pennyworth of hooks and a pennyworth of 'line' was all the apparatus needed to allow one to experience thrills such as are felt by the whale-fishers of the Northern Ocean. A wriggling and indignant worm was placed on the eel-hook and a weight, generally a leaden sinker pilfered from the lab, [was] attached to it to make it go to the bottom. Then the line was paid out till the bed of the Nore was reached and left there for several hours or overnight.

When an eel was caught and skinned, the skin was hung to dry on a tree, after which it was attached to the end of a whip for a whip-lash. The eel was handed into the kitchen to be cooked. Having the Nore so close to the school was a mixed blessing and Harden, himself an excellent swimmer, would not allow the boys to swim unless he was present. On the other hand, on Sunday afternoons in summer time, Wilson remembered 'we used to go up the river ... to the Bishop's Meadow and there disport ourselves to our heart's content in the "silvery Nore" but this came to the ears of our headmaster and the practice had to be discontinued'. The boys then sneaked off to bathe in the Pococke stream.

In winter the occasional snowstorm gave endless opportunities for sport and even Harden joined in the revelry. Wilson, a great admirer of Harden, recalls 'with what horror-stricken delight we watched our respected head come a cropper on the slide' during a snowy spell before Christmas 1909. It may well have been Harden who suggested paper chases on Saturday after-noons in the summer term. Among the approved pastimes were rugby and cricket. According to Wilson, the boys had to tog out for rugby practically every day but there was no proper coaching. The secondsets taught the rudi-ments of the game to the grabbers, while 'the masters paraded the field armed with their walking sticks, which they did not scruple to apply to the nether regions of such forwards as were not putting all their weight into the scrum, or to anyone who did not appear to be doing their best'.[4]

Like most long-established schools, Kilkenny College had its own slang, which in some cases overlapped with that of Mountjoy and in other respects was peculiar to Kilkenny. For instance, to work hard in Kilkenny was 'to stew', while in Mountjoy it was the familiar 'swot'. Dreadful to record, the Kilkenny boys called a girl 'a tart', while the Mountjoy boys called her 'a doll'. Among the obscure terms in Kilkenny was 'chaubles' for sweets and 'jot' for cake. The boys also had a repertoire of songs, including:

> Three weeks more, where shall we be?
> Outside the walls of old K.C.
> No more Latin, no more French,
> No more sitting on a hard old bench,
> No more tea in dirty mugs,
> No more cabbage full of slugs.

The end of the Christmas term in 1910 was marred by the death of a boy from an epileptic fit. 'Awful gloom and depression … fell on the school … At 6.30 a.m. on the day of the funeral – a cold, raw December morning– we filed past the coffin, laid on trestles in the school hall and afterwards marched two deep after the hearse.'

Considering that Wilson was only 18 when he wrote this memoir, it is clear that he was no ordinary schoolboy. Although Harden's boys had to finish their schooling in Mountjoy, he was a major influence on them and deserves some of the credit for their later success. Several of Harden's pupils later became headmasters. Edward B. Coursey distinguished himself in the First World War, being awarded both the Military Cross and the Belgian *Croix de Guerre*. A brilliant teacher of maths, he later joined Harden on the staff at The King's Hospital. He returned to teach at Kilkenny College and was given the role of senior resident master. In 1932, having coached the cup-winning hockey team, he was appointed headmaster of Galway Grammar School and continued in that post till 1948. J. J. Butler was also a long-serving principal. Appointed headmaster of St Patrick's Cathedral Grammar School, Dublin in 1919, he succeeded Harden as headmaster of The King's Hospital in 1928, where he remained at the helm until his retirement in 1961. Another of Harden's pupils, A. A. Hanbidge, reopened Dundalk Grammar School, which had closed in 1916, and was headmaster from 1921 to 1951.[5]

Two past pupils, graduates of the Royal Military Academy at Woolwich and veterans of both World Wars, were Major-General Desmond Harrison and Major-General Sir Harold Williams. Harrison, who also had a degree from Cambridge, served with the Royal Engineers, was engineer-in-chief with the Southeast Asia Command from 1943 to 1946 and director of fortification and works at the War Office in London from 1946 until he retired in 1947. Williams was chief engineer in the Indian Army from 1948 to 1954 and settled in India, where he was a pioneer of mountaineering and a noted orni-

Arnold Schwarzenegger, John G. Frayne, Joan Collins at the Academy Awards, 1983

thologist.[6] John Frayne distinguished himself in the field of electronics, specifically in sound recording. He was best known for his pioneering work in the development of the stereo LP record and in motion picture sound. He was also co-author of the first significant handbook on the art and science of recording.[7]

If a criticism can be made of Harden, it is that he trusted the boys too much and was often unaware of what they got up to. Clearly he had no idea that they broke bounds and risked their lives in dangerous pursuits, nor that there was a lot of bullying. As one who hated corporal punishment, he did not permit it to the prefects and came down hard on fagging whenever he found any incident of it. He would have been horrified if he had known about the ordeals. Given his academic interests, it was inevitable that Harden would not stay long in Kilkenny College. His departure was much lamented and he was remembered with great affection by staff and pupils alike, something which can rarely be said of headmasters of the time.[8] In 1927, upon his election as bishop, past pupils and officials of Kilkenny College presented him with his episcopal ring. Appropriately, a former pupil, the Revd Robert Watson, the then diocesan inspector of the Board of Education, made the presentation. He gave an account of life in Kilkenny College before and after

Harden's appointment and of the change brought about by his kindness and consideration for his pupils.

The Revd E. G. Seale was a headmaster in the same mould as Harden and profited from his predecessor's cultivation of an academic atmosphere. He had been headmaster of Cork Grammar School from 1908 to 1914 and had previously taught at Highgate School, London, and Wesley College, Dublin, where he had been educated. He was a gifted classics teacher, under whom boys reached a high standard in examinations. The inspired appointment of a distinguished successor to Harden bore fruit for, as Seale reported in 1917, the number of boarders rose to 80, 'an upward leap of thirty since the war began'.[9] In 1917, his last year at Kilkenny College, 95 per cent of the boys who sat the Intermediate Board examinations passed, compared to a national average of 61.4 per cent. Two first class exhibitions were awarded and six second class exhibitions; a medal in arithmetic and algebra and a special prize in Latin composition (for second place in Ireland); nine first class prizes and eight second class prizes. Notably, the boys achieved across the science, mathematical, classical and modern literary groups, one of them, R. M. Young, taking first class exhibitions in science and maths and the aforementioned medal.[10] This is creditable for such a small school and, according to the presentation speech at Seale's departure, constituted 'a record number of intermediate successes'.[11]

It is hard to reconcile this rosy picture with the view of E. R. Dodds, who was resident classics master in Seale's last term. Dodds thought that his colleagues had 'small interest in their work or in anything else and their morale was correspondingly low.'[12] It has to be borne in mind that Dodds had been expelled from Campbell College, Belfast, for 'gross, studied and sustained insolence to the headmaster'.[13] Perhaps, as he had just graduated from Oxford and was on his way to becoming a distinguished classicist,[14] he felt himself superior to anything in Kilkenny. 'The little town offered only two amusements. One could hire a boat on the River Nore and troll for pike (usually in vain). And there were two obliging – up to a point – girls whom one could escort to the local cinema and cuddle; we took turns at this exercise. Otherwise we sat about and talked of the shortage of jobs.' By his own admission, he did not cover himself in glory, for, one night, when he was on duty, he went into a noisy dormitory, only to see 'the leading trouble-maker' disappear under a bed. 'I lost my temper completely, dragged him out by the hair and administered a couple of really hearty cuffs. For this unauthorised assault I should no doubt have been sacked from any respectable English grammar school.' At the end of the term Dodds left to become sixth-form master at The High School in Dublin

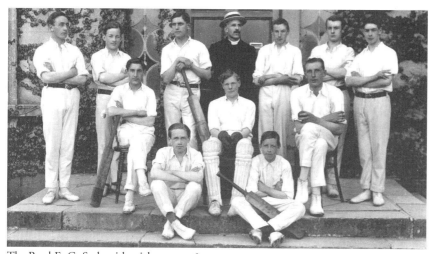

The Revd E. G. Seale with cricket XI, 1916
Back row, L to R: W. Smyth, J. N. Davin, G. C. Bryan, The Revd E. G. Seale, T .H. Porter, A.S. Troughton, A. G. Warren
Middle row: W. B. J. Sproule, W. O'Neill, Mr T. H. Blackburn
Front row: R. M. Young, C. J. Little

Seale's time as headmaster was overshadowed by the First World War. Many past pupils served, some of whom had relations in the school. The boys followed events as closely as they could and sang the war songs such as 'Pack up your troubles'. The newly-launched school magazine recorded the names of past pupils serving with the forces. Among them was Lieutenant John W. Salter, from Skibbereen. In July 1916 his parents received official notification of his death in action. A month later, however, the postman delivered an unthinkable surprise – a cheerful letter from John in a prisoner-of-war camp.[15] Such were the fluctuating emotions of many Kilkenny College families during the war and for some the experience was one of unrelieved tragedy, ending with the death or devastating disability of a son.[16]

Seale's stay in Kilkenny College was short, for in 1917 he was appointed headmaster of Portora Royal School, Enniskillen. Described by one of his Portoran past pupils as a 'headmaster of the real old sort, a clergyman, a classicist, a disciplinarian, but first and foremost a gentleman', the growth of Portora in the next two decades was due to his leadership and it can be assumed that Kilkenny College would likewise have prospered under his headship, had he not moved. There is no known extant description of Seale by a Kilkenny College boy, so we must rely on the same Portoran.

He was … a remarkably handsome and dignified-looking man. Yet he had a list of disabilities which should have made him a mere figure of fun. He had a club foot, his right arm was partially paralysed, there was a nervous twitch in his cheek

– particularly when he was angry – and he had a peculiar, almost barking voice. All of these infirmities we imitated when his back was turned but we feared and respected his presence and, when he was angry and stamped his foot and called us 'cads', it was like Jehovah thundering from the top of Mount Sinai. The soul of honour himself, he expected an almost impossible standard of honour from us …[17]

Seale's departure ended the best period in Kilkenny College's history since Baillie left in 1842. Harden and Seale were headmasters in the classical tradition and could have filled a similar position in a good English public school. One can only wonder if either of them could have maintained numbers and academic success in the face of the enormous difficulties of the 1920s and 1930s.

CHAPTER TEN

A new state, 1917-1952

The board which had chosen Harden and Seale to raise the profile of Kilkenny College made a very different appointment in 1917. Perhaps, due to the war, the governors found it impossible to find a successor in the same mould. It was a radical departure to appoint a young teacher in the college, a scientist rather than a classicist.[1] C. G. Shankey had been educated in the Incorporated Society schools of Dundalk and Mountjoy and had taken engineering degrees at the Royal University and Trinity College.

At his final prize day Seale had singled out Shankey, 'whose zeal, teaching capacity and force of character have for years been devoted to the best interests of the school.'[2] Perhaps it was a mixture of ambition and good connections (he was married to a daughter of the Provost, W. E. Thrift, a governor of the Incorporated Society) which led Shankey to write to the Bishop of Ossory, J. A. F. Gregg, to inform him that he was going to apply for the job. The bishop invited him to the palace to discuss it and, according to Shankey, 'promised no support; he must see the other candidates first … I learned later that he did …support me when the time came to make the appointment.'[3]

Shankey suffered an initial blow when eight boys followed Seale to Portora. He also had to cope with the difficulties caused first by the First World War, then by the War of Independence and by the foundation of the new state. Just one of the problems was that the Black and Tans took over the ball alley and dug a pit in the floor, where they serviced their lorries. Far more serious was the uncertainty and sense of isolation which pervaded not only Kilkenny College but all the Protestant schools and the entire Church of Ireland. While fears were eased by the stability of the first Irish administration, developments under the Fianna Fáil government of the 1930s, particularly the recognition in the 1937 Constitution of the special position of the Roman Catholic Church, led to greater anxiety. It was hard for Protestants to avoid associating the new state with Roman Catholicism, hard to establish that one could be Protestant *and* Irish, hard to be confident about the future. In consequence, Protestants tended to keep to themselves and be inward-looking.

One notable exception to this trend was Thomas Westropp Bennett, a

pupil of the 1880s. He was untypical of the Protestant gentry, for he became
a Roman Catholic and was active in nationalist politics at national and local
level before the First World War. His work with Horace Plunkett on the
board of the Irish Agricultural Organisation Society may have helped him be
elected for Cumann na nGaedhael to the first senate in 1922. He was
Cathaoirleach of Seanad Éireann from 1928 until its final sitting in 1936 and
strenuously resisted the campaign to abolish that body. In the 1930s he
chaired the first talks which led to the founding of Fine Gael. He was indeed
a rare product of Kilkenny College.[4]

Even before the First World War, Protestant schools were suffering serious
difficulties due to shrinking endowments and decreasing numbers. Numbers
had been falling for half a century but fell further in the twenties and thirties. First, there was the loss of potential pupils, due to the large number of
young men who perished in the war and who did not, therefore, have children. (This did not, of course, apply only to the Protestant population but,
because it was so much smaller in the first place, the effect was greater.)
Secondly, political events between 1916 and 1922 led a substantial number of
Protestants to emigrate, especially from country areas. While the Irish population suffered a decline between 1911 and 1936, the Protestant decline was
massive: from almost 250,000 to just over 145,000.

With Irish independence came a new Department of Education, which
centralised responsibility for both primary and secondary education.[5] One of
the main objectives was to increase the numbers going on to secondary
school. Rightly, there was concern that so many children had only a primary
education, the main reason being that most secondary schools were fee-paying and that parents could not afford the fees. The Intermediate Education
Act of 1921 took the first steps to establish local government scholarships,
which helped the gifted few but made little impact on the problem. Few
Protestant pupils tried for these scholarships, perhaps because of the lack of
identity with national and local politics. While Protestant parents faced further
financial pressure due to the fact that the population was scattered and most
pupils therefore had to board, there were various ways of financing pupils
within the Protestant schools. These ranged from scholarships to
Incorporated Society schools, which were awarded on the basis of academic
ability and financial circumstances, to an almost free education in The King's
Hospital, where boys were admitted on the basis of financial need.

From 1924 the Department introduced what purported to be a 'complete
reform of the secondary programme' but which in reality was far less than
that.[6] One area of reform was in financial assistance to secondary schools.

Payment by results was replaced by a capitation fee for each 'recognised' pupil, recognition being obtained by satisfying the entrance requirements of the school or by the new Primary School Certificate. The Department paid the major part of teachers' salaries and insisted that schools which received grants should employ a number of 'registered' teachers proportionate to the number of pupils on the roll. Before registering, a teacher had to take a degree from a recognised university, complete a year of teaching satisfactorily and pass an oral examination in Irish. The overall effect of this reform was very good: it provided a vital source of funding for schools and ensured that teachers achieved a higher level of qualification than had generally been the case.

Leaving and Intermediate Certificate examinations replaced those of the Intermediate Board. The curriculum had to include Irish, English, maths, history and geography, another language or science or commerce or (for girls) domestic science. Apart from making Irish compulsory,[7] the emphasis changed little from that of the Intermediate Board, in that it was still literary. The cost of providing facilities for science and the shortage of science and modern language teachers who could also pass the Irish oral worked against the development of these subjects.[8] Many schools, moreover, preferred to keep to the old, familiar subjects such as Latin.

The Department set the syllabi, conducted the examinations and had power to inspect the schools. It was thus able to influence the development of the secondary programmes but direct control of each school, including the appointment of teachers, remained with its governing body. While the new system was better than the old, it certainly was not 'a complete reform'. Over the years, the Department began to give grants to develop the teaching of subjects such as science and music but it was not until the 1960s that a radical rethink of secondary education took place.

The most obvious effect in a school like Kilkenny College was in the degree of financial security and in freedom from payment by results. Kilkenny already had graduate senior teachers, so teacher registration impacted less on the standard of teaching than in the average school, where many teachers had a shocking lack of training. On the other hand, Shankey found it hard to keep good masters, as many were promoted to senior jobs or head-masterships in other schools.[9] One of the problem areas was Irish, for very few Protestants were qualified to teach it. William Condell (Liam Ó Conaill) was in sole charge of Irish teaching in Kilkenny College for five years before his appointment in 1928 as vice-principal of Coláiste Móibhí, the Church of Ireland preparatory teacher training college. While teaching, he studied for a

Sports day, late 1920s

degree from Trinity, which he was awarded in 1927. Condell's preferred sub-ject was mathematics but it seems that, like many teachers in Protestant schools in the 1920s, he was 'persuaded' to teach Irish. His success must have been limited because, on his appointment to Coláiste Móibhí, the Department of Education observed that he could do no more than hold a simple conversation in Irish and would need an intensive course in the Gaeltacht.[10] Condell's case illustrates the difficulties which a school like Kilkenny College encountered under the new Department in the 1920s.

For most of his time as headmaster, Shankey had to make do with five or six full-time teachers, a few part-timers and two or three unqualified junior masters. Foremost among the senior masters were Dick Hendy and Francis Lipsett, both of whom spent virtually their entire career in Kilkenny College. At its height there were 75 to 80 boarders and a few day boys, some of whom were juniors entering at the age of eight or nine into second form. This preparatory school was run by the gentle Mrs Enid Shankey. It was opened in 1936 in response to the closure of the only Protestant preparatory school in Kilkenny.[11] Most boys started in third form, aged about 12, while the Intermediate Certificate year was called sixth form. In the early years, as Edgar Roe remembers, 'We had to go to the convent as the examination centre, where the supervising nun referred to the "young gentlemen from the college". As we went in and out, there was a nun standing at every door of the corridor to make sure we didn't stray!'[12] Later the boys sat the examinations in St Kieran's College. There seems to have been no contact with other Kilkenny schools, even on the sporting field, because St Kieran's College played Gaelic games. A few boys, who did not go on to Mountjoy, returned for a fifth year in order to prepare for the Trinity entrance examination. For some years there was a small number of girls, Deirdre Shankey and her friends being educated in the same classroom as the boys. Shankey bravely allowed the girls to play hockey with the boys. Maeve Shankey was also a pupil and, as Maeve Kyle, enjoyed many years of sporting success both as a hockey international, gaining 58 caps, and an Olympic athlete in Melbourne, Rome and Tokyo.

Shankey taught almost full-time and managed every aspect of the school. He was a committed and effective science teacher, many of whose pupils later became distinguished scientists and engineers. One of his early protégés was Edward Duthie, who worked in the Nobel prize-winning research team of Sir Howard Florey in the development of penicillin. Another past pupil involved in the development of medicine was Dermot Taylor, Professor of Pharmacology at UCLA, and an expert in the medicinal qualities of plants. Shankey was not among those principals who resented the Department's attempts to raise the position of science; he placed the subject 'in the front rank of humanistic studies'. On the other hand, he believed that 'much of the work in the laboratory could be done more effectively at the demonstration bench than by the boys themselves.'[13] Inside and outside the classroom, he was an awe-inspiring figure, strict and quick-tempered. While many, like Roe, had great respect for him, regarding him as 'very strict and fair and a good teacher', others were afraid of him.

Shankey occasionally held public canings in the big schoolroom, when the pupils assembled in silent witness. There was nothing unusual about this in schools of the time, for there were many fearsome headmasters in other Irish schools. Shocking as it seems, one must not judge caning by 21st century standards. Corporal punishment was part of the prevailing culture and many schoolboys of the time admit that, if they had complained to their father, they might have received another beating for getting into trouble. It is, on the other hand, not surprising that masters used corporal punishment liberally and the boys continued to indulge in rough practices. W. M. Abernethy (1923-29) recalls that 'the most distressing example of corporal punishment during [his time at the college] was when the whole school had to witness the public caning of three boys caught smoking'. Yet he felt that Shankey 'in all fairness … did not use [the cane] a lot' but remembered that many masters were heavy-handed in administering punishment.[14] Al Williams remembers that Shankey did not hold scores against his pupils: 'If you committed a crime, he punished you and, two minutes later, forgot it for ever.'[15]

'The Rt Revd the Lord Bishop Rafter' and ceremonial assistants at the Grabbers' Christening, 1929

Fagging was still the order of the day and, as Victor Griffin recalls, 'There were some ferocious prefects and other seniors, who took a sadistic delight in using the hockey stick'.[16] 'The Christening', formalised so that the head prefect dressed up as pope or archbishop, was in Roe's words 'awesome', in Griffin's 'cruel'. Some boys were deeply upset, while others cherished photographs of the occasion. It is clear that the headmaster and staff turned a blind eye to such activities but the Christening was eventually stopped, when parents complained. Such initiation ceremonies, common in boys' schools, would not be tolerated today. There was, of course a positive aspect of fagging, in that a senior boy often looked after the junior who fagged for him. Al Williams, for instance, happily remembers fagging in his first year for Jack Stanley as the basis of a good friendship.

For all that Shankey could be severe, there was a jovial and relaxed side. For many years he and his wife invited a few first-year boys to tea on Sunday afternoons until they had all been entertained. With his blessing, Mrs Shankey ran a stamp club in their drawing room. Al Williams recalls that 'on summer afternoons he and Mrs Shankey would sit outside, watching the boys play tennis and we would go up and talk to him.' On those occasions the boys saw an affable headmaster and, after they had left school, they found him friendly. As George Benn recalls, Shankey 'welcomed any old boy with open arms.'[17]

As to routine, Roe remembers:

Food was a bit scarce. Breakfast was porridge and plain bread, marg and tea. The elite (prefects) sat at the end of the tables and took a lot of the porridge for themselves, so juniors only got a little daub. It was the same at tea but you could bring your own jam. We were given jam at Sunday tea. In my time there was a change to Tuesday tea, with the introduction of 'tart' (a large piece of pastry). At dinner the masters were at the tables and gave you a proper helping. I was always hungry, so were most of us, but you were lucky if you had tuck in your box. We got parcels from home – bread and curranty cake. For supper, in the break in prep, we got cold milk in summer and cocoa in winter.

Not only were the boys always hungry: in winter they were also cold. During the war years, with severe rationing and a shortage of fuel, conditions were even worse, yet living conditions in school were far better than in many a home. In their spare time the boys might gather round the fire in the big schoolroom but the hierarchy still prevailed and first years had to keep to the lower half. Their formal dress did not help for, as Roe recalls, it did nothing to keep a boy warm:

> As juniors we had to wear Eton suits all day on Sundays. We called them 'bum freezers', because they had no bottom on the jacket. The collars would get a hard time while we were playing on Sunday afternoons and would be inspected by the master on duty after tea. You would be fined if the collar was dirty or bent. When you were about 14, you graduated to an ordinary suit.

Apart from any considerations of warmth, this garb made the boys stand out in the city. Perhaps that was what the school authorities wanted but Griffin suggests that it was a 'crazy' custom, which 'should have long been stopped'. Many boys hated the Eton collar and mortar board; hated being teased for wearing them and were glad to throw the mortar board into the Nore on their last day in school. For other boys, the Eton collar and mortar board offered a corporate identity and the jettisoning into the river represented a rite of passage. These relics were eventually abandoned after Shankey had left.

Epidemics were still a constant threat but in 1928 the governors bought a house opposite the college, part of which was used as an isolation infirmary. Despite using this and another 'sick bay', an outbreak of measles in 1931 spread and one boy died.[18] Until the advent of penicillin, there was always a real possibility that an epidemic would result in the death of one or more boys.

As to games, Mark Wilson had implied that rugby and cricket were played on the Bog in pre-war days.[19] By Roe's time, although many drainage efforts had been made and part of it was laid out as a hockey pitch, it was deemed too wet for use in winter. The actual playing field, to which the boys walked, was over two kilometres away, in Archer's Field on the road to

C. G. Shankey with rugby 1st xv, 1928-29
Back row L to R: W. L. Corrigan, W.M. Abernethy, J. A. Finnegan, P. H. Giles,
Mr C. G. Shankey, C. R. M. Macken, G. A. Sothern, C. P. Nicholls, —
Middle row: H. D. Meredith, C. H. E. Chamney, E. C. Ridgeway, H. T. Deacon,
H. M. Young
Front row: F. T. Baker, W. J. Daniels, J. W. Rafter

Bennetsbridge. There was one rugby pitch, one hockey pitch and a little corrugated tin hut to change in. Opposition was limited and the boys often travelled to Waterford for matches against Bishop Foy's, Newtown and Waterpark College. If the match was in Dublin, they would travel by train and have 'a great day out'.[20] As Kilkenny College always had small numbers, the rugby teams were usually beaten in the first round of the cup. It was, therefore, remarkable that two pupils went on to play for their country, Ernest Ridgeway, gaining five caps between 1931 and 1935, and Robert Agar, playing ten times, including one match in the grand slam season of 1948. The hockey teams did much better and occasionally won Leinster cups. Past pupils still recall the excitement in 1932 when, in only the second season of competing, the juniors, coached by Coursey, brought the cup to Kilkenny after defeating the holders, Avoca School 2-1.[21] Further success at junior level under Hendy led to a young team achieving a sensational senior cup victory in 1936 with all three goals in the drawn final and replay scored by N. H. P. Bovenizer.[22] It must also be remembered that numerous Kilkenny boys, such as S. W. Earle, E. J. Furlong and J. T. Sleator, played on senior cup-winning

J.C.T. hockey team, 1933-34
Back row L to R: Mr R. Hendy, J. H. Barry, R. H. Johnston, Mr C. G. Shankey,
E. D. Murdock, A. G. Wallace, S. McCullough, R. J. Rainsbury
Front row: S. A. Barry, D. V. Hutchinson, V. W. Rafter (capt), N. H. P. Bovenizer,
E. R. Huggard

teams for Mountjoy. An indicator of the standard of hockey was that a pupil
of the early 1940s, Edwin Hilton, later played for Ireland, winning three caps.
Handball was played in the ball alley, which was also used for drill in bad
weather. It was later turned into the Berkeley Memorial Hall. One of the
most enjoyable activities of Roe's time in Kilkenny College was scouting,
started by Brian Osborne, a junior master. Osborne was keen on theatre, so
the scouts put on shows in Lewis's yard, in the grandly-named 'Star Theatre'.
Although Kilkenny College was not renowned for cultural activities, a tradition developed of each class putting on a small play each year.

Many former pupils served in the Second World War. The Kilkenny
College diaspora provided soldiers, airmen and sailors for forces not only
from Britain but from numerous other countries around the English-speak-
ing world. At least a dozen past pupils were killed. A number of those who
survived had their career paths heavily influenced by the war and pursued
distinguished careers in the forces. James Wallace joined the Royal Air Force
in 1938 and was awarded a Distinguished Service Order during the war. As
air commodore, he held the third highest rank in the force and went on to
appointments as Deputy Captain of the Queen's Flight in 1960 and director
of public relations for the RAF (1964-67).

Scouts on the river bank at Maidenhall, Bennetsbridge, 1930s
L to R: E. W. Roe, A. H. Bruce, E. J. Doherty, I. Carter, T. J. Collier

Educationally and materially, little had changed by Shankey's later years, although fagging was diluted. Most pupils of the forties and early fifties, like their predecessors, enjoyed games and enlivened their daily life by such activities as eel-fishing in the Nore. Any change of routine or any treat was greatly welcomed. Food, or the scarcity of it was always on their minds, so one of the highlights of the year was the 'Old Boys' Scoff' at Halloween, when the boys sat down to a four-course dinner at the expense of their predecessors.

Most boys came from homes where money was in short supply and the better motivated made the best of the opportunities afforded by their education in Kilkenny College. The most striking case is of Ken Stanley, the fourth of eight children, who came first in Ireland in the Incorporated Society examination and was awarded a foundation scholarship. Aged 12, he was aware that even a foundation scholarship did not cover the full fees, so, on being told of the county council scholarship scheme, he decided to sit the examination during his first year. With help from Ian King, a junior master, he won a scholarship. Initially it was granted at the lower rate for those who lived within three miles of the nearest secondary school but Stanley, on his own initiative, wrote to Carlow County Council to put the case that he qualified for the higher rate, as there was no suitable school within three miles of

his home. Having won his point, his parents had to pay no more fees for his secondary education.

Shankey, who was highly respected in the community, mellowed in later years. For all the difficulties he faced, he turned out a number of boys who distinguished themselves in later life. Among these were Victor Griffin, Dean of St Patrick's Cathedral, Dublin (1969-91) and a leading liberal voice in the Church of Ireland, R. R. Hartford, Regius Professor of Divinity at Trinity College, Dublin (1957-62)[23] and E. J. J. Furlong, Professor of Philosophy and a Fellow of Trinity (1954-83). John A. Storey was an innovative headmaster of Masonic Boys' School (1944-61), succeeding an earlier past pupil, John Strettan.[24] Later another two of Shankey's pupils became headmasters themselves and well understood the inherent difficulties: Bill Tector of Sandford Park School (1985-89) and Al Williams of Bandon Grammar School (1972-93). Two pupils were noted bankers with the Bank of Ireland: George Notley became general manager and Jack Stanley was manager of the foreign and corporate division, later general manager and director, Northern Ireland.[25] Arthur H. Elliott was Commissioner of Inland Revenue in Northern Ireland. Hewitt Wilson was the most senior chaplain in the Royal Air Force from 1973 to 1980.

Shankey retired in 1953 and took up the post of secretary of the Incorporated Society. From a staff viewpoint, Ian King regards Shankey as 'an excellent headmaster'. One of the things which impressed him most was that Shankey was very supportive of the staff and fair in dealing with conflict, whether between members of staff, staff and pupils, or between pupils.[26] Norman Ruddock, whose appreciation of Shankey appeared in *The Irish Times*, wrote of 'a brilliant teacher and educationalist ... Few will forget his

Victor Griffin with President Mary Robinson, Dr Nicholas Robinson and Canon Gerald Magahy at St Patrick's Cathedral, Dublin, 17 March 1991

Hewitt Wilson

systematic science teaching, his clear and lucid explanation of the Old Testament in scripture class, his authoritative knowledge on the field of sport, or his justice and discipline, always tempered with love and mercy'.[27]

Shankey's time in Kilkenny is the first period for which the authors have been able to interview past pupils. With hindsight, past pupils of any school tend to have heightened memories, so that schooldays are viewed with 'rose-tinted spectacles' or the unpleasant aspects are exaggerated, as in Ruddock's memory of the college in winter as being 'not unlike the gulag camps in Siberia'.[28] It must be said that some of the liveliest accounts come from those with vivid memories and it is a rare person who can take a truly objective view. It is the historian's job to balance the disparate views of a school and its personalities.

CHAPTER ELEVEN

Into co-education, 1952-1979

Shankey's successor, Gilbert Colton, from Co. Offaly, had been headmaster of Villiers School, Limerick, since 1947.[1] George Coe, a member of his teaching staff, recalled 'a very benevolent and caring gentleman of the old school. He cared deeply about the happiness of all. He was always willing to give students a second chance.'[2] He was even-tempered and used the cane sparingly. Benevolent he may have been but he was sometimes angry, when he felt the boys had let him down. On one such occasion Lipsett was taking a Latin class in the room directly over the front door. When Lipsett was out of the room, order broke down quickly. One of the boys, who was being teased, 'flung a Latin grammar book at his tormentor, who ducked. The book went through the window and landed, with a shower of glass, at the feet of Bishop Phair, who was just then being admitted at the front door by Mr Colton.'[3] Retribution followed.

Colton 'knew exactly what to take seriously, when to turn a blind eye'.[4] He had 'an uncanny ability to turn up at the most unexpected moments'.[5] 'The fact that he seemed ubiquitous and omnipresent gave both pupils and teachers the uneasy feeling that he knew everything that was going on but, as George Coe comments, 'he was wise enough to know otherwise.' Ken Stanley, who had been a pupil under Shankey, was a junior master under Colton from 1956 to 1960. He maintains that Colton was 'an extremely good headmaster, who built the foundations for today's successful school but doesn't get the credit he deserves',[6] because Kilkenny College's meteoric rise under his successors has eclipsed his contribution. One must also remember that, although the position of the Church of Ireland in Irish society was changing during Colton's time at Kilkenny College, it was not he but his successor who benefited. Having suffered a lack of confidence and a sense of isolation since Irish independence, the church was gradually led to a more positive view. As far back as the 1940s, Professor W. B. Stanford had urged Church of Ireland people 'to take a sympathetic and active part in building the future of Ireland in freedom'.[7] Likewise, Dr Henry McAdoo encouraged them to involve themselves in the Dáil, the Seanad, local government, and in the cultural and educational life of the country.[8] It was significant that he and George Simms, two of the foremost figures in the church, were Irish speakers.

Gilbert Colton

The person in the pew is not much in touch with theological theory and it required the leadership of Simms to re-energise the Church of Ireland and to persuade it to resume a role in Irish society. It was a task which he began as Bishop of Cork from 1952 to 1956, in conjunction with McAdoo, whom he appointed Dean. By his commitment to civic involvement and to warming the chilly ecumenical climate, Simms transformed the image of the Church of Ireland in the Cork community and he proceeded to do the same in the much more influential position of Archbishop of Dublin from 1956 to 1969. By the time that he was elected Archbishop of Armagh, Church of Ireland people had a new confidence and were participating more fully in Irish society.

Over the years, this development had a major impact on the Protestant schools, as Roman Catholic parents started to send their children there and Protestant parents accepted the new mix of pupils. While, in turn, Protestant parents were less anxious about sending their children to the local school, the overall result was a considerable increase in numbers in Protestant schools. The effects were felt in Kilkenny College only in Colton's later years. Being a realist, he set out to keep the school open and tried to give the boys a good start in life, despite the limitations of their and his position.

A modest prospectus from his early years stated that the school aimed 'to fit the pupils, physically, morally and intellectually so that they may discharge their duties as citizens with honour to their religion and their school and with credit to themselves.' He did all he could to bolster that aspiration: he cited the heritage of a fine building, illustrious headmasters and distinguished past pupils; the introduction of hot and cold showers, 'the usual secondary school subjects' and 'a large and safe pool in the river where the boys may swim under supervision'.[9] These were indeed unexceptional facilities but they were the best he could offer. Colton could not offer a wide range of subjects, for he had only a tiny number of permanent senior teachers. Otherwise, like Shankey, he had to rely on a series of teachers, few of whom stayed long, and on junior masters. Typically the latter were aged 19 or 20 and were good students who would have gone to university, had finances per mitted. They taught a full timetable, took games and did duty for a modest sum, with full board. In theory they had the opportunity to study for an external degree from Trinity College, or later from the University of London but few found enough spare time to complete the course. Those who graduated moved to a better job; others moved to Dublin to gain the qualifications which would enable them to become registered teachers.[10] In time Colton abandoned the more esoteric claims of that prospectus, removing references to German and Greek, for instance, but celebrating the improvements which he made in his early years. Having settled into the job, he had the confidence to say under the heading of 'academic': 'a school is best judged by the men who leave its gates,' and that, as a training for life, discipline was largely administered by the boys themselves. While every pupil was conscious of the fine façade and the beauty of the tree-lined riverside setting, with the castle towering on the other side, Homan Potterton gives the finest literary picture of Kilkenny College in the middle of the 20th century, as befits one who was later director of the National Gallery of Ireland:

> The school building was a Georgian country mansion set down in parkland in the middle of a medieval city. … During my time there I came to realise that it was beautiful, and that architecture might strive for perfection, and that nature could be embellished by artifice. Rising through only three stories, the classical façade of the building is utterly plain, but adapted for Irish use by having the tall windows of the *piano nobile* repeated for extra light at ground level. A single flourish of extravagance … was a frilly trollop of a fanlight flaunting herself above the hall-door. Nature had encroached on all of this and a Virginia creeper that must have been well over a hundred years old … romped recklessly from one side to the other and up as far as a balustrade which capped the whole like a tiara perched on the brow of a debutante.
>
> The parkland in front of the building, which we called the Bog, was triangular in shape: on one side the school and then at an angle to it a walk of ancient pollarded limes called Swift's Walk. The River Nore, flowing the length of the park, formed the hypotenuse. The waters squeezed under the arches of St John's Bridge, grazed the walls beneath the castle on the far side, and – depending on the season – staggered or erupted over a salmon weir which formed a basin near the cricket nets.[11]

Against this was the inescapable truth that the school was grim, cold and draughty inside and that Colton had to make the most of outdated facilities. Like his predecessors, he taught *and* managed every aspect of the school, as Kilkenny College could not afford to appoint an administrator until the 1980s. Fortunately, Colton was a practical man, who could handle the finances and clear the drains. He upgraded the physical conditions for staff and students and, beginning with efficient showers, made real improvements. He involved the boys in the maintenance of both buildings and grounds and afternoons found him out working with the boys or doing repairs in the workshop. W. R. Grey, who taught English and French from 1954 to 1957, wrote at the time a vivid depiction of parts of the school. Remembered as a brilliant story teller and reader of literature, his words conjure up the atmosphere, instantly recognisable to anyone who was in the old college:

> The boys are standing in the boot hall, which is the name of convenience for that dismal vestibule with brown walls sheltering the large boiler. They enjoy the fullest benefit of the boiler's heat, or that heavy warm pungent odour of cinder which lingers poisonously in the hall, sometimes thickly, at no time ever gone. To this is added occasionally the stench of rugger togs soaked in rain and sweat and left on the rails to dry.[12]

He pictures, as master on duty, assembling for breakfast in the dining room:

> The yellow walls are cold, brilliantly lit by the morning sun pouring in the tall windows: there is no fire in the grate, because the room will be occupied for only short periods and the black frames round the engraved portraits of Berkeley and Congreve accentuate the spare, bleak effect. I wait by the fireplace under the silver cups, the prefects take up position at the heads of the tables, and the rank and file pour in, each clutching to himself his extra provision of sugar, butter, syrup or jam or whatever else he has culled from the privacy of his tuck-box.

Grey recalls that grace, said before and after meals, was sometimes modified, if the meat was under or over cooked, to: 'From what we are about to receive may the Lord protect us.'

Despite the perpetual shortage of money, Colton strove to maintain the vestiges of the school's educational and sporting reputation. He achieved a gradual increase in numbers, so that, even as a four-year school, numbers rose above 100. He also managed to raise academic standards and, in the 1960s, when Mountjoy's numbers had risen too high to leave space for Kilkenny College boys, established a six-year curriculum. Most of all, Colton kept the college open when many other small schools closed because of decreasing numbers. This achievement is considerable when one considers what was happening in Protestant secondary education in the Republic. In the four decades since the new Irish state was established the value of endowments had shrunk even further and the shortage of teachers and a rise in salaries caused further difficulties. What state aid there was did not enable the

Swimming in the Nore

schools to cope with traditional requirements, never mind new developments.

In 1961 the General Synod of the Church of Ireland was told that its schools were in a dire position. The next year the Synod appointed an Advisory Committee on Church of Ireland Secondary Schools, which took three years to come up with suggestions. The committee was adamant that Church of Ireland schools had to help themselves by amalgamations and closures and the raising of funds through the sale of redundant properties. The committee believed, however, that the only ultimate solution was for the state to fund the entire secondary education system.[13]

In 1966 the Minister for Education did indeed introduce 'free secondary education' but it did not amount to free education within the Protestant sector. The scheme, whereby an annual grant for each recognised day pupil would be paid to a school, which would not then be allowed to charge fees, was not considered suitable for the Protestant schools. Instead, a block grant was paid to a committee representing the Protestant churches, the Secondary Education Committee (commonly referred to as 'the SEC'). This grant was planned to give proportionate funding to Protestant pupils but was intended to cover the expenses of only 75 per cent of them because, initially, it was anticipated that the same proportion of Roman Catholic pupils would benefit from the scheme. This meant that SEC grants would be means-tested, which may have been fair but it imposed a major administrative burden and has remained a problem ever since. As boarding was so much part of Protestant education, in due course the Protestant churches managed to have the system modified, so that the block grant was increased and was applied to the needs of boarding pupils.[14]

The 'free' education system did bring financial relief to the Protestant schools, as did the introduction (in 1964) of capital grants to improve old schools and build new schools. These reforms were part of a radical review of education in Ireland, which was made possible by the rapid expansion of the Irish economy in the 1960s. It was only when the government grasped the necessity of underpinning economic growth with an educated workforce that it faced up to the dire state of education in Ireland. In 1962 it initiated the first scientific survey of education and the report, *Investment in Education*, showed just how bad the situation was. One of the worst features was the small percentage of pupils going on to higher education. Less than a third of pupils had any secondary education and only a quarter of those sat the Leaving Certificate.[15]

There were various remedies but no rapid way of producing an educated workforce. Free education and free school transport gave greater access, as did third-level scholarships; capital grants would become vital but had to go hand-in-hand with amalgamations of small schools; the reform of the Leaving Certificate curriculum was intended to make it relevant to the changing needs of the time, while vocational education received a huge boost. Over a period the reforms did work and Ireland achieved a much higher level of participation in secondary education.

The reforms, however, did not greatly help a school such as Kilkenny College, whose future remained in doubt. In fact, the Department's desire for larger schools which could offer a wider range of subjects and economies of scale made the future even less certain. In the late 1960s and 1970s a major reorganisation of Protestant schools took place, with amalgamations, closures and relocations. In addition, the recommendation which the Church of Ireland made in 1965, that schools would become co-educational, was adopted. The number of Protestant schools was reduced from 42 in 1963 to 28 (of which five were comprehensives or community schools) by the late 1980s. Thus, in Dublin, for example, The High School moved to the suburbs and amalgamated with the Diocesan Secondary School for girls; The King's Hospital took over Mercer's School, Castleknock and moved to Palmerstown; in an even greater change, Mountjoy School and Bertrand and Rutland High School for girls united as Mount Temple, one of the new Protestant comprehensive schools. The government's funding of Protestant comprehensive schools increased rather than decreased inequalities of access in the Protestant sector, with free education being limited to those living within reach as day pupils.

The Advisory Committee considered that only one Protestant school was needed in the southeast. If that were to become a reality, two of the three – Kilkenny College, Newtown and Bishop Foy's – would have to close. As Kenneth Milne wrote at the time, amalgamation 'is infinitely to be preferred to a lingering decline'.[16] The two Waterford schools merged on the Newtown site in 1967 but an amalgamation with Kilkenny College was never likely, as Newtown was run by the Religious Society of Friends and was committed to maintaining the Quaker ethos. One suggestion was that the Incorporated Society should close Kilkenny College and Celbridge Collegiate and open a new school in Carlow. This was vigorously opposed by Dr Henry McAdoo, Bishop of Ossory from 1962 to 1977. McAdoo knew that Kilkenny College would be in a strong position to serve pupils in the southeast if it became co-educational and improved its facilities.[17] The college was operating in outdated buildings and on a restricting site and its numbers were small. One of the factors which kept the numbers small was that it catered mainly for boys from farms, whose parents sent them to school for two or three years 'to get the corners rubbed off'. Most boys whose future on the farm was secure had little academic interest and Colton and his successor struggled to convince parents that the Leaving Certificate should be the minimum qualification.

McAdoo's support was vital to Colton in securing the future of Kilkenny College for, in 1972, they faced down the threat of closure and secured a merger with Celbridge. When the Incorporated Society announced that both schools would close in the summer of 1973, the only feasible alternative was to amalgamate them and Kilkenny seemed the obvious location. This solution had the great recommendation that they were both Society schools and many families sent their sons to Kilkenny and their daughters to Celbridge.[18] It is interesting that such an amalgamation had been considered but rejected by the Society after the Second World War, when there seemed to be a possibility of using Kilkenny Castle as a school.

In 1968, when the College playing fields at Archer's Field were closed, Colton had ensured that the Society bought Newtown House (a former hunting lodge belonging to the Statham family) and some 25 acres on the Castlecomer Road. While initially it was used for games and the house served as a dormitory for some of the boys, its importance lay in its potential. In 1972 it provided the vital space for accommodating the girls and, before he retired, Colton had obtained approval in principle for the construction of a

Newtown House

new school there. By September 1973, Newtown House had been renamed Celbridge House, where Miss Yates, her staff and girls would live, and a pre-fabricated kitchen and dining room had been erected; classrooms in John Street had been converted to dormitories for the displaced boys and some prefabs from Celbridge were installed in John Street as classrooms.

Colton and the headmistress of Celbridge, Miss Freda Yates, worked throughout the year to prepare for the amalgamation, ensuring that teachers taught the same parts of the various courses in readiness for joint classes from September 1973. Neither Colton nor Miss Yates had wanted this development but both worked tirelessly to make it a success. His apprehension about running a co-educational school was allayed by the firm and reassuring presence of Miss Yates, who had a wise approach to boy-girl relationships and was not afraid to deal with boys who were churlish. Many of the boys were hostile both to the girls and to the Celbridge teachers. Miss Walsh, who was a gifted English teacher, found it particularly difficult, as the boys tended to be dis-missive of languages, whereas they were more interested in maths, which Miss Yates taught.

The amalgamation was immediately beneficial in that the combined numbers made up one good-sized class. In the early years, more girls than boys stayed to do the Leaving Certificate, reflecting patterns that preceded the amalgamation. Soon there was a marked increase in day pupils, many of

Sports day, 1970s

whose parents were professional people with higher academic expectations. Colton and his staff had to push for better results and better results attracted more pupils. New subjects, such as biology and agricultural science, were introduced and numbers rose from year to year, so there was a constant need for more accommodation.

Before Miss Yates's arrival, Colton virtually 'ran a one-man-show', in which the staff took little responsibility. In her he found a 'lady principal', whose experience made her advice invaluable and he consulted her on all issues. The concept of vice-principals was little developed in the 1970s and neither he nor she had an office but, by the time she retired in 1991, the post was well established, Miss Yates's teaching hours had been reduced and numbers would have permitted her to have abandoned the classroom had she so wished. Meanwhile, his wife, Gladys, ran the housekeeping on a shoestring. The kitchen facilities, never good, became totally inadequate as numbers increased and the menus were limited and monotonous. As long as the Incorporated Society was in charge, it controlled the purse strings tightly and, as Miss Yates recalls, she had to seek permission to spend £5. In 1976 the Society handed over the management of Kilkenny College to a local board, with the Bishop of Ossory as chairman. This was part of the process by which the Society relinquished direct management of its schools and became a trustee body. It has maintained its interest in the schools and since 1992 has representatives of the individual schools as members. The income from the Society's endowments is still used to support the schools, both by scholarships and capital grants.

Freda Yates

When Colton retired in 1979, he might justifiably have looked back with satisfaction: first that he had kept the college open despite the many challenges; finally that he had set it on its way as an expanding co-educational school. It was no mean achievement.

CHAPTER TWELVE

Into a new millennium, 1979-2005

The final chapter gives a brief account of Kilkenny College under the head-mastership of Sam McClure and the Revd R. J. (Jack) Black. It is too early to attempt a thorough historical assessment of so recent a phase in the life of the college but it is clear that Black's arrival and departure illustrate the biblical truth that 'one sows and another reaps'. Just as Black benefited greatly from the developments carried out by McClure, so his successor, Philip Gray, benefited from Black's projects, the last of which was a new classroom block, opened in the third academic year after Black's retirement.

Under McClure and Black, the college changed almost beyond recognition. The move to a purpose-built school on the Castlecomer Road has been followed by an almost continuous building programme, a huge increase in numbers and a great expansion in the range of subjects, extracurricular activities and pastoral care. Many past pupils, proud of their heritage, send their children to a college which is very different from the one they attended themselves before the 1980s.[1] McClure, appointed headmaster in 1979, carried out the first part of this programme, handing over, on his retirement in 1996, to Black. Having been a senior member of staff at Newtown School, Waterford, for many years, McClure knew the area and its people and was used to co-education. He worked hard to raise academic expectations and to persuade boys to stay on for the Leaving Certificate. This effort was not just within the school, for he reiterated the message at every opportunity throughout the united dioceses. By the time he retired, with very few exceptions, first-year entrants stayed to sit the Leaving Certificate and went on to third-level education.

When McClure took over, there were 234 pupils; when he retired there were 673 and the school had to refuse places to nearly 100 applicants.[2] Even in 1979 the school was rapidly outgrowing the John Street premises. McClure's own quarters, which formerly occupied nearly half of the main building, were progressively reduced and at one stage he and his family lived above a bank in order to make room for extra dormitory accommodation. Initially he threw his energies into improvements and raised the money for the multi-purpose McAdoo Hall, the first new building at the college for many years. This was a major achievement, considering that the economic situation was poor and that he had to re-roof and restore the main building after a fire in October 1980. This disaster had a noted positive result, in that, on the initiative of Bishop Peter Birch, St Kieran's College offered temporary boarding accommodation for 65 boys and the arrangement fostered a closer relationship between the two schools.

Like Colton, McClure maintained a presence. He would walk around the college, seemingly appearing from nowhere but, in days when smoking was still tolerated, he deliberately smoked his pipe so that his arrival would be signalled! (He even advised his staff to do likewise.) Freda Yates, his vice-principal, describes McClure as 'a visionary', who soon developed a vision for a new school with larger numbers on the Castlecomer Road. Increasingly, he was convinced that it was too difficult and too expensive to run the school on two sites. It was indeed a logistical nightmare, with extra expense on maintenance, staff and transport. McClure was a political being, who manoeuvred skilfully to gain support from politicians for the project and to obtain the vital building grant from the Department of Education. With the purchase of extra land at Celbridge House, the prospect of the new school became a reality.[3] Perhaps the visit of the Taoiseach, Charles Haughey, to the burnt-out shell at John Street, was the catalyst in this venture. McClure toured new schools across the country, evaluating them and testing his ideas. He developed certain immovable principles, which he implemented with determination. Among them was provision for all classrooms to look out on the open air and for a warm and welcoming area at the entrance.

It was a two-stage process: first, the new teaching facilities opened on a green-field site in 1985 but the boys continued to live in John Street; secondly, that entire site was sold to the county council for its headquarters and a boys' dormitory block was built on the new premises. Government aid extended only to teaching facilities and the college was required to fund 20 per cent of these costs. Other developments had to be funded by the college, from revenue, grants and a successful appeal.[4]

It was a difficult decision to leave the old buildings. Even on his way to the signing of the contract with the county council, McClure was asking himself if he was doing the right thing. Bishop Noel Willoughby, who spoke at the ceremony, expressed the sadness they both felt at leaving the ancient campus but said that the decision had been much easier in the knowledge that the city 'would be enhanced by [its] restoration by the civic authorities'.[5] Willoughby was a son of the dioceses and knew the region and its people intimately. He had the common touch and was greatly liked within and

The Most Revd Donald Caird, Paddy Cooney, TD, Minister for Education, the Rt Revd Noel Willoughby, and Sam McClure at the opening of the new school

without the Church of Ireland community. As chairman of the board, he and McClure together recreated Kilkenny College as a diocesan school. McClure was a Presbyterian but, on coming to Kilkenny, he became a member of the Church of Ireland. This was not merely a strategic move, for he was an active layman and served as churchwarden in St John's.

While the new college was taking shape, it became obvious that there was an urgent need for reappraisal of the role of Protestant schools and the educational needs of Protestant families. The situation had changed greatly since the last appraisal in the 1960s and Canon Gerald Magahy, one of the leading educationalists of his time, set out the position clearly. As he acknowledged, the most basic question was: 'What is a Protestant school? Is it a school in which all pupils and staff are Protestants? If this is our criterion, then we simply do not have any Protestant schools.'

Numbers had increased because parents had come to realise the necessity of a secondary education and could now avail of grants and free transport; Protestant pupils were now distributed among fewer schools (14) and some schools now took in a sizeable number of Roman Catholic pupils. As Magahy saw, this raised the question: 'If Protestant schools keep their numbers up by welcoming Roman Catholic pupils, can they expect the government to continue to recognise the special needs of Protestant families and support them in any worthwhile manner?' Among the trends he examined was the changing attitude of Protestant parents, some of whom now felt that both boarding and denominational education were wrong, while others, 'when they see their neighbours' children getting into third-level education from the local school, which is free, ... query the necessity of paying high fees just to attend a Protestant school'.[6]

The key to understanding much of this is the changed situation in inter-church marriages. For most of the 20th century 'mixed marriages' caused a lot of bitterness and were generally regarded as a tragedy for a Protestant family. Under the *Ne Temere* decree of 1908 no such marriage was permitted without a promise to bring up the children as Roman Catholics. Not only did that prevent a couple from making their own decision about their children; it led to whole Protestant families dying out, with no-one to take over a farm or business. It is no wonder that Protestant families, feeling defensive, wanted their children to be educated with other Protestants, to the exclusion of Roman Catholics, for fear of mixed marriages. It is no exaggeration to say that mixed marriages posed a threat to the survival of the Protestant population of Ireland.

The ecumenical climate improved rapidly after the election of John XXIII as Pope in 1958. Under his leadership, Anglican-Roman Catholic relations warmed and the Second Vatican Council adopted a new approach to Christian unity. By 1968 an Anglican-Roman Catholic International Commission (ARCIC) was established, with Bishop McAdoo as co-chairman, and a similar commission on the theology of marriage and its application to mixed marriages, with Archbishop Simms as co-chairman. Painstaking work continued for years and a high level of agreement was achieved. Over some 30 years, partly by official relaxation of the rules, partly by the initiative of the laity, the 'mixed marriage' was transformed into an 'inter-church marriage'.[7] Today such marriages generally take place in the bride's church, with clergy of both denominations taking part; the couple determines the religious upbringing of the children, many of whom are baptised in the Church of Ireland and attend Church of Ireland schools.

In the context of this history, these advances are significant because they had a major effect on Protestant schools. In Kilkenny College McClure and Magahy produced a paper for the board, in which they posed the question whether 'the main purpose' of the school was to cater 'for all Protestant children in our catchment area who wish to come here' or 'for all pupils who can afford to come'.[8] The ultimate decision was a compromise which emphasised the needs of the Protestant community, while welcoming as many other pupils as could be accommodated. The paper recognised that 'more Roman Catholic families can afford a school which charges higher fees' so, for the sake of the Protestant community, McClure made it a priority 'to do all in our power to reduce running costs'. This was a delicate balance because 'the

Girls' Hockey SCT, 1993-94
Back row L to R: L. Threlfall, C. Roe, M. Treacy, L. Furney, R. Deverell, J. Williams,
A. Salter, E. O'Flynn, Mr A. Kerr
Front row: J. Phelan, J. Byrne, O. Rynhart, R. Cooper, R. Williams (capt.), L. Pollock,
L. Wynne, H. Williams, J. Watkins

more wealthy families wanted the best of all worlds: facilities, travel, choice
of extra-curricular activities, choice of subjects, better exam results.' The chief
method of reducing costs was the move to an 11-day fortnight, then to five-
day boarding. McClure saw this as a wise move, irrespective of financial considerations, for he had come to believe that pupils needed to maintain a close
relationship with their families and it was becoming more difficult to secure
adequate staffing at weekends. Over the years, as Protestant Aid stopped giving education grants and there began to be a shortfall in the Incorporated
Society contribution, the college set up an education trust fund to help needy
pupils and in 1997 established Kilkenny College foundation scholarships,
funded out of school revenue.[9]

The growth in numbers meant that the college could offer a wider range
of subjects to Leaving Certificate level and separate classes for honours and
pass candidates.[10] This was important, for McClure was determined that 'no
Church of Ireland child will be deprived of an education in Kilkenny College
... because he/she is academically weak'.[11] Schools which take only academically strong pupils obviously find it easier to produce excellent results. It was

a major achievement in Kilkenny College to maintain a non-selective intake and still enable the brightest pupils to gain entry to courses which demanded the highest points. The introduction of a transition year, with courses ranging from communications and journalism to cooking and community affairs, also gave opportunities for self-development.

McClure was good at delegating and knew that the expanding school could not be run as a one-man show. The administrative burden imposed by increasing numbers and by building a new school made it essential to relieve McClure of looking after the finances and maintenance and an administrator was appointed in 1984. McClure saw as a vital part of delegation the introduction of form teachers and year heads and, in his many appointments, looked for staff who were willing to contribute outside class.[12] In another radical departure, he did not have a headmaster's house built at the new site but lived off-campus. This meant that housepersons had greater responsibility. It worked so well for McClure that it has become the practice in Kilkenny College.

When McClure retired in 1996, there was an obvious successor. The Revd R. J. Black had been headmaster of Dundalk Grammar School since 1984, during which time numbers more than trebled. In appointing him, the board chose an experienced and proven principal of a provincial school and had once again an ordained headmaster. While there was no possibility of reverting to the policy of having a clerical headmaster, Black's appointment enabled the college to strengthen its position as a focal point of the united dioceses. Like McClure, Black took every opportunity to visit national schools, to address their parent-teacher meetings and speak at the Mothers' Union. It was undoubtedly an advantage that, as an ordained headmaster, he could be invited to preach around the dioceses. Likewise, for instance, when he visited bereaved families, as headmasters often do, he was seen to exercise a pastoral ministry, which tended to make people feel positively about the college.

From his early days as a parish curate, Black had taught religious education in various secondary schools and in the early 1980s was involved in drawing up a new common RE syllabus. He fostered the development of the RE department so effectively in Kilkenny College that it was selected as one of the pilot schools for the new syllabus. This went so well that a full class sat the first Junior Certificate RE examination and a comparable number went on to take it in the first Leaving Certificate examination. Religious education went beyond the syllabus: the Christian Union was encouraged and confirmation classes were given a prominent position, each class going on retreat.

Black was a qualified careers guidance teacher and had taken responsibility for that department in Dundalk when he was headmaster. In Kilkenny College he had to restrict himself to guidance for the sixth-form pupils. He also created a pastoral care structure, with a team comprising a full-time counsellor, house persons and the nurses.

It was highly significant that Black was invited by the Department of Education to include the college in a European secondary education assessment programme. Not only did it give him the opportunity to visit many countries to observe new techniques but it meant that Kilkenny College was involved in what was essentially a curriculum development project. McClure had previously applied to introduce a number of practical subjects but little progress had been made. Now the inspectors were aware of the curricular limitations in the college, so Black's application to introduce nine new subjects was well received. Pilot status was important and in 2001 Kilkenny College was selected as one of three Irish schools to take part in an OECD study on information technology in secondary schools and the Department granted an extra 50,000 euro for the following school years, in recognition of the college's pilot status in IT, RE and maths.

In his first year, finding that numbers were falling despite all the recent improvements, Black had identified the cause as a lack of provision for practical subjects such as woodwork and technology, coupled with a limited number of academic subjects. As Kilkenny College compared badly with local schools in this respect, parents were increasingly inclined not to send their children to the college. Convinced that the college was still the best choice for Church of Ireland parents, he introduced economics and applied maths, and upgraded physics. Black's contacts with the Department were vital to his single most important achievement, that of getting community school status for Kilkenny College. He pressed his case in the Department that the college served the entire Church of Ireland community of the southeast, irrespective of academic ability and was, in effect, a community school. Having won his point, Kilkenny College began to enjoy the advantages of a community school, in special treatment for pupils with special needs and in additional staffing for technical subjects.

His powers of persuasion in the Department of Education were remarkable. From 1996 to 2003 he obtained funding for a day-pupil centre and classroom facilities for business studies, economics and computers, home economics, guidance and technical subjects which are computer-controlled. While this provision had previously been made in the community-school sector, it was the first time that the Department had made it in a secondary

Jack Black

school. Also, in a joint project, the college funded an engineering and technology room, which Black persuaded the Department to equip as a pilot scheme, with a pioneering extraction system. He even managed to win funding for the dining hall space, on condition that it could also serve as classrooms.

In these years Kilkenny College paid for a new library, a second computer room and an IT link to all classrooms, a modern kitchen and a senior boys' dormitory. Even this phenomenal degree of development was not enough and in 2003, with no prospect of more funding from the Department, Black launched a fund-raising campaign for a girls' dormitory extension and a new classroom block and quiet room. These came to fruition after Black's retirement, with Yates House being completed in 2006 and the Jonathan Swift Building in 2007. The development of the music department[13] under David Milne was well demonstrated by a performance of his anthem based on the school motto, *Comme je trouve,*[14] at the opening ceremony, attended by the Minister for Education, Mary Hanafin. Before he retired, Black had won a commitment from the Department to equip the teaching block. This major and vital concession was further proof of official recognition that Kilkenny College occupied a special position. The college received more generous funding than other schools not only due to its community school status but because Black carried the point that it was attracting a significantly higher proportion of pupils who were eligible for the SEC grant than other Protestant schools.[15]

All this development was needed not only to provide facilities for technical subjects but also to accommodate extra pupils, for, during Black's time, numbers rose to 800. Although he realised that there was an inevitable loss of the personal touch, he believed that he had to extend the range of academic subjects to cater for the most academic as well as the least academic pupils. This required extra teachers and, in turn, extra pupils. By 2005 the college employed 146 people, excluding music teachers. It thus constituted a large business, which needed not only a chief executive (the headmaster) but also an administrator to assist him, by looking after finance and external maintenance. The appointment in 1999 of Peter Dukelow completed the

David Milne with
members of the
orchestra

transition to a professional, with a degree in economics and practical experience. Another innovative appointment was that of Aubrey O'Keeffe as deputy principal in 2002. When Freda Yates retired in 1991, she had still been teaching classes. Oliver Harrington, who had taught in the college for many years, became full-time vice-principal. When he retired, the Department had recently instituted the enhanced post of deputy principal. That post was open to applicants from any school and thus it was that a newcomer, O'Keeffe, was appointed. The development of a management team became a necessity and teachers were asked to take responsibilities, administrative and pastoral, which would have been unheard of in former times. One such member of staff, Simon Thompson, went from co-ordinating transition year to the position of headmaster of Midleton College, the first such appointment for a Kilkenny College teacher for decades. On the other hand, Black recognised that it was becoming increasingly difficult for full-time teachers to be heads of the boarding houses and moved towards full-time house appointments. While he admits that he did not know all the pupils individually,[16] his approach to the teaching staff was one of personal and regular engagement: meeting with each person regularly was time-consuming but he believed it was essential for keeping good communications. Through these meetings he kept himself informed about the activities which staff members organised. These ranged through a wide range of extracurricular activities and included an annual exchange with a French school.

In addition to a growing number teaching physical education, many teachers were involved in coaching sports. Noted successes included that of

Boys' Hockey SCT, 1998-99
Back row L to R: G. Walshe, H. Kelly, E. Bryan, L. Wilson, Mr H. Sharman
Second row: Mr R. Willis, P. Case, J. Gahan, D. O'Gorman, K. White, G. Greene,
G. Bourke, K. Williams, S. Ellis, Mr R. Harding
Front row: E. O'Mahony, G. Sharman, P. Hegarty, M. Magnier (capt.), L. Pearson,
S. Thompson, W O'Donnell

Rugby SCT, 2000-01
Back row L to R: P. O'Connell, J. Harvey, T. Langley, G. Greene
Third row: R. Porter, C. D'Alton, L. Deverell, R. Hanbidge
Second row: A. Deacon, N. Patterson, R. Bergin, C. Foley, B. Thompson, R. Gee,
B. Thackaberry
Front row: S. Holland, G. Roe, C. Peavoy, R. Jones (capt.), G. Jacob, R. Deverell,
Mr K. Clayton

Equestrian team, Hickstead, 2005
Back row L to R: G. Dunne, D. Johnston, V. Anderson, L. Farrell, C. Hogan, T. Walshe,
Jennifer Lalor *Third row:* D. Wilson, N. Walshe, C. Stanley, C. Gillson, Jessica Lalor, S.
Hutchinson, H. Lalor, R. Cahill, S. Milne, E. Sterling, L. Leon *Second row:* L. Harper, B.
Bambrick, J. Ponsonby, M. Connolly, F. Furnell, G. Dunne, D. Furnell, F. Scala, D. Mullins
Front row: S. Rafter, M. Hutchinson, M. van Amerongen, D. Brennan, J. Younghusband, J.
Liekens-Schurman, Mr P. Cuddihy (*chef d'équipe*) J. Brennan, V. Byrne, L. Butler, S.
Brennan, C. Younghusband, R. Hogan

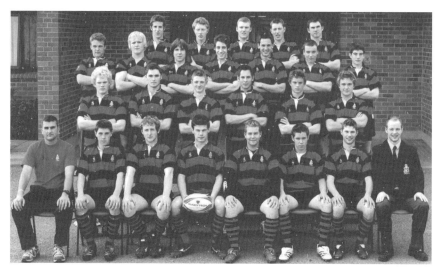

Rugby SCT semi-finalists, 2006-07
Back row L to R: W. Carter, S. Hemmingway, N. Copeland, J. McAssey, T. Dukelow
Third row: M. Brannigan, K. McArdle, M. D'Alton, S. Yates, P. Mahon, R. O'Driscoll
Second row: E. Seale, M. Ruddock, D. Ryall, A. Yates, G. Dunne, C. Rynhart
Front row: Mr J. Carter, C. Ronaldson, G. Beattie, B. Horan (capt.), K. Dagg,
C. Masterson, B. Braithwaite, S. Talbot

Philip Gray

the girls' senior hockey team in 1994, in winning the All-Ireland championship and representing Ireland in the European championships. The provision of an all-weather hockey pitch helped the senior boys to bring home the Leinster Cup in 1999 for the first time in 34 years. They again won the cup in 2001 and were finalists in 2002. While academic facilities had to take precedence, it was important to expand sports facilities as finances allowed. Under McClure and Black four rugby pitches, two synthetic and two shale hockey pitches, tennis courts and a sports hall were provided. A significant development was the move up to the top flight of Leinster schools rugby. While it met with resistance, this promotion represented recognition[17] of Kilkenny College's increased strength of numbers. Without it, the noted success of the 2001 and 2007 seasons, when the senior XV reached the semi-final of the Leinster Schools Senior Cup, would have been impossible. Among newer sports, there were noted successes in the equestrian department. College teams were victorious at the All-Ireland Schools Championship on three occasions and in 2005 Kilkenny College became the first Irish school to win the Schools European Show Jumping Championship at Hickstead.

Black was able to rely on support behind the scenes from his wife, Ollie. He was the first headmaster to be non-resident throughout his term of office and the first whose wife could have avoided involvement. Twenty years had brought about a major shift from the situation under Colton, when Mrs Colton was housekeeper and greatly involved in the day-to-day running of the college, to one in which it became so well staffed that any contribution from the headmaster's wife was a bonus rather than a necessity.

Black's most regular contact with the Board was with the chairman, the bishop. All three bishops during Black's time – Noel Willoughby, John Neill and Peter Barrett – were frequent visitors to the college but it was particularly helpful in Black's first year to have Bishop Willoughby as a confidant, for he 'knew everyone and everything about the school'.[17] The support of the board was essential to Black's success in fund-raising and obtaining substantial aid from the Incorporated Society for boarding facilities. One of Black's last innovations was to pave the way for a school management board. Under the Education Act of 1999 it became a legal requirement but it did not apply where a principal had been appointed before 1998. Despite being ill early in 2005, Black managed to put in place the mechanisms which allowed Philip Gray to implement a board of management, representative of the board of directors, parents and staff, with a facility for hearing the views of pupils.[19] Kilkenny College had travelled far from the distant supervision of its visitors, through control by the Incorporated Society, to regulation by a local board of governors and finally to shared responsibility on a democratic basis.

SECTION B

The Pococke School
(1763-1903)

CHAPTER THIRTEEN

Foundation

The Pococke School, Kilkenny, was founded by the will of Richard Pococke, Bishop of Ossory from 1756 to 1765. While the foundation of Kilkenny College and Celbridge Collegiate was in each case a philanthropic act among many initiatives by a major public figure, neither Ormond nor Conolly was greatly engaged in education. In Pococke's case, however, his foundation of a school in Kilkenny can be entirely explained by his career and background. An Englishman and a bachelor, a polymath[1] and a broadminded patron, his decision to devote his estate to establishing a school rather than to one of his other charitable interests suggests that his own experience of education was strongly inspirational.

He was born in 1704[2] in Southampton. His father, also named Richard, was then headmaster of the King Edward VI Free Grammar School in Southampton. His maternal grandfather, the Revd Isaac Milles, rector of Highclere in the northwest corner of Hampshire, had himself been educated at a school founded by Edward VI in Bury St Edmund's, in his native Suffolk,[3] and was running a school in his parish. From a young age, Richard Pococke attended his father's school but his father died of smallpox in 1710, aged 44, and his mother returned to Highclere, where Richard continued his education in his grandfather's school. Richard Pococke's upbringing in Highclere must have been more influential than his early years in Southampton. We have some record of the factors that shaped his character and learning: his grandfather's approach to education was in many ways far ahead of his time. We are told that 'in managing the business of his school, Mr Milles's great care was to breed the children committed to his care to sentiments and habits of truth and virtue, of piety and devotion, of good nature and friendliness, to one another, and to all men. The teaching and grounding them in the perfect practice of these, and the like principles and duties, he thought to be of far greater moment than all the knowledge of letters ...' He neither practised corporal punishment 'nor did he seem ever to endeavour to settle any great authority and awe towards himself in the minds of the children … He would frequently reason with them and represent to them the necessity of doing some things and the advantage of abstaining from others; and leave it to their own choice, after trial, which way they would act.' 'Both by precept and example,' he taught them 'to be humane, civil and kind to all, more especially to the poor, to whom he would sometimes, in a pleasant and artful way, lead the children to perform acts of generosity and charity.'[4]

If his mother had not brought Richard Pococke to Highclere, it is unlikely that he would have moved to Ireland, for it was there that he became acquainted with the family of the major landowner, the Earl of Pembroke. Although the earl lived in Wiltshire, he educated his sons at Milles's private school and, when he went to Ireland as Lord Lieutenant in 1707, he appointed Thomas Milles (Pococke's uncle) as his chaplain. It was advantageous for Thomas to accompany 'the father of his old school-fellows'[5] to Ireland, for he was consecrated Bishop of Waterford and Lismore the following year. A bachelor, who took a keen interest in his nephews, it was probably he who financed Richard Pococke's education at Oxford after Isaac Milles died in 1720. Soon after completing his BA degree in 1725, Pococke was ordained and quickly appointed to the precentorship of Lismore Cathedral by his uncle. He was not, however, required to reside in Ireland, so he could continue his studies in Oxford. The death of his uncle in 1740 did not alter Richard Pococke's connection with the diocese. His cousin, Jeremiah Milles, was precentor of Waterford Cathedral and, upon his resignation in 1745, Pococke took on that post in addition to his own. In the following year, the then Lord Lieutenant, the Earl of Chesterfield, appointed him Archdeacon of Dublin. As archdeacon, he became involved with the Incorporated Society. He was also active as a trustee of Mercer's School in Rathcoole, where poor girls were trained for service, the school having its own flax field for supplying the girls' linen spinning.[6] His attitude to charity schools can be seen from a later sermon to the Incorporated Society:

> The objects of the charity: the unhappy children of those who are depressed by the utmost poverty; and under this institution, from dirt and nakedness are kept clean and decently apparelled; from being ill fed and lodged are supplied with wholesome food and proper habitations; instead of being abandoned to an idle and dissolute life are accustomed to useful labour and a regularity of manners … all which particulars have a visible good effect on the mind and general behaviour, as well as on the health of the body, the reputation and the increase of property.[7]

Aware of the importance of practical training in the field of agricultural production, he maintained that it was essential 'not to direct to any particular profession only and always to breed some of them, a proper proportion, to those employments which relate to agriculture: otherwise, we may want hands in that most necessary and valuable profession'.[8]

In the years prior to his appointment as archdeacon, Pococke had undertaken extensive antiquarian explorations of the Middle East and other regions. In his new position his explorations were mostly restricted to Britain and Ireland. He wrote detailed descriptions of the many localities he visited, revealing a special interest in schools. The description of his tour of Ireland in 1752 mentions 16 of the Incorporated Society's charter schools, ranging from Strangford to Kinsale, the Erasmus Smith school in Sligo and Bishop Foy's school in Waterford. During his 1753 tour he took in the Society's charter schools at Carbury, Castledermot and Stradbally and in 1758 his tour included visits to the charter schools at Cashel and Dunmanway.

Pococke was, perhaps, particularly encouraged by the workings of the charter schools at Innishannon and Dundalk. Of Innishannon, where there was a close relationship between the charter school and a linen factory, Pococke wrote that he 'saw several children apprenticed from the charter schools and the workhouse in Dublin'.[9] At Dundalk he observed the connection between the charter school and the local manufacture of cambric.[10] Pococke identified himself with the Incorporated Society in reporting that Dundalk 'had forty of our charter boys'. The use of such a phrase suggests that he was an official visitor on behalf of the Society, as does his care ('I saw such of them as could be got together and gave them a small present and a word of exhortation').[11]

In September 1752, Pococke recorded in his journal that he 'came to Kilkenny, most pleasantly situated on the Nore' and observed 'a free school … with an endowment, if I mistake not of £120 a year, a house and pleasant meadows on the river; and it is the only one in Ireland that has some face of a public school, but the prices are risen so high, that it is feared it will fall in its credit …'[12] In March 1756 Pococke became Bishop of Ossory and moved to Kilkenny. During his time as bishop he was much involved in the restoration of St Canice's Cathedral.[13] It is probable that he had regular contact with, and some influence on, the running of Kilkenny College. He also established a linen factory at Lintown. He had taken an interest in similar ventures on his tours and it is likely that he was also influenced by Barry Colles, a pioneer in the development of linen manufacturing in Kilkenny. Colles was a brother-in-law of the Revd Mervyn Archdall, Pococke's trusted personal chaplain.[14]

After nine years in Kilkenny, he was appointed Bishop of Meath but died a few months later. He had made a will in Kilkenny in 1763 and a second will, as a codicil to the first, in London in 1765.[15] He left most of his estate to the Incorporated Society for the founding of a linen-weaving school in Kilkenny and stipulated that it was intended only for the education of Roman Catholic boys between the ages of 12 and 16. His family background in education must have had some bearing on this choice of bequest. Perhaps also we can see the influence of his grandfather in his decision to train the poor and marginalised in a useful discipline. Pococke also showed himself a man of his times in believing that the best way to help disadvantaged Roman Catholic boys was to provide them with a trade and make them good Protestant citizens. Given his limited objectives, as one historian put it, 'the bare possibility of embodying in Kilkenny College those he desired to succour could not occur'.[16]

The codicil, after some small bequests to his sister, a cousin and his servants, reads:

I do leave all the rest of my estate real and personal to the Incorporated Society in Dublin for promoting English Protestant Schools in Ireland, in trust for the uses following:
First, that the interest and rents be paid half-yearly to my said sister Elizabeth Pococke on her order, for and during her natural life, and then to Elizabeth Milles, spinster, of Higham Ferrars, for and during her natural life, excepting that I do leave to the said Elizabeth Milles four pounds a year English money during her natural life, four pounds a year to Jane Bingham, of Havant, spinster, during her life; and then I do leave all my estate real and personal for founding a school for papist boys from twelve to sixteen years old, who shall become Protestants, and to be bred in linen-weaving, and instructed in the principles of the

Protestant religion; said boys not to have been at any school before of any public, legal foundation, and particularly in none of the charter schools; to be apprenticed to the Society, after they are fourteen years old, for seven years, desiring that my manufactory house at Lintown, Kilkenny, if not disposed of by me, be applied for that use; and if the Society may think it better to sell one of my leases, I desire the produce may be disposed of in some government security; and if any other religion shall at any time be established than the present Protestant religion, I do then leave the whole for such time to St Patrick's Hospital in Dublin for lunatics, under the direction of the Archbishop of Dublin for the time being, and of the other governors of said hospital, to revert to the said Society whenever it shall be re-established for the purposes above mentioned. I do leave the Incorporated Society in Dublin the execution of this my last will and testament. I do leave all my manuscripts to the British Museum in London, to the governors or trustees thereof. The above will, written with my own hand on the 24th day of March 1765, I do desire may be looked on as a codicil to the other will, signed and sealed, as far as it differs from it, not having here in London convenient witnesses.[17]

Memorial to
Richard Pococke

CHAPTER FOURTEEN

The factory school

Little is known of the early history of the linen-weaving factory which provided the premises for Pococke's weaving school. Located on Green's Hill, on a site overlooking the Nore, the name 'Lintown' sounds like a contrived name to indicate a place of linen production. Spinning and weaving had long been done by agricultural families in their cottages but the industry only began to develop in the 17th century, in the face of English opposition to the Irish wool trade. After a period of increasing restrictions, exports of Irish wool were virtually halted by William III. While the British government would not tolerate Irish wool competing with English wool, it saw linen as an acceptable alternative for the Irish, so high-quality flax seed was imported and new looms were built. In the Restoration period the first Duke of Ormond, as Lord Lieutenant, gave incentives to Protestant immigrants to work in linen production. The contribution of the Quakers and the Huguenots was particularly significant in Ulster. Louis Crommelin, a Huguenot weaver of fine linen, did so much to improve the industry that the government appointed him to oversee its development in the Lagan valley. It was largely due to his work that the Board of Trustees of the Linen Manufacturers of Ireland was established in 1711 to encourage the Irish linen industry. By 1741 the industry had expanded almost a hundredfold and rigorous quality control was in place. Expansion continued throughout the 18th century, not only in Ulster but also in places like Kilkenny. Perhaps Pococke established and named 'Lintown' in the hope that Kilkenny could emulate Ulster's success. We do not know how effectively his original factory worked but it was many years before the Incorporated Society was in a position to set up the weaving school. The delay, caused by complications in the administration of Pococke's estate, made the task difficult, for the building fell into disrepair.

In setting up the Pococke school, the Society sought help from its existing presence in the city, the local committee of the Kilkenny charter school.[1] (This school, opened at Brownstown in 1745 for 40 boys, resembled that intended by Bishop Pococke, especially as the boys were engaged in spinning wool.) It was a bad decision to rely on the local committee, for it was totally incompetent. Its neglect of the charter school was exposed by John Howard, the noted prison reformer. Following an initial tour of charter schools in Ireland, Howard presented a damning report to the Incorporated Society in 1782, with particular censure of the Kilkenny charter school. One of his key revelations was that the local committee not only failed to report the deplorable state of the school but repeatedly commended the master for his work![2] Howard's continued visiting of Irish charter schools convinced him that local committees hid the truth about appalling conditions from the Incorporated Society which, in turn, concealed the facts in its annual reports. His conviction that a parliamentary inquiry was essential before the charter schools could be reformed was a significant factor in the establishment of the first educational commission in 1788.

The state of the Kilkenny charter school would not be relevant to this history were it not for the role which the local committee was given in the Pococke school. In March 1778 the local committee was informed that 'the Society observe …that the house and offices of Lintown have been left in great ruin and waste and desire to know how it came about and by whom done'.[3] The committee was asked to investigate and report what repairs were necessary to prepare the premises for the operation of a weaving school and to identify a contractor for the work. The following month, it was asked to supervise the repair and fitting up of the factory at Lintown. The work was to begin immediately but the procurement of looms was postponed.[4]

In 1781, the Society, with plans for 'five or six papist boys from twelve to fourteen years old to be immediately admitted',[5] appointed Edward Graham, the usher at the charter school, to be master at Lintown. It is implied that this appointment was due to his training as a weaver. It was reported that Graham 'expected the Society would allow him at the rate of £18-4-0 for his and his wife's salary and diet … and covering the … account for sundry necessaries provided by him for the looms there'.[6] The charter school practice was to be followed as to food and clothing. All these plans had to be put on hold, however, as further difficulties arose with regard to Pococke's estate. A seven-year delay ensued.[7] At last, in 1788, the local committee was asked to provide six bedsteads, with suitable bedding 'for the use of the children intended to be lodged in the factory' and the Bishop of Ossory was asked to advise about 'such particulars of furniture as his lordship shall judge necessary for the accommodation of the children intended to be lodged'.[8]

Although he drew a salary from 1781 until he left in 1788, it is not clear how Graham's weaving experience was put to use, for there were no boys to teach. His successor, Andrew Neelands, was appointed in January 1789. His salary was £40 per annum and he was paid £5-10-0 per annum for feeding

A linen weaver

and clothing each apprentice to be brought up in the factory.[9] On the arrival of Neelands, the first six boys were admitted, five of whom soon ran away and were replaced. In 1791 the Society approved the construction of an additional workroom with a loft, at considerable cost.[10] This might indicate that the operations of the factory were sufficiently successful to warrant expansion but there was no immediate increase in numbers. One of the reasons why it was difficult to achieve growth was that many boys ran away. The Society often pursued 'eloped apprentices', as the advertisement below shows, but it is unlikely that it was consistently successful:

> John Morrissey, aged between 17 and 18 years, slight made, fair hair and light complexion; and Thomas Duggan, of about the same age, stout made, ruddy complexion and black hair; these two apprentices eloped on 20 May last, from the factory at Lintown, near Kilkenny. All persons are cautioned against harbouring or … employing them. Any information respecting them will be thankfully received …[11]

One has to ask why so many boys ran away but, for lack of information, we can only guess that it was because of the harshness of the regime, the proselytising element, their unhappiness at being away from their families, or a mixture of the three. From an early stage the factory school was involved in weaving not only linen but cotton also.[12] There were various efforts towards the end of the century to establish a cotton industry in Kilkenny and the Incorporated Society obviously decided that the spirit of Pococke's will allowed them to do so even though cotton had not been mentioned. An advertisement in 1799 in a local newspaper read:

> A cotton factory is now completely established at Green's Hill, Kilkenny, where all kinds of cords, thicksets, velveteens, etc, are manufactured by some of the best mechanics of Manchester. Andrew Neelands, the proprietor, informs the shopkeepers, dealers, etc. that he has now a considerable quantity of goods ready for sale, which he is resolved to sell on the most reasonable terms for ready money only.[13]

This sounds impressive but the reference to 'the best mechanics of Manchester' points to the cause of the failure of the cotton industry in Kilkenny: its scale was never big enough to afford the technicians who could keep the machinery working. Those who came from England rarely stayed long and there was a lack of trained Irish mechanics to take their place. In the short term, cotton may have assumed greater importance, as can be seen from a statistical survey in 1802:

> There are 24 boys and as many looms now employed: the establishment is in a thriving way. Andrew Neelands, the master, carries on the business on his own account: he contracts with the trustees for the maintenance and instruction of the boys at £7 a year each, and they are apprenticed to him for seven years … At the Lintown Factory are made fustians, corduroys, velveteens and velvets, generally by 20 looms.[14]

The survey stated that the boys received schooling as well as training in weaving, although this may not have extended beyond religious education. The Society was always anxious to see that the boys were not only receiving religious education from the catechist but were also attending church. When in 1805 it discovered that many boys were absent from church, it considered this to be 'highly prejudicial to the interests of the institution' and maintained that it was 'the cause of the numerous and disgraceful elopements that have from time to time taken place'.[15] Moreover, the Society was adamant that boys who did not regularly attend church would not receive the usual grant on leaving. The Society was inclined to interpret the instructions in Pococke's will as an exhortation to proselytise. Its narrow view is evidenced by the peculiar case of William Farrell in 1805. He had been nominated for admission to the factory because, although both his parents were Protestant, they had died many years before and he was reported 'never to have been instructed in the Protestant religion but from the time of the death of his parents [was] always in the hands of papists'.[16] He was, therefore, admitted even though he did not strictly qualify according to the terms of Pococke's will.

James Pounds was appointed usher in February 1805, with particular responsibility for teaching. From an early stage he was under pressure from the Society to raise the educational standards, his salary of £20 per annum carrying a 'gratuity of ten pounds per annum, provided his conduct and attention to the improvement of the children shall be such as to merit the same'.[17] In November 1805, the Committee of Fifteen observed that 'the specimens of the children's writing are very indifferent' and threatened to fine the usher. In January 1806 Pounds was again warned that 'unless a visible improvement takes place in the writing of the boys next quarter, he will be fined'.[18] Later that year the committee fined him £2-10-0, not allowing him 'a bounty … in consequence of the shameful bad specimens of the boys' writing' and spoke of a further heavy fine for 'neglect of his duty … if improvement does not immediately take place'.[19]

In May 1806 Andrew Neelands was dismissed. There are no details of his offence but the board maintained that it was 'indispensably incumbent on them … to protect [the factory] not only from the contagion of immoral example but the scandal attending the suspicion of such immorality in the master'.[20] Neelands's dismissal was not an unusual measure by the Society, nor did it prevent him from obtaining a similar position, for in 1814 he took charge of the House of Industry in Kilkenny.[21]

The next master was James McKowen. The visit by the commissioners of the Board of Education in August 1808 found 28 boys (all but five from Co. Kilkenny), who were considered remarkably 'robust looking lads'. Although the boys received tuition in spelling and arithmetic as well as religious education, 'coming from the looms … [they] never had steady hands for writing'. The report provides a rare description of the structure of the factory:

> The house contains two dormitories, one 36 feet by 18, the other about 30 feet by the same; in the first there were ten beds, in the latter eight, (the master's apartment was contiguous to this, the usher's to the former), both are lofty and well ventilated … There is a good school-room, 28 feet long by 20 broad, which is also used as the dining hall. There are two working rooms, placed one within the other, the length of both nearly 50 yards; they are rather below the level of the street, and contained 21 looms, besides several wheels for winding cotton on, with a sufficient space between each, and a broad passage along the centre of the rooms; both are thoroughly ventilated by a great number of windows at both sides.[22]

It seems probable that the boys were still weaving linen and cotton. While they could have been spinning and winding the cotton, the reference to wheels for winding suggests that it came into Lintown ready-spun and that the boys were winding it prior to weaving. It is, however, possible that cotton manufacture had already been abandoned and that the cotton was being woven into the warp of the linen, as this was a common practice in the production of heavy linen. It is difficult to imagine that linen and cotton weaving both continued in an orderly way under McKowen's mismanagement. James McKowen ran into serious debt and was dismissed in 1816 for gross misapplication of the Society's money. His successor was John Armstrong, considered by the Revd Elias Thackeray, the Society's visitor in 1817, as 'likely to prove a very useful servant of the Society'.[23] While Thackeray saw that the physical state of the school was bad, he reported favourably on the education under McKowen but he may have been over-optimistic, for in 1818 he complained about Armstrong's neglect. By then Armstrong had been dismissed for fraudulent accounting.

So bad was the situation – the boys 'were mainly in rags' – that when Thomas Burrowes, the usher at Lintown, was promoted to succeed Armstrong, the Society provided a suit of clothes for each boy, so that 'the new master might not sink under difficulties caused by the mismanagement or misconduct of his predecessor'.[24] In 1820, the Revd William Lee, the Society's visitor, found that the educational standards of the 16 boys at Lintown were, with few exceptions, 'singularly and lamentably deficient'. He reported that there were only two hours of class a day and that there was 'a very striking inferiority in every respect in reading, writing and acquaintance with ... the Bible and ... religion'. Describing the factory as being in 'as bad a condition as can be conceived', he looked forward to its relocation.[25]

In 1816 the Society had begun to explore the possibility of relocating the factory to a six-acre site on the charter school lands at Brownstown. The opinion of the Attorney General was sought and was favourable to the idea. In 1817 the Kilkenny charter school for local boys was suppressed and replaced for a short time by a girls' school. Once the girls had been removed, the way was clear for the transfer of the factory school from Lintown and this was approved by the Society in February 1819.[26] At Brownstown there was 'an excellent school-room, 30' by 18', and three dormitories'. The apartments of the master and usher were 'most judiciously placed' in the centre of the house to be close to each of the dormitories.[27]

The move of the Pococke factory school from Lintown to Brownstown did not improve the efficiency of the operation. From 1822 to 1826 Burrowes employed a foreman to instruct the boys in the weaving business. One official visitor was not, however, impressed with Burrowes. James Glassford, one of the commissioners of the Royal Commission of Irish Education Inquiry, inspected the school in October 1824 and reported that 'the plan of the establishment is very defective so far as concerns the education of the children. The time of the master is engaged with his farm more than with the school and his object and interest in the weaving department … is to make the most from the work of the boys on his own account.' Burrowes admitted to Glassford that 'he only superintends the school and leaves the teaching to his brother' and his brother 'who has no remuneration, leaves it chiefly to one of the apprentices, the latter evidently unfit and without due authority'. Burrowes's brother was absent at the time of the visit, as he was sitting examinations at Trinity College. Burrowes himself was not always on duty at the school either, owning 'a small property … in the county of Carlow, which he cultivates himself and which requires his occasional absence'. The only aspect which won Glassford's approval was the scripture teaching of the catechist, the Revd Peter Roe, whose diary shows that he attended regularly.[28]

Despite the censure, Burrowes remained at the Pococke until 1829, when James Pounds was appointed. If, as seems probable, he was the former usher at Lintown Factory, the society was either forgiving or forgetful, as he had not given satisfaction. Pounds had been master at Ardbraccan charter school for 18 years prior to its closure in 1828. Although there was an increased intake of boys in the following year, the growth was not sustained. While the factory was credited with providing a competitive weaving service for the local poor, 'who had turned their little patches of land into flax gardens',[29] it faced increasing difficulties and the Incorporated Society came to acknowledge that 'the experiment did not succeed'.[30] In 1840, acting on legal advice that 'there appears to be ample grounds for asserting that this charitable fund cannot be beneficially administered in the exact manner prescribed by Bishop Pococke's will,'[31] it effected a major change by abandoning the industrial training and making the Pococke a straightforward school. At the same time it gave up all ideas of converting Roman Catholics and made the Pococke 'absolutely and exclusively a Protestant institution'.

This change was a belated recognition that proselytism did not work. The commissioners' report of 1825 had shown that it had brought the Society's schools into disrepute and caused bitterness in the Roman Catholic population. Roman Catholic bishops then spoke out, condemning the schools as 'the very germs, the roots of the Protestant propaganda' and complaining about the 'immense sums of money given by parliament to gain over proselytes'.[32] The 1825 report and the resultant cut in government finance spelt doom for the charter schools. The Incorporated Society had to reorientate its entire educational facilities and abandon any idea of converting its pupils. Some schools were closed, others suffered a reduction in numbers and in 1840 the Pococke School changed from an industrial school for Roman Catholic boys to a conventional school for Protestants.

Only five boys are mentioned in 1840,[33] which suggests that the number had fallen to that figure. There was, in any case, ample proof of the failure of the Pococke as it was constituted. The local committee decided that this change required that 'the master should be a person of higher literary attainments than the present master and be responsible for both the management of the institution and the instruction of the youth committed to his care.' In recognition of Pounds's 'fidelity' and 'the loss of a situation which he had every expectation of holding during his life',[34] he was granted a generous pension but its payment was delayed because he was in debt to the Society. Recalling his last three years at Brownstown, he explained that 'the number of boys so decreased ... he was at a most serious loss thereby in as much as that there was the same attendance, consumption of fuel and in some cases of food required as if the establishment was complete'.[35] In the summer of 1840 the boys of the factory were removed and each received £5 and a suit of clothing.[36] The looms were sold off. Whereas the educational tradition of Richard Pococke was to continue in Kilkenny as 'the Pococke Institution' or 'Pococke College', the industrial legacy of his original factory at Lintown was brought to an end.

CHAPTER FIFTEEN

New identity, 1840-1859

In order to fit out Brownstown as a proper school, William Pidgeon, agent of the Incorporated Society, was asked to visit in the summer of 1840. Following this, William Farrell, the Society's architect, was sent to draw up specifications for necessary repairs. Farrell's plan gives an insight into the probable use of the rooms in the decades that followed.[1] By January 1841 work had progressed enough to allow new pupils to be admitted. To equip the school the following articles were ordered: 1 set of fire irons, 24 spoons, 24 knives and forks, 24 delft plates, 24 tin porringers, 2 pots, 2 tubs, 12 pairs of sheets. A list of books and maps ordered for the school is a helpful indication of the Society's intentions for what was to be taught there:

> 6 Murray's Reader, 6 Murray's English Grammar, 6 Pinnock's Geography, 1 Jackson's Bookkeeping, 3 Bonycastle's Mensuration, 3 Bonycastle's Algebra, 12 Carpenter's Spelling Books, 4 Gough's Arithmetic, 1 Johnson Dictionary, 12 Bibles, 12 Prayer Books, 1 map each of the World, Europe, Asia, Africa and America.[2]

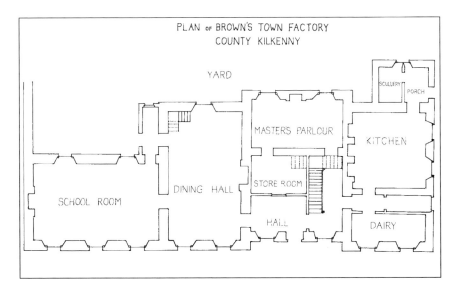

Plan of the Pococke School, 1840

The first master of the academic school which succeeded the factory was Richard Jessop. He had previously been on the staff of the Dundalk Institution, so he would have been aware of the experiment initiated in 1839 by Elias Thackeray with regard to the charter school in Dundalk. Thackeray proposed to make the Society's boarding schools more efficient by introducing a competitive system that would see clever children elected to the free places. He also suggested renaming the improved schools as 'institutions'.[3] If Jessop had aspirations to implement Thackeray's ideas in the Pococke School, he did not stay long enough to have any noticeable effect, resigning after a year. Alexander Hanlon was appointed master in July 1841. Like his predecessor, he moved from the Dundalk Institution. The son of a Clare farmer, he was one of the few Society masters to have been brought up in a Roman Catholic family. Through an education at Ennis College (funded by the Erasmus Smith Foundation) and at Trinity College, he became an Anglican and there is no suggestion that his religious background was an obstacle in his chosen career. In his first year there were eight foundationers, with an additional four in the following year. Of these only a handful were boarders. A Society deputation in June 1842 found that the younger boys in the school were 'well instructed in mathematics, arithmetic, English grammar, history, geography and the church catechism, bearing in consideration the short time they have been in the institution'.[4] Hanlon's time in Kilkenny was far from easy, as the process of establishing its reputation as a school proved slow. In July 1842, he appealed to the Society for quick payment of money due to him:

> I need not say how anxiously I will expect the decision of the committee on those bills, especially as … notwithstanding the strictest economy, it takes my salary and every shilling I can get to support the establishment, which might be owing to my having only three boarders as yet and also to my having expended considerable sums on the farm without having yet got any return.[5]

In October 1842, the local committee expressed regret 'at the very disgraceful state of the bedding, not caused by any neglect on the part of the master but by the very great deficiency in the supply afforded to him'. For the 17 pupils there were only 17 coverlets, 29 pairs of sheets and 15 bolsters. There was also concern that 'no place has been provided where the boys can wash themselves, so that they are obliged, even in this inclement season, to do so at the pump'. Both situations were rectified promptly with an immediate new supply of bedding and a washhouse with 20 basins by the end of December.[6]

Early in 1843, the Bishop of Ossory suggested that 'the Pococke Institution … might … by a very slight alteration to its rules … serve the purpose of a training school for masters … and supply … a very pressing want.' He, therefore, proposed that the maximum age of admission of pupils on the Pococke foundation be extended from 12 to 16 and this change was approved.[7] That year Hanlon moved to Santry School to manage a revised system of education. What was termed a training school opened there in February 1844. It received boys from the Pococke and other Society schools for three years' preparation to be schoolmasters. The entrants were to be existing pupils on the foundation who were the best at answering and the best behaved.[8]

Soon after replacing Hanlon in December 1843, John Turner asked the Society for a supply of books: 'There are no copies of geography with the exception of a few Pinnock's catechisms, there are no arithmetics except four copies of Gough's which has long since discontinued to be regarded as a good one … There are no histories of England. There are no Euclids.'[9] We can thus deduce some neglect before Turner's arrival but also his eagerness for the boys to succeed in their learning. In 1847 the Society expressed 'regret and disapprobation' after the annual deputation found that 'the clothing provided by Mr Turner is decidedly inferior to that in use in all their other schools'.[10] An incident the following year suggests that the boys did not get enough to eat. Two boys were expelled for theft and several other incidents were investigated. Many cases involved the theft of food, one of the boys admitting to 'breaking into the storeroom through a small glass window, which he broke for that purpose, and stealing at sundry times loaves of bread and eggs'.[11]

Turner was appointed to Dundalk Institution in 1853 and John L. Booth was appointed master, on the basis that he had already served the Society for 15 years as an assistant master in Dundalk Institution. The recruitment subcommittee believed that 'promoting a well-conducted assistant to the rank of a master in one of our institutions will have a beneficial effect in stimulating our other assistants …to increased attention and exertions in the cause of education.'[12] The educational commissioner's report in 1856 concluded that:

> This is in every respect, a well-managed school. The answering of the pupils in parsing, geography, arithmetic, algebra and English history was such as I have rarely met with. They not only know the rules and their application but answered with steadiness and confidence. It is impossible they should have acquitted themselves so creditably without great application on their own part and careful instruction from their master. What, it appears to me, the advanced state of instruction in this school particularly illustrates is the advantage of regular and uninterrupted study.[13]

The boys' petition

This may seem splendid but it cannot be reconciled with what happened a year later, when the pupils' complaints about conditions in the school led to Booth's dismissal. While rebellions and 'barrings out' were common, it was extraordinary that the foundationers at the Pococke School in 1857 expressed their dissatisfaction with the master not by rebellion but by writing a letter to the Society. Signed by 22 pupils from fifth to first year, it reads:

> The humble petition of the boys on the foundation … showeth that the undersigned are entirely neglected – first, in their education, it being wholly left to their own efforts; secondly, with regard to their food, which in respect to quantity and quality is much inferior to what they understand they are allowed; they … wish an investigation in the course of which several other irregularities will be developed … and if you will be so kind as to accede to that request, they shall as in duty bound, ever pray.[14]

It is equally extraordinary that the secretary of the Society, the Revd Richard Ardill, took the letter seriously and that very day went to Kilkenny to investigate, bringing with him a committee member, the Revd J. H. Stubbs. The next morning, they conferred first with the catechist, the Revd Vernon Drapes, 'as to the most prudent mode of acting in a matter of such deep importance to the well-being of the establishment and of extreme delicacy,

the master being, as it were, upon his trial and his own pupils being his principal accusers.' Ardill, clearly anxious to make the inquiry fair, asked Drapes
to record the proceedings and spent five hours hearing the statements of the
boys and the master.

The boys brought five charges against the master, relating to insufficient
instruction, diet, clothing and bedclothes, and the moral character of the
master. Several boys spoke but, most serious of all, Ashmore Fulton (senior
monitor), 'states that he never was instructed in any branch whatever, that
there is no school at all, that the boys are allowed to do just as they please.'
Booth's reply to this was that he taught the fourth year boys and that they
were to teach the juniors. James Wilson, one of the fourth year boys, alleged
that David Burleigh (a third year boy) 'was beaten severely at night when in
bed during vacation without having his fault enquired into.' Booth's response,
that 'he does not recollect having beaten a boy these three years' was not
allowed to stand, as Wilson retorted that 'no person could forget it who had
his senses about him at the time' and one of the boys who had not signed the
letter corroborated his evidence:

> Elliott Cairns (boarder) states that he recollects the circumstances of a mug
> having been broken at dinner during Mr Booth's absence from home; that Mrs
> Booth charged Burleigh with having broken it; that he denied it twice respect-
> fully, addressing her each time as Ma'am; that he was then charged with telling a
> falsehood and that in denying this charge he did not speak respectfully or call her
> Ma'am; that on Mr Booth's return, he (Mr B.) pulled Burleigh out of his bed at
> midnight while asleep and beat him severely with a cutting whip.
>
> Mr Booth, having been asked by Mr Stubbs whether he wished to say any-
> thing further in reply to the complaints brought against him, stated that some of
> the charges are untrue; that others are exaggerated; and that with reference to the
> rest, he will correct what is amiss and take care that no ground of complaint be
> given for the future.[15]

The subsequent report read that the boys:

> all reiterated their complaint openly and fearlessly and with the appearance of
> perfect truth; nor did they contradict themselves in any part of their examination
> upon the statements they made. ... It appears that the system by which the business
> of the school is carried on is very bad, or more properly, there is no system at all,
> no regularity in the order of instruction, no fixed or appointed time for almost
> any branch of study.[16]

The report concluded that Booth had irretrievably lost the boys' respect
and that his management of 'so very important an institution as the Pococke'
fell short. Booth wrote to defend himself, maintaining that he fed the boys a

better diet than the Society prescribed, and 'the proof of the success of my system is contained in the fact that, at the various diocesan examinations of schoolmasters, those trained in the Pococke School have always excelled'. Claiming that boarder numbers were 'constantly increasing', he asserted that the disturbance would not have occurred if the Society had responded to his frequent applications for an assistant. He alleged that 'the whole matter is a conspiracy', asking, 'Am I, after having been twenty-two years under the Society, to have my character destroyed on the evidence of such boys?'[17]

The board dismissed him and moved quickly to appoint a successor. Space does not permit a more detailed account of this episode, which is extraordinary in many ways: firstly, in acting so promptly on the boys' complaints, although this may be explained by the fact that Ardill had recently received 'reports prejudicial to the character of the master';[18] secondly, in believing the boys rather than the master; thirdly, in acting so speedily in dismissing him, for educational authorities were notoriously slow to act in such cases. According to Booth's second letter, the school was 'in a state of insurrection'[19] since the inquiry, which would have lent urgency to the Society's decision. The whole affair ended in less than a month and William H. Engledow was appointed master, ironically with an assistant master to help him.

It is impossible to know whether Booth was sinned against or sinning. On balance, given the care with which Ardill approached the issue, it is probable that Booth had become slack and that the Society was wise to terminate his appointment. The incident makes it hard to believe Ardill's assertion to the educational commissioners that 'we have now no such thing as an elopement either in the boys' or girls' schools'.[20] On the other hand, the incident does support a claim which Ardill made to the educational commissioners in relation to another school, that 'if there were misconduct or undue severity exercised by the masters, the boys would make their complaints to the catechist or members of the commission visiting the school'. Ardill specifically stated that masters had 'no authority to inflict corporal punishment, except so far as a pandy [*sic*] on the hand. If a boy is punished, it is, perhaps, by solitary confinement, or by reporting him to the Society.' Pressed by the commissioners that there should be a formal Society rule to that effect, Ardill replied:

> Where cases of insubordination occur, the master reports it, and I then write such a letter as he might read to the assembled school, requiring that an ample apology should be made by the offending party, or that his conduct should be brought under the consideration of the board, when the consequence would be his dismissal, in all probability. This system, invariably, has the desired effect of producing a reformation and an apology.[21]

The confidence in the good relations between masters and pupils in the Society's schools must have been severely shaken by the situation in the Pococke School. Engledow, however, gave satisfaction and the Society gave short shrift to the boys, who continued for some time to complain about the conditions. An Englishman, Engledow had previously taught in his native Durham and had had responsibility for boys at the cathedral school there. He had moved to Dublin and was studying at Trinity College. He had been an unsuccessful candidate for the mastership of the Society's school on Aungier Street but had made a very favourable impression and this led to him being chosen to solve the crisis in the Pococke.[22] He must have been successful in restoring order at the Pococke, for two years later he secured the mastership of the Incorporated Society's leading boys' school at Santry. Although he was a relative newcomer, Engledow's ambitious plan for education, extending to agricultural chemistry and surveying,[23] was probably the factor which set him apart from the other candidates, such as the long-serving Turner. The appointment turned out well and Engledow remained in Santry for many years. The Society chose well in the appointment of Engledow's successor at the Pococke School. John Blair Browne became headmaster in 1859 and steered the school for its remaining years as a separate school.

CHAPTER SIXTEEN

Furthering the boys, 1859-1903

John Blair Browne, from Co. Down, became headmaster in 1859 and gave the Pococke a long period of sustained stability. By this time, 'the great object' of the Incorporated Society 'was to fill the vacuum between the higher and lower classes of society; to afford gentlemen of small means a convenient opportunity of having their sons or their daughters carefully and well educated; and at the same time to preserve to the parents ... that feeling of independence which it is our desire always to cherish'.[1] Browne was a respected assistant master at Santry School and may have been educated there.[2] One of his former Pococke pupils, Samuel Hawkes, later wrote to the Society from his teaching position in England expressing appreciation of Browne as a teacher:

> He spares neither time nor energy in furthering the boys, his mind is stretched to the utmost in the performance of his duties, he is not only continually concerned on the intellectual advancement but is also warmly and intensely engaged in moralising all who come under his care, teaching both by precept and example. The quickness with which he detects and extirpates everything which might eventually prove injurious to spiritual growth is wonderful, the leniency with which he treats all personal annoyances exemplifies his good desire, for forgiveness on his part is always ready, though severity might be dealt with justice.[3]

A register of pupils survives from the early years of Browne's headmastership. One of the most successful of those pupils was William J. Richards, from Clonmel, who went to India as a young man in 1871 to work with the Church Missionary Society. During 35 years in India he worked on the revision of the Bible in Malayalam, an important language of southern India, and was awarded a doctorate of divinity in 1891 in recognition of that achievement. Another past pupil who had a successful career on the sub-continent was William Booth, a respected mathematician at the University of Calcutta and an educational administrator in Assam.[4]

At the beginning of Browne's time, the Society began to benefit from the funds of a substantial additional endowment, by the will of Anne Gorman.[5] Boarding fees for boys who were not on foundation scholarships were an important source of income for the school. (Pococke fees, at £25 per annum in 1872, were considerably less than those for Kilkenny College, at £45.[6]) Foundation scholars were elected by competitive examinations from the counties of Kilkenny, Wexford, Waterford, Cork, Kerry, Limerick and Tipperary.[7] Significantly, whereas much of Pococke's intention had been abandoned, disadvantaged boys regularly won scholarships, with a steady intake from the Protestant industrial schools of Cork and Tralee.[8] There were some 40 schools sending candidates for the Pococke. A letter describing the competitive examination was written to the children's page of *The Irish Times:*

Dear Granny,

It's such a long time since I wrote to you last. Isn't it? Well, I hope you will excuse me, as I was very sick the greater part of the time, and also I was studying hard for an examination for entrance to Pococke College, Kilkenny, the course of which I will tell you about just now. My father and I started from the barracks at 4 o'clock in the morning and drove to the railway station, which is about 12 miles distant. When we arrived there we had only a wait of about five minutes, and after a pleasant ride of one hour we arrived at our destination. The examination commenced at 11 o'clock, so we had three hours to have a look at the city. After having spent the greater part of our time in the city, we started for the college, which is about a mile or so outside it. When we arrived there we were met by the parents of some other competitors and the boys themselves. We all chatted together for some time, and then at the hour appointed we had to go in, our parents being allowed in with us. The first part of the examination was in scripture, and any boy who did not take 50 per cent in that subject was disqualified from the other part of the examination. There were eight candidates altogether, and of these one was disqualified from the secular part of the examination, which comprised reading, writing, arithmetic, grammar, geography of Europe (principally that of the British Isles), first book of Euclid, algebra, English composition. We were examined in the greater part of the subjects by word of mouth. We got an essay on bicycles. I think I did it very fair. After the examination was over we got out for a while till the marks were counted up. We were then called in and the result read out to us. A boy from Cappoquin took first place and I took second. We all went to the railway station, and saw each other off. I arrived home at half-past ten o'clock, fairly tired after my long day. Dear Granny, as this is my fourth attempt to win a hamper, I hope it will be as successful as I was at the examination …

From your affectionate grandson,

Albert Keegan[9]

When an educational commissioner visited the Pococke in October 1879, the school was found to be providing a 'high class English and mathematical education' for 53 pupils, 'the answering of the senior class in grammar, geography, Euclid and algebra' being 'very creditable'. The schoolhouse was reported to be 'kept in perfect repair, owing … to the exertions of the headmaster, at whose suggestion all the improvements [were] made'. The commission did, however, follow up a criticism made by the previous commission in 1857 that the Society's schools needed to be regularly inspected 'by a person acquainted with the ordinary necessities of an educational establishment'. The lack of inspection had allowed neglect in the areas of 'discipline, classification of pupils, cleanliness, etc.' and one effect in the Pococke was that 'the non-foundation boys were much behind the foundation boys'.[10]

The report was favourable enough to permit the following piece in the *Kilkenny Moderator* in 1882:

> There are few scholastic institutions in Ireland which can compare with the Pococke Institution in efficiency and usefulness and this is proved by the number of well-taught and thoroughly-qualified young men whom it sends out year by year into so many departments of the public service … When once a boy gains admission to the Pococke, he may, by his own diligence and good conduct, rise to almost any position of trust and honour for which his talents are found to qualify him. We could point to many, both at home and abroad, who are reflecting credit on this institution in which they received their education.[11]

A contemporary publication lists the subjects taught:

> The course of instruction includes the higher branches of mathematics, bookkeeping, surveying, navigation, English, grammar, composition, history, geography, mapping and drawing. Classics, French and drawing are taught at an extra charge of four guineas each. In addition to the foundation scholars, the regular boarders average thirty. They enter as hall-boarders at twenty guineas, or as parlour-boarders at thirty guineas each. Day pupils are taken at four guineas.[12]

Browne maintained that 'the first principle he taught his boys was brotherly love'.[13] If this was his approach, one can well believe his report that all were 'terribly upset' when a newly-appointed teacher of science and art died from an overdose of a medicine 'he had been in the habit of taking for many years'.[14] Browne's evidence to the educational endowments commission in November 1887 details the academic reputation of the Pococke. One recent day pupil had moved to the Pococke from Kilkenny College 'to be ground up in science'. Browne told the inquiry that 86 of his boys had passed civil service examinations (they got the first three passes in the British Isles), one had got a high place in the Royal University of Ireland and a great many had passed in science. The list went on to include many who gained passes for the College of Surgeons and others who had gone to England as mathematical masters. The school had for some years been connected with the South Kensington Department of Science and Art but, even though as many as 76 boys passed in a year, Browne had decided to end the link.[15] As to supervision by the Incorporated Society, Browne explained that the local committee had been discontinued because the same gentlemen appeared on the committee for the Model School and they were not allowed to act for both schools. Although the secretary of the Society visited the school frequently, Browne would have preferred to have a new local committee to support his work as headmaster.

The school continued at Brownstown until the retirement of John Blair Browne as headmaster in 1903 but the future was increasingly uncertain. As part of the Society's rationalisation in the 1890s, a sub-committee was appointed in December 1898, to 'consider the details of the amalgamation of the Collegiate School with the Pococke School'.[16] (The Collegiate School was the successor of Santry School and had been relocated to Portarlington a few years before.) The sub-committee found the Pococke School 'in an excellent state of repair' and suggested how it could be modified to accommodate the pupils from the Collegiate School.[17] That their recommendations were not implemented was probably due to the Society's unwillingness to invest considerable amounts of money in the buildings at Brownstown.

In March 1901, another sub-committee was appointed, 'to consider the possibility of effecting some union between Kilkenny College and the Pococke School, to form one strong school instead of two weak ones'.[18] The committee included the Bishop of Ossory and Richard Langrishe, a Kilkenny past pupil and prominent local figure, both of whom knew each school well. The proposal was feasible, as an amalgamation between a Society school and a non-Society school had been provided for in a scheme under the 1885 Educational Endowments Act for the management of the Incorporated Society endowments.[19] By the end of April 1903, all the formalities of the amalgamation were complete and the Society proposed that the boys from the Pococke School would begin in Kilkenny College after the summer vacation. Browne was awarded a pension of £300 per annum, partly calculated on the basis of his 51 years of service, partly on his expenditure on the substantial improvements he had made at Brownstown.[20]

One past pupil, writing more than 20 years later, provides a detailed account of the character of Browne's school to the very end:

Rugby team, 1897,
with H. B. Morton,
seated left

It was to [the Pococke] that the writer found himself consigned by train, as a very small boy, some twenty-three years ago. A kindly policeman showed him the way to its portals, and Mr John Blair Browne, who was then headmaster, extended to him his usual formula employed on such occasions, of 'Welcome, little man'!

The 'little man' found himself in trouble right from the first tee, so to speak. A perfectly brutal system of 'fagging' was then in operation. No slave on the cotton plantations of Kentucky was one whit more in the power of his masters than the 'Last Set Dogs' – the modern 'Grabbers' – were in the power of the 'Head Set'. Unremitting hardship, bullying and toil were their lot. Here is a sample: a big member of the Head Set was in the habit of coming into the dormitory at night and proclaiming peremptorily 'Last Set! On the floor!' Nine shivering urchins hopped out of bed and stood, scantily attired, in a line. 'About turn,' was the next order. They 'about-turned'! They did it smartly; it paid to be smart! 'Count toes,' went on the suave voice of the tyrant. We 'counted'! If inspection revealed that any unlucky wight had his knees bent during the process, he generally was sorry for himself. He had reason! But in any case our 'drill instructor' then proceeded to go along the line, and deliberately 'whale' each and every member of the squad with a set of plaited thongs, which he had ingeniously contrived for the purpose. Then the command 'Back to bed'! The last man in – and I was generally last – had some practical experience of the meaning of the proverb 'Devil take the hindmost'. During this wanton and utterly futile exhibition of cruelty, did any of his own set interfere? Not one! I could tell of equal cruelties perpetuated by others of them. I have been severely beaten by a blackthorn stick across the shoulders by one of them for an utterly trivial offence. None of us ever cared much to see the headmaster coming round the place; but many a time his unexpected appearance saved some unfortunate from being half-murdered.

The entry upon a second year was like the opening of paradise. It relieved one of the grinding and degrading tyranny of the past year. One watched with a philosophical eye the newcomers being put through the mill! One had achieved independence! It seems a fitting place to say something of the methods of Mr Browne, the headmaster. He was a most dignified-looking man, always wearing a large black beard and a black frock coat. The sight of him struck terror into the evil-doer's heart. He rarely caned a boy. He hated to do it. But most of us would have preferred to be flayed alive rather than come under his flashing eyes, and hear the tones of his voice in reproof. Someone would have broken a window. 'Now, boys! Who broke that window?' No answer. 'I see! Get to your books. Evening school will commence in future at 4 p.m. instead of 5 p.m., till further notice.' Curiously though, if anyone 'owned up', he was generally 'let down' with practically no sentence at all. But if he could not discover the perpetrator of any crime, however venial, J. Blair Browne invariably punished the whole school severely, by stopping a holiday or by extra school hours. It was often very hard luck – but people did not care to own up much to 'Johnnie'! His gaze was too petrifying!

Sunday at Pococke was truly a dreadful day. Sunday School from 10 to 11; march into town to St John's Church at 11.30; dinner; afternoon Sunday School, 3.30 to 4.30 p.m.; march into church at 6.30; tea; and then a religious lecture by Johnnie from 8 to 9.20 p.m. That final lecture is still spoken about with bated breath by old Pococke boys. Most people grow fidgety with a sermon – even a good one – if it lasts more than twenty minutes. But Johnnie's sermons were not good ones! And they lasted an hour and twenty minutes each – in addition to the other religious teaching instilled into us throughout the day. It is a striking testimony to the innate good that is in human nature that quite the majority of old Pococke boys are not atheists! Some of them are even clergymen!

There was a lighter side to life in Pococke. I spent many happy days there. I was unfeignedly sorry to exchange it for the civilised and humanising influence of Mountjoy School.[21]

The retirement of John Blair Browne as headmaster was not an absolute watershed, for his legacy continued. Boys whom he had begun to shape continued their education in Kilkenny College and Mountjoy School and no doubt drew on their experience of his guidance. Many of his past pupils had distinguished service either in the church or in education, probably the two spheres of society which Browne cared about most.[22] J. B. Leslie, rector of Kilsaran, Co Louth, from 1900 to 1951, left a lasting legacy to the Church of Ireland in compiling the succession lists of clergy, a work frequently cited in

The front of the
Pococke School

this history. It is likely that many Pococke boys fought in the Boer War and World War One but the Incorporated Society totals of past pupil servicemen did not include schools that had closed. To date, three Pococke past pupils have been identified as casualties of the First World War: William Howe, Henry Mulholland and Richard Murphy. Browne considered Howe 'one of the best boys all round that I have ever had under my care – he has excellent abilities and is most industrious and his conduct since he came here has been all that could be desired.'[23]

Most of the Pococke boys began a new school year in September 1903 at Kilkenny College. The eulogy in the local newspaper read: 'Down to the last moment of its existence as a separate school … the old Pococke College, Kilkenny, maintained its prestige, and recently the list of honours and passes won by pupils of the college … bore strong testimony to the truth of our assertion'.[24]

SECTION C

Celbridge Collegiate School
1740-1973

CHAPTER SEVENTEEN

Foundation and early years

William 'Speaker' Conolly founded by his will a school which later came to be known as the Collegiate School, Celbridge. Born in 1662 to a family of moderate means in Ballyshannon, Co Donegal, he rose far beyond his origins to be one of the most powerful men in Ireland. Having studied law in Dublin and become an attorney, he was first elected member of parliament for the borough of Donegal in 1692. His marriage in 1694 to Katherine Conyngham connected him to the most important families in west Ulster[1] and he used her substantial dowry to expand his portfolio of landed estates. In the following years he became very wealthy, largely by successful land speculation.[2] In public life, his drive and ability enabled him to achieve political dominance by holding three posts which were never held simultaneously by any other man: those of Lord Justice of Ireland, First Commissioner of the Revenue and Speaker of the House of Commons. With access to the highest echelons of government, control of proceedings in the House of Commons and unparalleled opportunities for patronage, Conolly became arguably not only the richest but probably the most influential man in Ireland.

In the 1720s he built Castletown House in Celbridge.[3] Ireland's most important Palladian house, there is still argument as to its architect. It seems that the Italian architect, Alessandro Galilei, produced a grand design during a visit to Ireland in 1718-19. Galilei was back in Italy by the time that Conolly was ready to proceed, so a new architect had to be found. As Patrick Walsh says, 'It seems likely that Conolly sought advice from a number of local connoisseurs including the philosopher, George Berkeley ... and the architect, Thomas Burgh.'[4] It is uncertain how much of Galilei's design was followed but the façade is almost certainly his, while the wings and colonnades and probably the interior layout were designed by Edward Lovett Pearce. It is further proof of Conolly's power that he could call on Burgh, the Surveyor General, the outstanding young architect, Pearce, and the cultured philosopher, Berkeley, to help him in his project. In turn, Conolly was influential in securing for Pearce the commission for the new Irish House of Commons in College Green.

In 1729, shortly before he died, Conolly was planning to establish a charity school near Castletown, was apparently in the process of buying the requisite

William Conolly

land and was discussing a building design with Thomas Burgh.[5] The fact that the school was built to close the western vista from Castletown suggests that Conolly envisaged it as another physical memorial to his life, an idea that is supported by his consultation of Burgh. There were already three charity schools in Co. Kildare, one of which was in Celbridge, but Conolly's proposed school differed from these and other charity schools in that it was to be residential. His foundation of the school was a worthy philanthropic act but he also had an eye to posterity. His desire to secure his reputation is reflected in the wording on his tomb: 'He made a modest though splendid use of the great riches he had honestly acquired.'

Conolly's belief in the value of education was undoubtedly coloured by his personal experience but also reflected the contemporary desire to establish charity schools which would train the children of the poor for useful employment, so that they would not be a financial burden on the parishes. While this was the sole reason for setting up charity schools in England, in Ireland there was the further purpose of winning over 'popish' children to Protestant and English ways, in the hope that rebellions would cease. Conolly must have known about the wider movement which led to the establishment of the Incorporated Society in 1734 but pressed ahead with his own scheme. In his will Conolly left:

> the sum of £500 to my dear wife Katherine Conolly, to my dear nephew William Conolly, to the Right Revd Arthur, Lord Bishop of Clonfert and Kilmacduagh, to the Right Hon. Marmaduke Coghill, to Thomas Marley, Attorney General, and the Revd Mr George Marley, vicar of Kildrought, to be laid out by them in erecting a convenient building in or near the town of Celbridge in the county of Kildare on such spot of ground as shall be set out to them for that purpose by my said dear wife and nephew for the reception of forty orphans or other poor children. And I do likewise give and devise the sum of £250 yearly to be issuing out of the manor town and lands of Rathfarnham in the county of Dublin and on the appurtenances thereof to my said wife Katherine Conolly, to my said nephew, etc ..., the survivor or survivors of them and the heirs of such survivors for ever upon trust and in confidence that they lay out and expend the said sum of £250 yearly in maintenance and education of forty such orphans or poor children under such rules, regulations and directions as they or the major part of them shall think proper in the instruction of such children in the linen or hempen manufactures or in husbandry ...[6]

Conolly placed the chief responsibility for the school on his wife and nephew, William, because he and Katherine had no children. The trustees acquired the land which he had chosen and in 1733 William donated another 50 acres beside the school, to add to the original foundation. By 1737, according to the annual report of the Incorporated Society, he had begun 'a building of 120 feet square ... This building, which by computation will cost near £1,500, is to stand in a court of 400 feet square, surrounded by a wall ... and the work is in such forwardness that it will probably be roofed before next winter.' Whereas the design might well have been by Thomas Burgh, his death in 1730 meant that another architect must have shaped the project.

One conjecture is that Isaac Wills, who was in the circle of Burgh, was involved.[7] It is notable that the Society, which had no formal connection with the foundation at this stage, took an interest in it because it was 'directed nearly to the same ends and purposes [as] the charter schools'.[8]

Louisa Conolly

Although she was in her late sixties, Katherine took a close interest in the school for some years and added £50 per annum during her life. She died in 1752 and William died the following year. While he had lived mostly in London, his son, Thomas, inherited and lived at Castletown from 1759. Thomas was not much interested in the school but his young bride was. She was Lady Louisa Lennox, the teenage daughter of the second duke of Richmond, and had been living for some years at Carton House, near Maynooth, with her sister, Emily, Countess of Kildare. Although she was English, by the time she came to live at Castletown in 1759, she had learnt a great love for Ireland and the Irish from her brother-in-law, the Earl of Kildare. In her thirties she became very involved in charitable work in the locality[9] and set up a local industrial school for boys. So impressive was her commitment that one commentator wrote: 'The virtues of Lady Louisa Conolly have peculiarly endeared her to the surrounding inhabitants. To use the language of scripture, she lives to humankind more than to herself.'[10]

Remarkably little is known about the school in the 18th century but it did attract further support. A large sum of £1,000 was left to the school by Arthur Price, Archbishop of Cashel, who died in 1752. Price's father had been vicar of Straffan and a friend of Conolly. Through this friendship Conolly became Arthur's patron, appointing him his personal chaplain in 1705 and securing the parish of Celbridge for him. Arthur had a fine house built for himself at Oakley Park, Celbridge, in 1720 and it is often suggested that its architect was Burgh. As one of William Conolly's executors, it was appropriate that Arthur Price later signified his approval of the aims and operation of the school by his sizeable legacy. Much of the information that is available comes from a cash book for the period 1785-95, which is preserved with the Incorporated Society records. From this source, we can glean the names of those who nominated the girls for admission: some men but typically ladies, such as Louisa's sister Emily (by then Duchess of Leinster) and Emily's daughter, Lady Bellamont. During this period a fee of £2-5-6 was paid for each admission. While the Incorporated Society in 1737 had anticipated that Celbridge would in time be able to take 100 pupils, the commissioners of education stated in 1788 that the school house had been designed for 40 girls but there were only 17.[11] The viability of the school in 1785 can be partly measured by reference to the annual rents itemised in the accounts:

Endowment of the Speaker William Conolly	£250
Endowment of the late William Conolly in land, bearing rent	£60
Endowment of the present Thomas Conolly, during the lives of Joseph Henry and Lady Louisa Conolly	£50
Endowment from Joseph Henry	£15
Annuity upon the sum of £200 given to the school by the late Theobald Wolfe	£9
Total	£384[12]

This money financed the operation of the school of 40 children under the care of a mistress and an assistant mistress but there were 50 girls at that time, as two cows enabled an extra ten girls to be supported. The farm and garden not only produced food for the staff and pupils but its surplus helped to balance the books. The accounts show regular expenditure on garden seeds and, after a byre and pigsty were built in 1790, the farm had additional livestock. The produce of the farm added variety, colour and extra nutrition to the otherwise simple diet of the girls. Even so, a large proportion of the school's funding went on food. A memorandum of a year's consumption to the end of April 1791 includes the following amounts:

salt fish	£0-11-6
8 geese	£0-14-8
meat (from the butcher)	£66-11-3
oatenmeal	£11-14- 0
potatoes	£7-16-0
pease	£8-17-1½
hops	£1-12-6
malt	£6-6-0
wheat	£69-15-10
butter, milk & buttermilk	£39-11-9½
	£213-10-8

It seems that the girls were quite well fed and clothed and had two pairs of shoes each, the school paying for a new pair of shoes for each girl every year. This may seem generous but an average girl would have grown out of a pair of shoes before the end of a year. It may have been Celbridge to which Elias Thackeray was referring a generation later when he commented:

Girl working at a garter loom

> In one female [charter] school the children every day had clean shoes, well black-ened. These children had always two pairs of shoes in use. This useful practice might be universally enforced; by daily change, the shoes would last longer … and habits of neatness would be acquired from the daily cleaning … which would accompany them in their apprenticeships and after they had entered into life.[13]

A local woman made their dresses and their blue and white linen petticoats. The dresses varied in colour from time to time: in 1785 they were green, with scarlet cuffs, in 1791 they were orange. The girls knitted their own blue and white worsted stockings.

There were two schoolrooms in 1785, so there was ample room for two teachers. Mary Taylor was on the staff, presumably as mistress, in 1783.[14] She resigned as mistress in 1789 and appears to have been succeeded by Katherine Holt, with her husband Joshua. While it seems likely that a female assistant was employed, the only wages mentioned in 1785 for another teacher are for James Collison, the writing and reading master. In addition to reading and writing, the girls were taught to spin, weave and to pencil calico.[15] Garter looms were made for the school by a carpenter at 6s 6d per loom, amount-ing to a total of £3-5-0. The income from the girls' work also went to offset the costs of their education. Some of the girls received a loom when they left, so that they could make a living; others went into service and received a set of clothes. On one occasion Lady Louisa noted that she had bought these herself, which shows how close her involvement was.

All that we know about the school in the late 18th century comes from this, the only surviving internal record of the time. There is no record of how the school fared during the 1798 rebellion, in which Celbridge suffered a lot of damage. It must have affected the school, for there were both rebels and soldiers in Celbridge. The soldiers were just as dangerous for the local people,

Thomas Conolly

for they had free-quarter and made daily threats to burn the town. Many houses were burnt and the church was destroyed. The Conollys were devastated to find that some of their servants were rebels or sympathisers.

The turn of the century brought serious developments for the Conolly family, which had an inevitable impact on the school. When Thomas Conolly died in 1803, he left 'considerable debts, mortgages and judgements due on the estates'.[16] Although he was by inheritance the richest and most influential man in Ireland, he lacked his great uncle's management skills and became embroiled in a lawsuit with his sisters over his mother's will: hence the difficult situation which afflicted his widow. Lady Louisa had to devote most of her time to running those estates and had, therefore, to reduce her involvement in the school. The commissioners of the Board of Education, nevertheless, found that the school was still well run.[17] Estimating that the maintenance of the children, excluding salaries, cost about £10 each, they expressed the hope that, in the future, a contingency fund could be established to cover expenses arising from sickness and repairs and to allow an increase in numbers.

In 1809 Lady Louisa proposed to transfer the management of 'the Celbridge Charity School' to the Incorporated Society.[18] The proposal came at a time when the Society was considering the recommendation of the Board of Education that it should close several of its schools, in the hope that by 'contracting the number and enlarging the size of the establishments all the valuable purposes of the institution [would] be more effectively obtained, that the management [would] be rendered more easy and the permanent annual expense considerably reduced'.[19] The Society realised that the process would be helped by taking over Celbridge, as it could 'accommodate with ease 150 children; and consequently, when properly fitted up, [would be] sufficient for the reception of all the females now in … Monivea Nursery and Loughrea and Castlebar Schools'.[20] Its committee reported that the Society 'expended in sundry necessary repairs, furniture, etc. and in building a new school-room, dining-hall and dormitories at the school of Celbridge, between

5 January 1811 and 5 January 1812, £2,394-7-6'.[21] Repairs and additions were sanctioned at Celbridge and the Society's school at Santry for three reasons:

1. That both establishments possessed considerable endowments … that of Celbridge, 531 acres of land in perpetuity, together with a rent charge of £309 per annum …

2. Because both establishments, being in the vicinity of Dublin, were within easy reach of inspection from thence.

3. Because the suppression of Loughrea, Castlebar and Arklow schools, which were all appropriated to the reception of female children, rendered it necessary to provide additional accommodation for children of that sex in some of the remaining schools.

Furthermore, the committee felt the investment was fully justified as the works had 'not only advanced those establishments (previously extremely incommodious) to a state of comparative convenience, comfort and respectability but have provided additional accommodation for 100 children' and 'when the funds of the Society shall enable them to build suitable infirmaries, each of these schools will be completely commodious and healthful establishments for 150 children and present a striking contrast in appearance and real comfort to their former state'. When the Society took over Celbridge there were less than a hundred girls.[22] In that year 17 girls were transferred from the Society's school at Castlebar, which was being closed and by the end of 1812, with the works completed, there were 154 pupils.

The transfer to Incorporated Society management was formalised by a deed of 28 September 1811.[23] The parties to the deed, in addition to the Society, were Nathaniel Clements, the Earl of Leitrim, Lady Louisa Conolly, the Revd Patrick Sands, vicar of Kildrought, John Joseph Kenny of Straffan and Edward Pakenham. As well as the transfer of property, the deed made specific provision for the nomination of pupils by 'Lady Louisa Augusta Conolly … and every future and successive lord of [the] manor of Castletown'. This right of nomination was a power to recommend 'any child whom she or he may think proper, not being deformed, maimed or unhealthy nor under the age of six years nor above the age of ten years and who has not been removed from any other school for misconduct'. The maximum number of Conolly nominations was stipulated to be 30 girls at any one time. It was further agreed that whenever one of those girls left the school or died, the lord of the manor could nominate another child instead. These girls were mostly to be selected from the family estates.[24] The Incorporated Society was to select all the rest of the children to be admitted

Castletown House

to the school. A large local committee, comprising members of the local aristocracy and gentry, was formed on the recommendation of Lady Conolly. Thus the school at Celbridge entered a new and more secure phase as a charter school.

CHAPTER EIGHTEEN

Stability, 1810-1859

The Incorporated Society applied the rules for the charter schools to Celbridge, thus introducing a rigid regime. The new rules adopted in 1809 make for chilling reading, the worst feature being the tendency to refer to a child as 'it'. The Society took a ruthless approach to 'idiots and others afflicted with evil, scald and scrofulous disorders' and to those who were 'notoriously addicted to such heinous offences as lying, swearing, stealing, etc or remarkably idle'. It held a negative view of children, instructing the ushers to superintend their conduct at all times, 'to pay strict attention to their morals, correcting them for improper behaviour, for slovenliness of dress, or inattention to the care of their clothes, etc.' The rules for masters, mistresses and ushers were also daunting, although there were incentives in the form of bonuses and promotion.[1]

The Society appointed a married couple as master and mistress at Celbridge. John and Bridget Boyle came from Farra School, near Mullingar, where their work had pleased the Society, so they knew how to implement the system. Boyle farmed the land and was allowed to keep any profit from the children's work, after paying the Society 20 shillings per annum for the labour of each child. While this system was abused in many schools, the Society and the local committee consistently commended the Boyles' regime in Celbridge. The girls were well prepared for a practical life in domestic service, farming or needlework and were, by and large, easily apprenticed when their time was up in the school. This happy situation was a marked contrast to that in many of the Society's schools, where the masters wanted to keep pupils when they became old enough for their work to be economically profitable and provided such a poor education that the children were, in any case, hard to apprentice. Boyle kept good records of apprenticeships and their success, and the register shows that many of the girls went into service with the aristocracy, while others were apprenticed to some branch of the clothing trade.[2] In 1826 one of Boyle's pupils was appointed assistant usher. This was, in effect, a vote of confidence in his own ability. Martha Neill, who entered the school in 1812, was later promoted and served as usher until 1848. Likewise, girls were regularly apprenticed to John Boyle to train as servants.

The education the Boyles provided consisted of the three Rs, 'scripture history and the principles of the Protestant religion'.[3] The same schedule was laid down for all the charter schools. Many hours were set apart for labour, when the girls worked at 'spinning, plaiting straw, dressing flax, knitting stockings and mending their own clothes and other useful branches of female industry.'[4] The last reference is to taking turns

> in the kitchen, the laundry, the dairy and the bakehouse, in milking the cows and cleaning the milk vessels, in scouring and cleaning the hall, the dormitories and every other part of the house, in filling the water cistern, feeding the poultry, weeding the garden and haymaking in the proper season, in waiting at the master's table and in attending the other children in sickness.[5]

This labour filled 4½ to 5 hours a day depending on the season, while 4½ were devoted to teaching. From 1 March to 1 October the girls got up at 6 o'clock and went to bed at 9, for the rest of the year they got up half an hour later but went to bed an hour earlier.[6] These times reflected the hours of daylight, for there was no point in getting up too early or staying up too late in the days before electric lights. One of the horrific aspects of the timetable is that they did not have breakfast for two or three hours after getting up! They had to clean the school and endure an hour and a half of class before they had anything to eat. It comes as a great relief to read that, at least, they were allowed a short period of play after breakfast and dinner. It is, of course, true that life at home would have been no easier.

Another worrying aspect of the daily schedule is that the girls had to look after other sick children. That inevitably put them at risk, though the school's isolation gave some protection from the major epidemics which raged through the city from time to time. The girls' health depended on a number of factors, including diet and exercise, cleanliness, both personal and in the kitchen and school generally. The fact that only 28 deaths are recorded in the register during the Boyles' time suggests that Celbridge was healthier than most of the Society's schools. Of the 28, probably 14 died of tuberculosis[7] but there is no evidence of a significant outbreak in the school.

The Society laid down the same rules for diet in all its schools. Breakfast consisted of porridge and a pint of milk or buttermilk, although wheaten bread could be substituted on Sundays. On Sundays and Thursdays each girl had ½lb (225g) of meat, exclusive of bone, and 2lb of potatoes. That may seem a large amount of potato but it must be remembered that no other vegetables and no dessert was offered. On Mondays and Fridays, the menu was soup (made with stock from the previous day's dinner, with added leek,

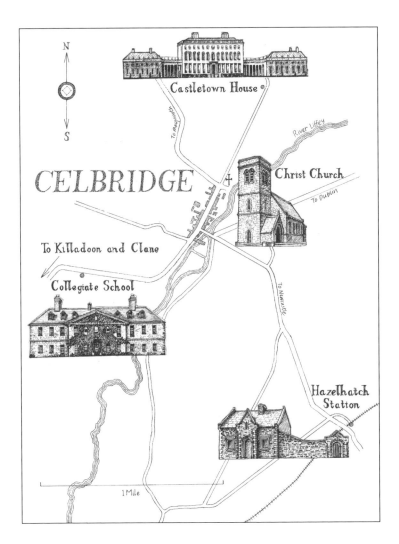

Celbridge

turnip, carrot and cabbage) and bread; on the three remaining days dinner was merely bread or porridge with milk. Supper alternated between bread and milk and potatoes and buttermilk. It is hard to be sure how the diet compared with the average diet in the sector of population from which the girls came but in the charter schools which followed the rules the diet was probably as good, if not better, than they would have received at home. Temporary alterations to the dietary were occasionally made when necessitated by widespread crop failure around the country[8] but the girls in Celbridge probably continued to benefit from extra food supplied by the farm.

As to cleanliness, the mistress, as in all charter schools, was to see that rooms were swept every day and washed once a week; that 'the children have clean linen twice a week, that their hands and faces be washed at least morning and evening, and their heads carefully combed every morning; that their hair be kept close cut; that clean sheets be put on their beds the first Sunday in every month, and each bed filled with 28lbs of fresh dry straw, regularly each quarter-day.'[9] Readers may shudder at the thought of the bedding but the Society believed at the time that the provision was good.

In 1819 the Society adopted the suggestion of the Revd Elias Thackeray (one of its most enthusiastic supporters) that boys and girls from the charter schools should be selected for training in Dublin as ushers, to qualify them for appointment as teachers in the Society's schools or in other schools. The Kevin Street School was modified for this purpose and in the next five years 11 girls were sent there from Celbridge, though it should be noted that not all of them went on to teach.

As we have seen in the introduction, the government began to challenge the Incorporated Society from the 1820s. The educational commissioners who reported in 1825 found in the charter schools what Kenneth Milne has described as 'a mixture of maladministration and corruption, to some extent endemic in the running of such institutions at that time, but exacerbated by the fact that the schools were, for the most part, remote from central supervision, and laboured under such economic restraints that exploitation of the children in their care by master and mistresses was temptingly easy'.[10] As part of their inquiry they asked Thackeray whether Celbridge was one of three 'marked exceptions' to the deplorable state of the schools. He replied that it was 'better than any others', pointing out that the local committee was the best and most conscientious.[11] This comment supported the opinion of the Revd William Lee, the Society's visitor for 1819, that Celbridge was the best school of its type in the country.

It is rare to hear the views of a pupil as far back as the early 19th century, so it interesting that the evidence of a past pupil, Susan Davis, appears in the report. She had been in Celbridge from 1812 to 1823 and recorded that she had been treated very well. She doubted if 'there was ever a better master or mistress than Mr and Mrs Boyle'. We do not know on what basis she was asked to give evidence, so it is impossible to say how reliable a witness she was but we do know that the Society was consistently pleased with the Boyles' work. During their time six girls ran away, which is not a large number for a school of that size. While all may have been well in Celbridge, the days of the charter schools were numbered. When the government cut financial support, the Society had to close schools and cut the numbers of pupils. Overall numbers fell from 1,500 in 1828 to 536 in 1838, with 287 in just five boarding schools and 249 in five day schools. Even in Celbridge the fall was dramatic.

January 1828	134
January 1829	148
January 1830	120
January 1831	102
January 1832	105
January 1833	89
January 1834	72
January 1835	59

Numbers in Celbridge School, 1828-1835 [12]

In 1832 the Society had more than 150 girls aged 16 or over, for whom they saw no prospect of apprenticeship. It decided that one way to reduce that number was to use government aid to help them emigrate to Australia, where there was plenty of work. In September 1835 as part of the scheme 13 girls from Celbridge sailed from London for Tasmania.[13] Although there is no evidence that further girls were sent to Australia, it seems to have been considered. In 1842 the mother of one of the older girls, Martha Macdonald, having heard that more girls were to be sent to Australia, wrote to the Society, asking for her daughter to be returned to her, as 'I dread the very idea of separation from my dear child to a place where most probable [*sic*] I never again should behold her in this world'.[14]

The diet had changed little by 1838, when the local committee complained that it was inadequate. It received from the Committee of Fifteen a stern reply redolent of Dickens's Mr Limbkins in *Oliver Twist*: 'As the charter schools are designed for the religious education and support of the children of the poor natives of Ireland, it is not deemed expedient to nourish such children in a way which … may make them discontented with their lot'.[15] Apart from this instance, there is a noticeable lack of complaints about the diet in Celbridge, whereas there were frequent complaints in relation to many charter schools.

An example of the strict discipline and seclusion in operation at Celbridge was the case of Margaret Nugent, who in 1842 was discovered to have been 'carrying on a correspondence by letters and private interviews with a young man in Celbridge'. The annual report of the local committee detailed the response:

> As soon as this violation of the rules of the institution was detected, the girl was instantly separated from her companions and she still remains locked up in a secluded apartment until the determination of the Society is known … [They]

regret that the confinement to which she had been subjected seems to have made no salutary impression on her. The remedy to prevent a repetition of such irregularities that suggests itself is to remove the offender as soon as possible and to such a situation as may preclude her return to this neighbourhood; together with all those elderly girls who may have been her accomplices and to maintain (if possible) an increased degree of vigilance and superintendence over all the rest as well during the hours of recreation and study and to interdict them from all recourse to those parts of the playground which are contiguous to the public road.[16]

In 1841 the Society, mindful of 'the necessity of bringing the expenditure of the Society within its income', introduced new limits to the number of foundation scholars in its schools, specifying 62 as the maximum number for Celbridge, of which 30 were to be received on the Conolly Foundation.[17] There were gradual changes in the admissions policy. Since the Society takeover, all the candidates except the Conolly foundationers had been elected by the board. In 1846, in an attempt to ensure that entrants were 'children of intelligence', it was decided that they should be elected from the county's scriptural schools, after examination in prescribed subjects. It was further ordered that girls should stay for four years only, to 'prevent the Society being burdened, as at present, with women who years ago should have been ... supporting themselves and contributing to the support of others'.[18] The Society's deputation of 1850 reported in relation to the examination that 'the anxiety evinced by the parents who were present that their children should be admitted formed a striking contrast to the indifference that was manifested two years ago'.[19] Another positive step came in 1853, when the Society raised the age of entry to ten. Sadly the Conolly family ignored this rule and continued to nominate girls as young as four or five until the 1880s, all without any test of ability. Obviously it was extremely difficult to educate girls up to 18 when the youngest were only four years old.

When Mrs Boyle died in 1850, Miss Mary McKenny (her daughter from a previous marriage)[20] took her place but died early in 1851 and was succeeded by her half-sister, Miss Anne Boyle. She took sole control when John Boyle died the following year. His death was deeply regretted by the Society and the local committee, which recorded that his service in Celbridge, in conjunction with his wife, had been:

a blessing to the country, by training up so many young people in the paths of religious knowledge and virtue. His life was a practical illustration of the purity of his principles ... In the management of the Society's farm, which is now in the most improved state, Mr Boyle employed the girls in those industrial works which so conveniently fit them for useful situations in the country districts, and the best proof of the value of that combined system of education is that the children are readily apprenticed.[21]

Under examination by the Society's deputation in 1853 Anne Boyle's teaching and management passed with flying colours. With her tuition, the girls had made new clothes for themselves, which the local committee thought were excellent. Not only did they make and repair the dresses of Miss Boyle and the family but they often were given similar work by the local gentry. In a cloistered existence, it was very rare for the girls to go on an outing and it must, therefore, have been a great excitement to be taken to the Great Exhibition in Dublin in September 1853. The catechist explained:

> this laudable indulgence originated with Giles Shaw, one of the members of the local committee ... By his liberality on the occasion ... a special railway carriage was provided for the children and tickets of admission presented to them ... and he devoted several hours for the express purpose of pointing out to the children all the most attractive objects of art and industry.[22]

The educational commissioners of the 1850s found that, although some girls went on to become teachers or governesses, the curriculum in Celbridge still did not extend beyond the three Rs, needlework, knitting and vocal music. In questioning the secretary of the Incorporated Society, the Revd Richard Ardill, they were told that the girls were no longer taught farming practices and the only industrial instruction now given to them was in needlework.

The Great Exhibition, Dublin, 1853

Masters were no longer charged for the children's labour and apprenticeships had been discontinued in all the Society's schools, except for the occasional Celbridge girl who was apprenticed as a servant. A small number of girls still went as servants in the 1850s but employers did not wish to burden themselves with the restrictions of an apprenticeship. In any case, the way forward for Celbridge was to educate its pupils for a better life. It was probably in recognition of a changing situation that the Society had discontinued the 'marriage portions of £5 apiece to deserving girls in the female boarding schools'.[23]

Asked if there was a teacher training scheme for girls, Ardill said that there were monitresses who taught the junior classes and who were then promoted to the position of teachers, for which they were paid as usheresses and, where possible, were placed in schools elsewhere. The Society report for 1853 had already suggested that a formal training class could be established in the school and in 1857 a special committee was set up to explore the possibility. It advocated a more comprehensive system of instruction for 'such girls as from their abilities and aptitude for teaching are likely to reflect credit on the Society's teacher training class'.[24] The commissioners pursued the point and recommended that teaching standards should be raised to enable it to become a training school for school mistresses.[25] The girls in the training class were to act as monitors so that they would get teaching practice. They were also to gain practical experience by superintending the domestic tasks. They were to have a different dress from the other girls. In order to implement this change, an extra teacher was appointed but the experiment was soon discontinued. In 1859 the new secretary of the Society wrote to Thomas Conolly that it had proved 'unattainable and the original intention of fitting the girls as household servants was determined to be adhered to'.[26] This retrograde step flew in the face of reality, as an increasing number went to the Kildare Place Training School.

Perhaps the main reason for the initial failure of the training class was the difficulty of raising standards due to the way the Conolly Foundation operated. One wonders if another reason for its failure was opposition from Miss Boyle, who in 1858 submitted her resignation, for 'want of bodily strength to discharge such arduous duties'[27] and finally retired in 1859. Late in 1858, the Society's secretary raised with her an alleged case of 'unduly severe punishment', when a girl was reputed to have been 'placed in irons'.[28] Although this was a serious matter, there is no further reference to the matter. Her retirement ended half a century of supervision by the Boyle family.

One other aspect of the school was explored by the educational commissioners. When Ardill said, 'I cannot speak too highly in praise of the local committee at Celbridge, who take the liveliest interest in the management of the school', he pointed out that there were several ladies who were active members and that the school would not be as good without the committee's input.[29] An ensuing discussion on possible conflict between an active local committee and the Society may well indicate why local committees were allowed to lapse.

The local committee had been supportive of the Boyles, who had brought a period of stability to the school and enabled it to survive when many charter schools were closed. By 1859 the kind of education they provided was outdated and a new headmistress was needed who could steer the school in a more academic direction.

Memorial to John and Bridget Boyle

CHAPTER NINETEEN

Gradual change, 1859-1909

The Incorporated Society faced many difficulties in finding headmistresses who could develop Celbridge as an academic school. In the next 50 years there were eight headmistresses, the last 15 years being a period of particular instability. Between 1894 and 1909, one headmistress resigned on her marriage but two resigned due to illness and one died before she took office. In the latter period, as Celbridge had become a much more academic school, such changes were problematic, as they threatened to halt the progress which had been made.

Miss Sarah Crawford, who was appointed headmistress in 1859, had been highly thought of as mistress of the Ranelagh School in Roscommon. She seems to have been a gentle and caring teacher and the Society was pleased with her work in Celbridge. Soon after her arrival, she ordered wine and extra food for girls who were delicate, at a cost of 1½d per person per day. While the Society was initially reluctant to allow this, it was probably at her request that in 1861 it increased the daily allowance by a halfpenny to sixpence, 'to allow the children a third dinner of meat each week'.[1] She also gave the girls skipping ropes and hoops to play with, perhaps for the good of their health, perhaps just for fun. The girls must have felt a considerable loss when she

The front of
Celbridge school

became ill and died in 1864. It is possible that her illness was the same as that which caused five girls to spend as many as 83 days in the Adelaide Hospital, Dublin, in that year.[2]

Miss Crawford's sister, Eliza, who had previously deputised for her in Celbridge, came with their mother, Mrs Anne Crawford, to fill her place on a temporary basis. (Mrs Crawford had been mistress in Roscommon after Sarah left.) In February 1867, Eliza Crawford wrote to the Society proposing an arrangement which would allow her mother and herself to retire from the charge of the school and recommending the appointment of Miss Anne Sexton as headmistress. Miss Sexton, who soon married Eliza Crawford's brother, was considered 'a lady very qualified' to be headmistress. Eliza Crawford wrote: 'In prospect of the close relationship in which I hope to stand to Miss Sexton through her marriage … it is part of our proposed arrangement that I shall remain at the school and assist as heretofore in the care of the children'.[3] This proposal was accepted and the new Mrs Anne Crawford became headmistress.

Anne Crawford served for nearly three decades before retiring in 1894. Strangely, the Society took the retrograde step of replacing her with 'a matron' rather than a 'mistress'. The position was advertised as being open to well-educated members of the Church of Ireland, either widows or unmarried (aged 35 to 45), with experience as matron in a similar institution.[4] In September Miss Bessie St George was elected, 'her chief duties to be the purchasing of the necessary food and clothing for the children; the keeping of the accounts; the conducting of the correspondence with the office; the superintending of the education given in the institution as well as the establishment generally …'[5] Although the Society had placed the emphasis on her managerial rather than her educational role, Miss St George approached the job as a conventional, if less than academic, headmistress. Before the end of 1894, she had written to the Society with new ideas for the school, including the establishment of a branch of the Girls' Friendly Society, the formation of a drill and callisthenics class, and cookery classes.[6] All three recommendations were adopted, once the cost of employing a drill instructor was ascertained. Miss St George had argued that 'the girls have no physical training, they walk and carry themselves very badly and several of them are occasionally subject to hysteria, doubtless the result of insufficient healthy exercise'; that 'these evils could be obviated or lessened by regular drill' and that 'it would be an amusement to the girls'. Sergeant William Hinch was appointed drill instructor to give classes to the girls two days a week.[7] He was an exceptional male presence in the highly seclusive school and it is safe to presume that he was not appointed without careful assessment of his suitability for such an environment.

Judging from the supercilious tone of this letter, it is not surprising that Miss St George's time at Celbridge was not an unmitigated success. Drill, which the local committee found excessive, was not a wise idea, being by no means the best form of physical exercise for girls. At the same time the local committee felt that the household work was too hard for the children and interfered with their studies.[8] Household work was a hang-over from the days when the girls were prepared for service and continued in the 20th century, with each girl having minor duties.

Either Miss St George was unwell when she took the job in Celbridge or she contracted a serious illness soon after arrival. This had an inevitable effect on the school and the local committee commented in October 1895 that 'the general management and teaching of the school has not maintained the efficiency which it should have done during the past year. Out of the twelve candidates sent forward to the Training College … only three succeeded in obtaining places – a much smaller proportion than usual'.[9] Many years later Canon Henry Kingsmill Moore, long-serving Society governor, recalled his first visit to the school:

> I did not see the mistress. She was an invalid, and it seemed as if everything there was in keeping with her invalidism – ill-kept walks, no flowers, a great kitchen garden just coaxed into feebly producing a few vegetables … Manifestly, however, there were possibilities. The avenue of limes and many other features showed that it would not be difficult to make the school a place of beauty.[10]

The Society, although sympathetic to Miss St George, regretted 'that in the interest of the school they feel themselves bound to call upon her to send in her resignation'.[11] A sub-committee was appointed to prepare for the recruitment of a new 'lady superintendent'. This title followed a report by the local committee, which suggested that the school needed a lady superintendent, a housekeeper, a teacher for the training class and a music teacher. The local committee thought that the lady superintendent should 'have supervision of the entire work of the school and take a certain share in the teaching'.[12] The sub-committee, however, chose to designate the four leading members of staff as headmistress, first teacher, matron and music teacher. It also decided that the headmistress would be 'responsible for the educational work as well as for the general supervision of the establishment'. It further recommended that a reward scheme would be introduced for the staff: 'in cases where candidates for the Training College gain 70 per cent or over,' a bonus should be given to each of the teachers.[13]

Illness remained a worrying prospect for teacher and pupil alike, as tuberculosis, diphtheria, typhus and typhoid fever, smallpox, measles, all common killers, were still endemic. There were some things which the Incorporated Society could do to foster good health: ensure good food and hygiene, provide adequate ventilation and outdoor exercise, and isolate the sick in a separate room. From time to time measures were taken in Celbridge. For instance, in 1873 the Society increased its dietary and clothing allowance for each girl at Celbridge and Roscommon. An extra halfpenny a day would be provided for feeding each girl. The total cost of the increases was about £500.[14] The diet may have been fine but that other bugbear of boarding schools remained – bad drains. A number of dangerous diseases, including diphtheria and typhoid fever, owe their origin to such problems and in 1877 there was an outbreak of typhoid fever, in which one pupil died.

Miss Augusta L'Estrange was appointed headmistress and her sister, Frances, music teacher. The two began work in Celbridge at the beginning of December 1895.[15] At the end of that year the Society decided to admit a limited number of fee-paying pupils. A prospectus was issued, stating that the fees would be £26 per annum for those under 12 years of age, £28 for the 12-15 age group and £30 for older girls.[16] Another part of the effort to improve the school was the construction of a new dining hall and lavatory. Just as the Misses L'Estrange arrived together in Celbridge, so did they depart together. On the same day in November 1897 both of them submitted a letter of resignation with the same reason – both were soon to be married. The local

Aerial view of
Celbridge school

committee commented on the 'marked improvement in the working of the school effected by Miss L'Estrange' and the Society wrote of the loss 'of her valuable services' and of their satisfaction 'with the admirable manner in which she … fulfilled the arduous duties devolving upon her and with the results of her successful efforts for the prosperity of the pupils'.[17] Miss Annie McCullagh, who had been a respected member of staff for some years, was appointed. Described by Kingsmill Moore as 'a head who gave of her best and threw her whole heart into the interests of the school', she served until ill-health forced her to resign in 1909.[18] Miss Georgina Osborne was appointed in 1909 but died suddenly before she took up office.[19]

Educational standards in Celbridge rose considerably during the late 19th century, a time when there was increasing engagement between the Incorporated Society and the government. In response to the 1881 educational commissioners, the Society stated that Celbridge girls 'were known as some of the cleverest and best-taught children in the Kildare Street Training School' and became school mistresses 'who were highly prized in the country and had gained great success'.[20] That commission reported that Celbridge was 'in every respect a well-conducted establishment and that the girls' education was 'well suited to qualify them as teachers in elementary schools'.[21] That was the vital point of the more academic approach. A training class was re-established in 1886 and roughly half of the first intake went on to the Training College. The training class continued to produce a steady stream of recruits, so that by the late 1890s there was a noticeable increase in girls going to the college and a small number of girls went straight to teach in local church schools.

In order to facilitate this development, there needed to be a bigger pool from which to select girls and the selection process had to be more thorough. The admission policy was broadened in 1859 to allow girls from Co. Wicklow to compete for places and in 1865 the Dublin parishes of Clontarf, Drumcondra, Glasnevin and Rathmichael were included.[22] The annual examination took place in the parochial school in Celbridge, which was a restrictive factor and it was not until 1906 that the Society established centres throughout the country and changed the format from an oral to a written examination.

The position of the Conolly Foundation remained a barrier to progress. The Conollys were not interested in equipping their girls for life as teachers but wanted simply to prepare them for service, as had always been the case. The further standards rose for the Society's girls, the greater the gap between the two groups, which posed considerable problems for the teachers. Another problem was a financial one, for the Conolly Trust was not paying its way. In 1889 the Society began to examine its legal obligations. A report by the Society's law agents considered whether the Society was 'bound in law to keep 30 children on the Foundation of the Celbridge Institution if the income annually arising from the Celbridge Trust funds should be insufficient for the purpose' and decided that the Society 'can never be held answerable beyond the amount which is afforded by the trust fund'.[23] In November 1897 Mrs Sarah Conolly, arguing that 'at present the girls on the Conolly Foundation … are being unfitted for domestic work by being taught music and French and the branches of an intermediate education', proposed a new scheme for the Conolly Foundation:

> I have been long desirous that the Conolly endowment at Celbridge School shall be devoted more to industrial training of the girls whom I nominate than previously; more especially as the standard of education has been raised so high in Celbridge School. With this end in view I would venture to propose that two houses in the village, belonging to the Castletown estate … should be so altered as to make them suitable for school premises in which the Conolly children should be located. They could attend the Celbridge National School and be educated there free of cost. When they have passed through the fifth or sixth standard I would propose that they should be retained in what may be termed the boarding house for a period not exceeding two years further to be trained in domestic, laundry work, etc.[24]

Responding to Mrs Conolly's proposal, a sub-committee of the Society drew up a draft scheme in January 1898 for the Society to acquire the interests of the two houses and fit them up as a school. This would have meant the end of Conolly girls at the Collegiate School, in which there seemed to be a demand for places. A Society statement on the Conolly Foundation read:

> While there has been recently a marked decrease in the number of candidates for boys' scholarships, there has been no such diminution in the number of competitors for entrance to the school at Roscommon or to the training class at Celbridge. At every centre where examinations were held this year, many well qualified girls were unable to secure the places which they eagerly sought. If the committee could grant five times the number of free and assisted scholarships that they intend to offer next year, it cannot be doubted that all would be readily filled by girls to take full advantage of the benefits allowed by the Society for their foundationers.[25]

The scheme fell through because it was too costly, as did the next plan, to send the Conolly girls to Ranelagh[26] but the problem was at least partly solved in 1901, when it was agreed that candidates for the Conolly Foundation would have to pass a simple examination and would pay fees of £10 per year. The necessity of this can be appreciated from the figures. In 1901, the total annual income from the Conolly endowment was £240-4-4. Between 1898 and 1901 the average annual expenditure on Conolly Foundation pupils was £439-1-1 (for an average of 15 pupils). This meant that expenditure amounted to approximately £200 a year more than the net annual income from the endowment.

Celbridge had for many years concentrated on giving a grounding to girls who would become teachers and in the 1890s 'was fast becoming the main source of supply of well educated female candidates'[27] for the Training College. The process by which Celbridge entered the Intermediate Board system seems to have begun with the inspector of endowed schools' report in 1895-6. He recommended that the school should not concentrate solely on preparing girls for the Training College but should enter them for the Intermediate and South Kensington Department of Science and Art examinations, pointing out that payment by results would mean added income.[28]

Although the Incorporated Society report of 1898 praised 'the excellent work' of the school, with eight pupils winning Queen's Scholarships to the Training College and with many successes in the examinations of the General Synod Board of Religious Education, Celbridge had to appoint a number of more highly qualified staff before it could take part in the Intermediate system. The school joined the system in 1901 and girls sat for the preparatory and junior grades the following year but it was not until 1908 that they first sat the senior grade.[29]

The move to join the Intermediate system followed developments in the Society, which adopted a new and reinvigorating constitution in 1894. As a result, while Santry School was closed, premises were bought for Mountjoy School and in Celbridge a new classroom and new dormitories were built in 1896. Having joined the Intermediate system, further improvements were required and in 1903 a science laboratory was built. In 1907 the Celbridge numbers rose to 100, mainly due to the closure of the Ranelagh School, Roscommon, which led to the transfer of girls with their teacher, Miss Margaret Thornton. Entry into the system did not reduce the numbers going to the Training College, in which 28 per cent of entrants in 1908 came from Celbridge. The Society's reluctance to accept that the increase of numbers required additional teaching resources placed an extra strain on Miss McCullagh's fragile health. She maintained that '[no] headmistress could now satisfactorily combine the duties of teaching and overseeing everything'.30 The fact that she had been attending sanitoria in Germany almost certainly indicates that she was suffering from tuberculosis. She resigned in 1909 in order to seek further treatment.

In the same year the school received a favourable report from two inspectors of the Intermediate Education Board. English, which was 'excellently taught throughout the school', came out best.[31] What the school now needed was a new headmistress of long tenure, who would establish high academic standards. This was exactly what it got with the appointment of Miss Emma McClelland.

CHAPTER TWENTY

Academic progress, 1909-1942

Emma McClelland

The appointment of Emma McClelland as headmistress was an inspired one.[1] She was cultured, up-to-date with the latest educational thinking and had benefited from experience in Europe and America. Thanks to her vision and drive, the school achieved a remarkably academic standard. Perhaps the best description is by Anna O'Connor, her past pupil and successor. Many years later, she recalled her early impressions of Miss McClelland:

> Of one supreme authority we were very conscious, although as yet we had little direct contact with her, seeing her on the platform at assemblies for prayers, morning and evening and at the head of the table in the dining hall at meal times. Miss McClelland, headmistress, was an impressive figure, dressed usually in a long, fashionable gown of saxe-blue silk, admirably fitted to her slender figure and emphasising her lovely, delicate complexion, blue eyes and snow-white hair (white prematurely, not through age, as we thought) … Her standards in all things were very exacting – lessons, manners, speech, conduct, etc., must conform to an ideal pattern. She was much admired and respected by the more thoughtful of us who responded to the challenge of her oft-repeated slogan: 'Aim for the stars and you may reach the top of the trees.'[2]

Although results had been good under her predecessor, they improved conspicuously in the early years of Miss McClelland's regime.[3] The papers printed lists each year of the top girls' schools in the Intermediate examinations and Celbridge regularly featured. The best year was 1915, when Celbridge came fourth after Loreto College, St Stephen's Green, Dublin, Victoria College, Belfast, and Dominican College, Eccles Street, Dublin.[4] At that time science and Latin were being taught but before long they were discontinued, except that Latin was still offered to any girl who was hoping to enter university. While French and German were both taught with particular success, girls won prizes in every subject which was taught and attained first, second or third places in Ireland. For instance, Anna O'Connor won a first class exhibition and a German composition prize at junior level in 1918 and a French composition prize at senior level in 1920 and Dorothy Fulcher won a first class exhibition at junior level in 1918, a first class exhibition and two first places at senior level.[5] Both later returned to Celbridge as outstanding language teachers. The proficiency in modern languages enabled two of the most outstanding students to win distinctions at Trinity College, Winifred Bradshaw becoming a Scholar in 1922 and Anna O'Connor following in her footsteps in 1925.[6] As far as can be established, Dorothy Osborne was in 1919 the first Celbridge girl to graduate from Trinity. She was followed by Annie Aldworth and Elizabeth Green. Presuming that those girls at Trinity were all studying the humanities, Violet Guy was remarkable in that she took degrees in medicine and then dentistry in the 1920s at Queen's University, Belfast. Celbridge Collegiate could be justly proud of these achievements.

When Miss McClelland became headmistress, she had a teaching staff of eight, one of whom she had taught in Rochelle School, Cork: Miss Helen Batwell was typical of the kind of teacher on whom Celbridge depended. For over 40 years she devoted her life to the school, firstly as a teacher of music, later also as a teacher of French and maths. According to Miss O'Connor, 'an inspector who knew her work repeatedly cited the school's results in this subject as a proof of the ability of girls to excel in mathematics'. Such was her commitment that in her spare time 'she was more likely to be found coaching hockey or tennis, checking on the school stationery or peeling potatoes in the kitchen'[7] than relaxing. This tribute was intended as a mark of praise but one could suggest that the atmosphere in this isolated girls' school might have been better if its dedicated staff had taken time to develop their own interests.

At the end of 1919 Miss McClelland resigned as headmistress, due to ill health. The board in accepting her resignation referred to 'the high tone and all-pervading *esprit de corps* which resulted from Miss McClelland's influence'.[8] Miss Dora Cox, French and maths teacher and one of the long-serving members of the teaching staff, took charge of the school pending a permanent appointment. Her short time as acting head brought new opportunities for the girls, including the introduction of hockey (Miss McClelland apparently thought the game too dangerous).[9] No new appointment was necessary when Miss McClelland recovered her health and offered to return to work.

The introduction of compulsory Irish after 1922 brought a serious challenge, as Celbridge was still the leading school from which girls entered the Church of Ireland Training College. The government found it extremely difficult to secure enough candidates for national school teacher training, so it set up secondary preparatory colleges, where the focus was on the Irish language. After the establishment of a Church of Ireland college, Coláiste Móibhí, in 1927, many Celbridge girls transferred there after the Intermediate Certificate. That proved the surest route to the Church of Ireland Training College. Another option was to stay in Celbridge and avail of the government's pupil-teacher scheme, established in 1926 to draw recruits from secondary schools into primary teaching. This scheme worked well in Celbridge but ultimately was discontinued because the standard of Irish in secondary schools remained insufficient. Although priority was given to candidates from these two sources, it was possible to gain entry through the Leaving Certificate and Training College entrance examination alone. It is greatly to the credit of Miss McClelland and her staff that Celbridge rose to that challenge and remained the best source of well-qualified students for the Church of Ireland Training College.[10] In this way, it is no exaggeration to say that the Collegiate School made a significant contribution to the survival of the Protestant community in the new state, in providing a supply of national school teachers. As Valerie Jones wrote in *A Gaelic Experiment*:

> Had [the national schools] disappeared, the survival of the Protestant community in the 26 counties could have been in jeopardy, for the church was dependent on its primary schools to build up a strong sense of Protestant identity and to pass on its teaching to each new generation in an overwhelmingly Catholic environment.[11]

Considering its pivotal role in supplying national school teachers, it is not surprising that Celbridge continued to produce good results in the new Leaving and Intermediate certificates. Nearly every year some of the girls won scholarships and secured a national first place in particular subjects. Again the extent of good teaching is indicated by the fact that these firsts were achieved in English, French, Latin, geography, history and maths.[12] In maintaining high standards Miss McClelland gave a decisive lead and managed to 'infect others with her enthusiasm'.[13] According to Anna O'Connor's glowing recollection, the teachers were:

> professional women of integrity and devotion [who] spared no pains in serving us, not alone by teaching their subjects with absorbed interest, but by caring for us in every way, giving ungrudgingly of their time and talents to instruct, amuse, cultivate

us … The most memorable thing about the teachers was their cheerfulness … They collaborated wholeheartedly with Miss McClelland in her design for high achievement in everything and anything undertaken. Their free time was scanty, their remuneration small, their recreations rare. No one had a motor-car, no buses travelled the roads, a visit to Dublin involved cycling to Hazelhatch or driving in a pony-cart; no late hours were tolerated. But when fine weather came they did enjoy their tennis, and tea in the charming teacher's garden, so beautifully kept by faithful gardeners.[14]

In her pursuit of academic excellence Miss McClelland had a valuable ally in Canon Henry Kingsmill Moore, principal of the Church of Ireland Training College from 1884 to 1927. For years she worked towards the building of a library. It came to fruition in 1937, when Kingsmill Moore laid the foundation stone, proclaiming: 'How the large sum necessary was accumulated is a mystery only to be explained by the unique influence of our great headmistress whose name the library appropriately bears.'[15] After his retirement, Kingsmill Moore remained an influential figure in the educational world and it was clearly beneficial that he took an active interest in Celbridge as a governor. A noted amateur botanist, he was also deeply involved in Miss McClelland's improvements to the school grounds and gardens. The most spectacular aspect was the creation of Kingsmill Moore Park in the field in front of the school, while the wrought-iron Mayne Gates, presented to the school by the Revd W. J. Mayne, secretary of the Incorporated Society, made for an impressive entrance. Kingsmill Moore presented a large collection of ferns, which was cared for by pupils and staff, chiefly by Miss Fulcher, until their eventual transfer to Celbridge House in Kilkenny. It was obviously important to Miss McClelland to have lovingly cultivated gardens round the school. It marked Celbridge out from almost every school in Ireland, greatly enhanced the environment for staff and pupils alike and led to a lifelong interest in gardening for many. Like all other developments, however, Miss McClelland's role was as a catalyst. The suggestion that she might have gardened actively was greeted with derision by her past pupils, who cannot imagine her dirtying her hands!

It was typical of Miss McClelland that she dressed for dinner in the evening and expected the teachers to do the same. There was a formality, which extended from starched napkins at table for the pupils, to their uniform. Although it changed somewhat over the years, when Anna O'Connor was a pupil:

> the full indoor uniform consisted of a navy blue serge skirt and close-fitting jacket of the same with a sailor collar adorned with its three or four white strips, and the V-shape at the neck filled in by a white modesty-vest; long black woollen

School group, 1940s

stockings and black house-shoes; a holland pinafore (off white) for weekdays, and a white dotted muslin one for Sundays, each held in by a black leather belt to which were fastened one's keys and a small purse for pocket money. Everyone wore long hair in two plaits, tied with broad navy ribbon and pinned up side by side at the back of the head, the two bows of ribbon then standing out at each side like small wings. Neatly done, it looked very pretty. Hair was well looked after, for a rule required that it be given the traditional hundred brush strokes each night.[16]

There was another, less palatable side of school life, however. Before going to bed at night, each girl had to fill her washstand jug with water for the morning. The jug stood by her bed at night and 'many a frosty morning ice had to be cracked'.[17] Mostly the girls had to use outside lavatories, where the roof leaked. One of the striking aspects of the school is that the girls lived in very much the same conditions at the end of Miss McClelland's time as they did when she arrived. Young people of today find it hard to believe how isolated the girls were at the Collegiate School, less than a century ago. There were very few cars, so most pupils travelled by train to Hazelhatch station, two miles away and from there to the school by pony and trap. The girls would not see their parents again until the end of term, unless they received a visit on the one afternoon in the term when parents were invited. Even then, the parents were 'almost searched' for forbidden sweets but, much to the satisfaction of the girls, they did smuggle them in.[18] Even worse, not only was there no half-term holiday but there were no Easter holidays either, with the second term of the school year extending from January to the summer.

The girls saw very little of the outside world, for their main ventures out of school were daily local walks or their Sunday walk to church. In recalling this in 2008 at the age of 93, Hilda Carter (Mrs Thompson) wrote a fine example of 'the Celbridge script', which girls were taught and which many retained for life:

> Sundays. We walked in line to Christ Church, Celbridge, the smallest at the front to the largest at the back. I was the smallest for two years. When we came to the village there was no talking. All mouths had to be closed in case we'd catch a germ!

The long-standing rule about keeping one's mouth shut in the village was aimed largely at the prevention of tuberculosis, though the school was not entirely free of it.[19]

At this time there were no day pupils, through whom the girls might have contact with the local community and, as Hilda Carter has said, 'there was no occasion for men or boys'.[20] The girls were not allowed to correspond with boys, even with their own brothers.

They amused themselves by playing games – hockey, cricket,[21] tennis, basketball, badminton, table tennis and lacrosse at various times – but never played matches against other schools. Some kept individual gardens and helped in the school garden. In 1915 they had started a handwritten school magazine, *The Celbridgite*. Miss McClelland may have been the driving force, for it frequently featured fashion drawings, articles and poems by her. Although it was a worthwhile enterprise, it seems to have faltered after a year but was revived about 1924 and continued somewhat sporadically until the closure of the school in 1973. An extraordinary element of subversion is seen in a handwritten book compiled during the First World War. *Celbridge Jingles Grave and Gay* contains ditties, written by a number of girls, some of which are outrageous. One cannot help wondering if they were composed as an antidote to the approved pieces for *The Celbridgite*. The girls cannot have intended members of staff to see stanzas like the following:

> Our ladyship Clell, the head of the staff.
> With her sausage roll and notions
> And long thin neck like a young giraffe –
> She is atrocious.
>
> Miss Cox, known far and wide as 'The Hen'
> With her fuz-buz wig and scowl.
> She talks through her teeth: 'dis', 'dat' and 'den'.
> Oh, preserve us from feather fowl.[22]

The girls may have been isolated but they did know about major developments in the wider world. *The Celbridgite* carried regular items of 'war news', as they tried to keep up to date with the progress of war. For them this was not just some far-off war like those of which they learned in history class but one in which they were intimately involved, for many family members were fighting in the trenches. There was constant anxiety, heightened when close relatives were killed in action. One unforgettable day at dinner a girl opened a letter from home and read of the death of her soldier brother.[23] There were also occasions of pride, as when Gladys Ritty learned that her brother had been awarded the Military Cross. In response to the war:

> Many girls knitted socks and scarves of khaki wool to be sent to the front through the agency of the Red Cross. One year, when the Synod examination results came and revealed that many prizes had, as usual, been won, the winners were asked to sacrifice the prizes so that the money could be given instead to the Red Cross to provide comforts for the soldiers. This was done without grumbling, though some girls may have had private feelings of frustration and loss. Austerity in general living conditions had to be practised everywhere, at school and elsewhere. No sugar in our tea; no white bread, all flour being of a greyish brown hue because, for economy reasons, it had to retain much of the wheat roughage; sweets were few and seldom seen, and no tuck, was allowed. You can imagine with what relief we heard in November 1918 that the armistice had been signed and that we could look forward to better things.[24]

Likewise, in 1916 the Easter Rising featured in *The Celbridgite*. It is safe to assume that the girls derived their political opinions from their teachers but their background was such that they naturally regarded it as a 'dreadful rebellion' and expressed their 'thankfulness that it has been thoroughly quelled'.

The magazine carried a report that the Rising had caused a bread shortage in Celbridge, adding 'thanks to the splendid work of the teachers ... we

Advertisement,
The Celbridgite, 1916

were spared all such experiences'. A clever advertisement for 'Ireland's Best Bakery' makes it clear that Miss Dora Cox and Miss Eleanor Wiber, the domestic economy teacher, had baked for the school.[25]

The girls' isolation was not caused by the war, for it continued throughout Miss McClelland's years as headmistress. While it was undoubtedly due in part to the school's geographical isolation, it also emanated from her attitude. Such isolation was not good and contrasts sadly with the situation in Rochelle School, Cork, where the girls were positively encouraged to go to concerts and other cultural events and to take part in parish and community activities. Such isolation inevitably fostered inward looking and the pettiness that can lurk in an all-female establishment.

There were regular dances, for which the girls sometimes dressed in their finery, but no outsiders were permitted. There were occasional dramatic performances, including an elaborately costumed *Hiawatha*, for which the sets were designed by Mícheál Mac Liammóir. He was not yet famous but the director clearly had a discerning eye in choosing him as designer. That this production occurred in May 1923 shows the extraordinary nature of Celbridge Collegiate. While the country was still wracked by the civil war, the school went on as if nothing untoward was happening. The same edition

The cast of
Hiawatha,
May 1923

of *The Irish Times* which reported that 'a large number of guests attended a very successful display given by the pupils', consisting of 'scenes from *Hiawatha,* selections by the school orchestra, physical drill displays and an operetta', carried numerous reports of burnings and lootings. The report on the display is followed immediately by one on an attempt to blow up the Nenagh to Dublin train. It seems that Celbridge worked on the principle that the show must go on![26]

One cannot help feel that Anna O'Connor's recollections of Miss McClelland were softened by the years, for many pupils were much less positive. While the more academic seniors admired her greatly and appreciated her many attempts to broaden their horizons, juniors were often fearful. Hilda Carter, who was the smallest girl in the school for her first two years, recalls that 'You rarely met her in the corridor but, if you did, you stood back and curtseyed. You'd be terrified to learn anything from her.'[27] In many ways the whole regime was over strict. Hester Walsh recalled 'all the times I was put "on silence" in those tender years.' One day, 'standing on the stairs in the long queue for "Black Jack" (our insides shone like our outsides), I began to hum a pretty tune. "You go on silence for six weeks"' was the dreaded response.[28] This was not an isolated incident but a common punishment, remembered by most past pupils. One other instance shows how the school, at its worst, resembled Lowood School in *Jane Eyre.* One morning, as the girls stood in prayer lines, Eunice Lochner showed a new manicure set to the girl next to her. Her punishment was silence for one month, a silence in which she could neither speak nor be spoken to.[29] Occasionally, the girls stood up for themselves, usually with disastrous results. Freda Lochner recalled that in her second last year her class rebelled against the strict rules on tuck. One day they raided the sweet cupboard and 'helped themselves to chocolate. Being honest, they left the money for it and this was their downfall. They had a pact to say nothing unless the Bible was brought out. They kept silent until forced to swear on the Bible.' It would appear that, as a result of this incident, all the girls involved left the school.[30]

Some girls found the atmosphere oppressive, escaping at the end of their school career as if from a prison, but many were content in the knowledge that life at home was severely restricted and that the good education they received in Celbridge was a passport to a better life. The latter formed the core of the past pupils' association, established in 1931, with Anna O'Connor as president. It had an active social programme in Dublin but the highlight of the year was the reunion, hosted by Miss McClelland.[31] Its commitment to helping the school was noted by Kingsmill Moore: 'Probably nothing attests the influence of Celbridge more than the loyal way in which past pupils rally to Miss McClelland's call. A large proportion of the fund for the library whose foundation stone has just been laid came from them.'[32]

In later years Miss McClelland spent most of her time upstairs, leaving a small number of senior members of staff to run the school. Elegant as ever, the pupils still believed that her dresses were the latest from Paris. Perhaps she mellowed over the years for one of her last pupils, Freda Yates, recalls 'If she met you in the corridor, she would give you two bars of chocolate, one for yourself and one for the handyman's dog!'[33] This is the first period for which

Fashion drawing by Emma McClelland

there are numerous extant past-pupil recollections.[34] One of the consistent themes that runs through to the departure from Celbridge in 1973 is the stark contrast between the lovely tree-lined avenue, attractive stone façade and spring bulbs and the bleak interior of the school. The overriding theme, however, is the personality of Miss McClelland and the tone which she set in the school. It is not surprising that she was succeeded by one of her brightest pupils and greatest admirers, Anna O'Connor.

CHAPTER TWENTY-ONE

Towards amalgamation, 1942-1973

Anna O'Connor was a Scholar of Trinity College and a senior moderator in French and German, who subsequently lectured on the teaching of Irish in the school of education and was awarded an M.A. for her work there. While headmistress she was influential in the wider educational world, particularly in the teaching of Irish. Appointed to the Council of Education by the minister for education in 1952, she was also a founder member of the Joint Managerial Body, the umbrella group which represents the management interests of voluntary secondary schools. This tiny indomitable person 'ruled with a rod of iron',[1] taught her own subject very effectively and was much more involved in the daily routine than Miss McClelland had been. Valerie Giles's recollection of her in the 1960s is very typical:

Anna O'Connor

Miss O'Connor was a small lady, who always wore grey clothes and black, laced-up shoes. Her white hair was worn in a bun and her spectacles were perched on the end of her nose. We were terrified of her. Students had to stand back against the wall and not move when she came along the corridor. We always hoped that she wouldn't stop to talk to us, as she used to speak in Irish. If we wanted to go out with our parents on a Sunday we had to line up after lunch … and ask permission in Irish from Miss O'Connor.[2]

As a past pupil returning to a school which was suffering along with the rest of Ireland the privations of the Second World War, she made no radical changes. While steeped in the Celbridge tradition, she was not a slave to it and, after a few years, stopped the teaching of 'the Celbridge script' (a writing style still distinctive of the older Celbridgite, shown in previous chapter) and relaxed some of the petty restrictions of former days. Matches against other schools were at last permitted, Easter holidays were introduced and, in a major concession to the chill of the school during the war years, girls were allowed to bring back a hot water bottle and a rug for their bed. They continued, however, to suffer in the cold, particularly from chilblains, which made walking and writing agonising. They got short shrift from matron and with poor nutrition and long, unbroken spells at school, it is not surprising that one year there was such a severe outbreak of infectious diseases that few girls managed to sit the Intermediate exams. Lapses in hygiene in the kitchen did not help, though they were no worse than in any other establishment of the time. Nuala Carter vividly recalls one of the girls holding up by the tail a mouse which she had pulled out of the soup pot![3]

Like her predecessor, Miss O'Connor focused on academic achievement and decorum. Academic standards remained high, particularly in Irish. She was a brilliant teacher of Irish, under whom it was the norm to take the higher paper in the Leaving Certificate. On a less positive note, she was a formidable presence in the classroom, as were many of the older teachers, so that girls were nervous of making mistakes, for fear of ridicule. In 1950 a confidential Department memorandum showed that less than half of the Protestant secondary schools prepared pupils for the Leaving Certificate, and that only 79 out of 3,584 pupils took Irish at Leaving Certificate level. Of these, less than 50 per cent of the boys but 85 per cent of the girls passed. Six girls obtained honours in Irish in the Leaving Certificate examination. (These figures are flawed, because they ignore the fact that many pupils received only one or two years of secondary education.) The memorandum acknowledged that Irish was taught to a high standard in such schools as Alexandra College, the Diocesan School for Girls and Celbridge, recognising that the Collegiate School provided a high proportion of students at the Training College.[4] In fact, more girls in Celbridge took the higher level than in any other Protestant-managed school.

Few girls went on to university, the number being limited largely by the financial circumstances of the girls' families but also by the fact that the school could only afford to offer a limited range of subjects, with none of the sciences. The lack of Latin denied the girls entry to Trinity but from 1955 a pass in maths was accepted instead of Latin. This made it easier for Celbridge girls to enter, although arrangements were sometimes made for one or two girls to take Latin. Celbridge girls found it easier than pupils from most

Girls modelling their dressmaking, 1951
Back row L to R: Kathleen Hobson, Joan Culbert, Joan Roe, Shirley Kingston, Iris Rusk,
Joan Levis (hidden), Kathleen Groves, Ina Stanley, ?Josephine Shannon (hidden).
Front row: Marina Earl, Winifred Bryan, Sylvia Stanley, Joan Rothwell, Ena Kingston,
Carrie Jeffers, Grace Tomkins, Violet Shannon
Miss B. O'Beirne is standing at the back.

Protestant schools to gain entry to the National University, for which a pass
in Irish was required. At the time, however, few pupils from Protestant
schools wanted to go to the National University. The point is proved by the
circumstances in which Sheila Deacon went to University College, Dublin in
1949: with Miss O'Connor's encouragement and by taking Latin as an extra
subject, she won a sizarship in Irish to Trinity. A local schoolmaster in Co.
Wexford pointed out to her father that she might qualify for one of the three
county council scholarships for university. Her father was not inclined to
apply, so the schoolmaster applied on her behalf and she was successful. As
these scholarships were not tenable at Trinity College, she went to UCD
where she studied happily. The story provides another instance of the reluctance of the Protestant population in the first decades of the new state to
engage with local authorities.[5]

    There were a few ways of funding oneself through Trinity: the most obvi-
ous was to win a sizarship or an entrance scholarship but Celbridge did not
have the resources to teach extra courses, which, in the latter case, required a
seventh year. Gladys Ruddock was awarded a bursary in 1955 under a scheme
to boost the numbers of Protestants training to teach in Protestant secondary
schools. In return, she had to agree to teach in a country school under

Girls on a school outing to Killiney beach, 1950s
L to R: Myra Bryan, —, Elizabeth Jacob, —, —, Wendy Slack, —, Anne Blennerhassett,
Heather Lewis

Protestant management for five years after graduation.[6] From 1960 she taught in Celbridge, where she received 'an excellent training' from Miss O'Connor:

> She ran a very strict and organised ship. During my first year she supervised many of my classes and always gave very positive and helpful criticism … You knew you had to have all your lessons well planned and you had to give regular homework assignments. She was also a stickler for punctuality: at 5.01 p.m. you were late for a 5.00 appointment.[7]

In the 1960s Miss O'Connor enabled a small number of girls to return for a seventh year to prepare for the Trinity entrance scholarship. After a year in which she acted as a junior mistress, even teaching Form 1 maths, Avril Copeland won an entrance scholarship in Irish. It is to Miss O'Connor's credit that she challenged academic pupils to abandon the well-worn paths to nursing and Guinness's and to aim for university. She was also astute enough to know that their chances of success were greatest in Irish and to persuade them to her viewpoint. As before, most girls became primary school teachers, nurses or secretaries, though a few subsequently became missionaries in Africa. Several girls were later ordained, including Olive McDonald (the Revd Olive Boothman), Hazel Minion and Jean Valentine (the Revd Jean Wynne). In 2007 Olive Jeffers (the Revd Olive Henderson) was the first Celbridgite to become a rector.[8]

In some ways educational policy was advanced. Long before field trips became popular, they took place regularly in Celbridge, when the girls were taken on foot to see archaeological features or historical remains. Miss O'Connor also was able to secure celebrated public figures to speak. Few girls have forgotten the privilege of hearing Samuel Beckett on his works, Dr Owen Sheehy Skeffington marking the 50th anniversary of the 1916 Rising, or Archbishop George Simms giving his captivating lecture on the Book of Kells. On the other hand, the school retained its isolation from the outside world. In Miss O'Connor's early years, the girls still had no access to the radio or to newspapers but later there was a radio in the schoolroom and a newspaper. Exceptional news was relayed by members of staff and Nuala Carter remembers that the girls celebrated the end of the war 'with an enormous V, made of chestnut blossoms'.[9]

As to discipline, Celbridge was particularly strict but it must be remembered that most girls' schools then retained a rigid discipline which is almost unimaginable today. Gladys Ruddock's prevailing memories are of 'order and organisation and marching and waiting around'.

> We lined up after class to put our books away in lockers, which were checked daily by the teachers on duty. We lined up with our desks along the corridors in class order before marching in to prep. This often took half an hour and we had to wait in silence to be ordered in. At the end of prep, we marched out again in class order to bring our books to our lockers and our desks to our classroom.[10]

The worst part of the rigid organisation seems to have been the Sunday morning pre-church inspection parade, after which the girls marched to the front square and waited in silence for Miss O'Connor to arrive. All this routine depended on supervision by the teachers. In addition they had to check each week on the girls' hair, hands and nails, their clothes and shoes and the neatness of their clothes cupboards. The girls were certainly trained to be tidy and organised! Table manners were considered important and were taught by the older students, as each table had a mixture of students from each year. 'Often at meals, if the talk was too noisy, the whole school would be put on silence, which meant eating your food and hearing every chew.'[11]

When the class of 1963-69 met in 2007 to pool their recollections, their prevailing memory was of fun, laughter and enduring friendships but one severe incident rankled.

> At the beginning of the third term of our first year all our class were caught talking
> – for the second or third time – after the silence bell at night. We were marched
> up to Miss O'Connor then and there in our pyjamas and dressing gowns. For

Cricket team, 1955

Back row L to R: Miss M. Case, Irene Hoffman, Annie Hunter, Emila Devine, — Mitchell, Audrey Payne, Frances Mitchell
Front row: Carrie Jeffers, Deirdre Latta, Gladys Ruddock, —, Valerie Hobson

this crime we were given the punishment of not being allowed out for the rest of term, or of having any visits from our parents – and remember this was the beginning of term! As far as I was concerned she might as well have told me I was being sent to outer Siberia for the rest of my life. I went back to bed and cried for most of the night.[12]

The shock was so great that this girl became ill and spent most of the term recovering at home, while the others remained gated. Occasionally a girl decided to run away but rarely got far before she was caught. On one occasion, third formers watched as one of their form-mates climbed over the wall into a field, only to see her dash back with an angry bull in pursuit![13]

It was not only the teachers who were strict: juniors also had to reckon with the prefects. In her first letter home since joining Form 1 in 1960, Helen Coe wrote as follows.[14]

We have right fun up the in the dorm at night when the prefects are at prayers, our prefects is terribly bossy in the morning she says at 7 o'clock:- "get up at once! strip those beds, turn those mattresses," & when we are in the washroom she shouts:- "Hurry up!" now som

The girls found any change in routine exciting. One of the favourite events was the annual Halloween dance, which in Miss O'Connor's time was attended by boys! The boys came from Kingstown School, where she had taught until her appointment as headmistress. Used to dancing with other girls at the usual Friday night dance, this occasion was both a pleasure and a torture. 'The most embarrassing thing that could happen on the night was for Miss O'Connor to take you by the hand, lead you across the floor to some boy or other. Then she would introduce you to one another, whereupon you were expected to dance together.'[15] In later years girls were permitted to bring a brother.

When Gladys Ruddock returned to teach, she soon expanded the games department. During her days as a pupil, Celbridge had at least abandoned the custom of internal matches only and managed to enter a couple of teams in Leinster cups. Now, with Miss O'Connor's support and her own coaching, Gladys soon had four or five hockey teams playing matches on a Saturday. This development brought the girls into regular contact with other schools and gave them a welcome break from the narrow confines of school. Gladys learned a lot from Anna O'Connor which was useful in her later career as principal of Alexandra College – 'Miss O'Connor was meticulous down to the last detail in everything she did. Long, hand-written lists were produced for every occasion, so presentation of events and finish were very important. However inexperienced the staff on duty were, they couldn't go wrong.'[16] This approach was essential, considering that Celbridge was always short of money and the Incorporated Society controlled the purse strings. Two representatives visited the school every year to inspect the books and examine schemes for expenditure. 'The pig profits' paid for many items and projects: the gardener/handyman fed the kitchen waste to the pigs, keeping half of the profits for his trouble, while the other half provided the headmistress with 'a slush fund'.

Miss O'Connor retired in 1967, with a high reputation as a headmistress. Her successor was a national school teacher[17] with no experience of teaching in a secondary school and a boarding school at that. Miss Mary Taylor's approach was very different from her predecessors. For the first time in living memory, Celbridge had a headmistress for whom life was more than the Collegiate School. Although she was a strict disciplinarian, much to the surprise of staff and girls alike, she was not omnipresent and allowed the girls much more rein. A young and fashionable woman, Miss Taylor wore her skirts to her knee and immediately rid the girls of their old-fashioned long, navy pleated skirt, shirt and tie. In came grey A-line skirts, which could be as much as six inches above the knee, grey jumpers and open-necked shirts in a

Mary Taylor and staff
Back row L to R: Miss E. Bonar, Miss T. Rock, Miss G. Ruddock., Miss F. Yates,
Miss E. Walsh, Miss V. Jackson
Front row: Mrs K. Fay (matron), Miss C. Flynn, Miss M. Taylor, Mrs E. Scully,
Mrs V. Ring

choice of pastels. The tie was gone. While the girls were bemused by the contrast with Miss O'Connor, they appreciated the new uniform and improvements in the food which Miss Taylor oversaw.

Miss Taylor was the first headmistress who managed to enjoy a social life outside school and that had implications for her continued headship. One of the stipulations of the Incorporated Society was that a headmistress had to resign if she was getting married. In accordance with this, Miss Taylor left after two years and Miss Freda Yates was appointed headmistress. If the Society had wanted an outsider in 1967, it now made a wise decision in opting for a past pupil, who was a long-serving member of staff.[18] In committing Celbridge to her capable and safe hands, it secured the services of the person who, more than anyone else, would guide the move to Kilkenny College and the introduction of co-education.

In its last years, Celbridge was a much more relaxed school. This reflected the style of Misses Taylor and Yates and of many of the newer staff. Outstanding among these was Miss Elizabeth Walsh, 'a generous and stimulating teacher' of English. Always careful to maintain a life outside Celbridge, she 'provided a practical example of public spirit and moral responsibility' and raised awareness in the girls of issues such as apartheid.[19] Miss Yates was full of commonsense, even-handed and approachable. For the first time there was a small number of male, non-resident teachers and there were married women, who only stayed in on their duty night. One of these was June Stuart, remembered not only for her teaching of French and Spanish but for 'making us laugh and cheering us up'.[20] Typical of the changing atmosphere, she enlisted the help of her husband, William, to work on the stage and lighting for the shows which she helped to put on. She (and her mother, Audrey Orr) worked wonders with costumes and make-up, raiding her wardrobe and his for items of clothing. Plays and musicals

Freda Rountree

were an important part of school life. Among the most memorable were an outdoor production of *A Midsummer Night's Dream* and a week-long production of *The Playboy of the Western World* in 1971, with Miss Walsh as director. These and musicals, such as *HMS Pinafore*, were a great source of fun. The girls also took part in inter-schools debates and attended dances in other schools and in the village. Incidentally, relations with Kilkenny College were such that an annual joint school dance was held in these later years. All this would have been impossible in earlier days. In the summer of 1971 there was huge excitement when a BBC Panorama crew came to the school while making a documentary which featured Protestant schools in Ireland. As Celbridge was one of only two girls' schools[21] which played cricket, the BBC filmed an internal cricket match and then played a friendly match against the girls. The kind of girl that emerged from this atmosphere spoke volumes of the approach of the staff and the prevailing attitude of the times. Almost any career path looked possible. Freda Barber (Mrs Rountree), for example, made a huge contribution in a short life to the cause of cultural preservation, serving as chairperson of the Heritage Council from 1995-1999.

In the 1960s, with numbers stable, the Incorporated Society built a new senior classroom for the seniors and reorganised other classroom and dormitory facilities. Just as the new classrooms were ready, numbers ominously began to fall. By 1970 Celbridge was suffering from its geographical isolation and lack of public transport, which severely limited the number of day pupils. No-one envisaged the vast expansion of the town which has subsequently occurred and therefore no-one could imagine a large increase in numbers. Another factor was the pace of change in education at the time. The Department of Education was now demanding better teaching facilities and the expansion of numbers to give economy of scale and enable a larger range of subjects. Even had the Department offered generous funding, Celbridge faced the same problem as other schools in elegant but outdated buildings: that of expanding and modernising without spoiling the environment. It was not only the classrooms which were inadequate: so were the dormitories, wash rooms, the kitchen and staff facilities. Even the headmistress had only a bedroom and sitting room on the first floor and had to share a bathroom with other teachers. The school was, therefore, not considered viable in the long term.

The announcement in October 1972 by the Incorporated Society that both Celbridge and Kilkenny would close in 1973 came as a great shock. When Miss Yates was interviewed for the job of headmistress, she had asked about the future of Celbridge and received a reassuring answer. It is greatly to her credit that, although the Society had not shared its thinking with her, she accepted its decision and worked tirelessly to implement the chosen solution of amalgamating the two in Kilkenny.

There were three possibilities for Celbridge: closure, merger with a school such as The King's Hospital or merger with another Society school. It would have been a travesty had the school been closed. The second option was a possibility at one stage, for the headmaster of The King's Hospital seriously considered buying Castletown House as a new campus and would have been interested in incorporating the Collegiate School.[22] Amalgamation with Kilkenny College rather than another Incorporated Society school was the obvious solution, as many families sent their sons to Kilkenny and their daughters to Celbridge. It also had the great advantage of providing the basis of a co-educational school.

While Celbridge was then the stronger school and had much better results, the announcement of the move to Kilkenny came as a relief. At first the girls were 'speechless'. Then curiosity took over and they invited the Kilkenny College boys up for a hockey match and a debate. This was such a success that they invited the boys a second time for a Scripture Union barbeque, 'which was an even greater success'.[23] Girls in Forms 1 to 5 were invited to transfer and most of them (68) did, along with Misses Yates and Walsh. While most other members of staff found jobs, Miss Yates was concerned for two and persuaded the Department of Education to agree that they would be employed ex-quota in another school. The two schools ensured that classes learned the same parts of courses, so that a good start could be made in September 1973. Miss Yates also made many trips to Kilkenny during the school year, working out the accommodation requirements for the girls at Celbridge House (originally Newtown House). At the same time, she was determined to make the last year in Celbridge special. Thanks to the whole-hearted support of staff, pupils and past pupils, it was a year to remember. Among the highlights was a production of *The Boyfriend*, for which the girls learned the tango and the Charleston from Mrs Stuart.

The other highlights were organised by the past pupils' association and began with a farewell dance at Easter. A marquee, draped in the old school colours of red and navy, was set up on the Mound. An eight-piece orchestra provided the music and, at the end, 450 guests sang 'Auld Lang Syne'. In the summer term a pageant, scripted and produced by past pupil, Emily Barber (née Bolster), featured 'Life in Celbridge through the years'. She took the approach of 'laugh and be proud', so the tone was positive rather than sad. The pageant was presented at the last meeting of the past pupils' association to be held in Celbridge, on 26 May 1973 and, finally, on 10 June a thanks-giving service was held in Christ Church, Celbridge. The special preacher was the Archbishop of Armagh, Dr George Simms, who had taken a close interest in the school over many years. The organist was a Collegiate girl, Valerie Horan, and the overflowing congregation found it an emotional but fitting end to the separate existence of the Collegiate School, Celbridge.

Conclusion

The Collegiate School, Celbridge presented a pageant in May 1973 on 'Life in Celbridge through the years'. If such a pageant were to be produced in 2009, to reflect life in the three schools from which the modern Kilkenny College evolved, it would be colourful and dramatic. Cameos might include today's pupils, boys and girls, conducting a computer-aided experiment in a science laboratory; then rushing to the playing fields for hockey, rugby or camogie. Contrasting cameos would present their predecessors: Kilkenny College boys 300 years ago, debating in Latin, part of the classical education which would equip them as leaders of Irish society. Moving on a century, little boys in rags, wearily labour on the looms of Pococke's weaving school; in the farmyard in Celbridge School, girls are feeding poultry, milking cows and bringing in the hay.

Moving through the hard times of the 19th century, the pageant would include 13 Celbridge girls boarding a ship for Australia in 1835, while Kilkenny College boys fished in the Nore to supplement the meagre diet produced by the college kitchen. Next, the set would be like a court room. The Incorporated Society officials are hearing the case made in 1857 by the Pococke foundationers against their headmaster, John Booth.

On to 1915 and a chance meeting of a Kilkenny College boy and a Pococke boy at the battlefield of the Somme, while in Celbridge the former's sister is knitting socks for the war effort. A year later, teachers in Celbridge are baking bread and discussing the food shortages caused by the 1916 Rising. On to 1923, with Kilkenny boys relating their adventures on the journey back to school after the Easter holidays, in the midst of the civil war. Meanwhile the girls in Celbridge are dressing up as American Indians for a production of *Hiawatha*.

The last sequence might have boys standing centre stage, dressed in costumes appropriate to different periods.

> Enter stage left Andrew O'Callaghan, brandishing the rod. All cower in fear.
> Enter John Mason Harden, smiling gently at the pupils. He holds a pack of cards, inviting the boys to join him in a game. All exit right.

The tiny figure of Anna O'Connor stands centre stage, issuing quiet commands in Irish, as girls march on and off stage repeatedly. All exit right.

Boys and girls in the current uniform stand centre stage. Enter Philip Gray, in academic gown, with referee's whistle in hand. The crowd cheers when he exhorts them to 'play a fair game' and 'uphold the honour of Kilkenny College'.

Kilkenny College has had a chequered existence. It has experienced the sublime and the abysmal. In the first years of the 21st century it is better equipped to serve Irish society than at any stage in its history. At every stage the college has faced particular challenges. Forcible closure was the challenge of the 1680s, a crumbling building constituted the problem a century later. At one point in the 1880s there were no pupils but a century later the challenge was to accommodate the ever-rising numbers on a new site. In 2008 the college suffered the enormous shock of Philip Gray's cycling accident and, at the time of writing, is facing the challenge of continuing his dynamic work in his absence. Kilkenny College is justly proud of its history. In the names of its buildings it commemorates distinguished past pupils and significant figures of recent times. It is this awareness of its goodly heritage that promises well for the future.

APPENDIX A

Statutes of Kilkenny College

These statutes are preserved in the Department of Manuscripts, Trinity College, Dublin (TCD MUN/P/1/2365). They were made on 18 March 1684 to come into effect on 25 March 1685. 25 March was at that time the first day of the new year and, therefore, both dates were, by our reckoning, in March 1685.

Statutes, orders and constitutions, made appointed and ordained by the Right Noble James, Duke, Earl and Marquis of Ormond, Earl of Ossory and Brecknock, Viscount Thurles, Baron of Arklow and Lanthony, Lord of the regalities and liberties of Tipperary, Chancellor of the universities of Oxford and Dublin, Chief Butler of Ireland, Lord Lieutenant General, and General Governor of Ireland, Lord Lieutenant of the County of Somerset, the Chief Cities of Bristol, Bath and Wells, one of the Lords of his Majesty's most honorable privy council of his Majesty's kingdoms England, Scotland and Ireland; Lord Stewart of his Majesty's Household and Westminster, and Knight of the most Noble Order of the Garter, founder of a grammar school at Kilkenny, in the Kingdom of Ireland, for the due government and managery and improvement of the said school, March the Eighteenth in the year of our Lord one thousand six hundred and eighty four.

IMPRIMIS. It is by these presents constituted and ordained, that there shall for ever be a Master constantly resident and attending the duties of the said School, who shall at least be a Master of Arts either here in Ireland or one of the universities of England, a person of good life and reputation, well skilled in humanity and grammar learning, loyal and orthodox, who shall take the oaths of allegiance and supremacy, and conform to the doctrine and discipline of the Church of Ireland as it is now established by law, and that Edward Hinton, Doctor in Divinity, be hereby confirmed to the place and office of Master of the said School.

2dly. That the Master shall be nominated and chosen by James, Duke of Ormond, his Grace, Founder, Patron and Governor and the heirs male of his body that shall be successively the Dukes of Ormond, Patrons and Governors of the said school, within the space of three months next after every vacancy, who by writing under the hand and seal of the respective Governors being recommended to the Visitors and by them examined and approved of as able and sufficient both for religion, learning and manners, upon certificate of such examination and approbation of the Visitors to the Governor shown, the said person so approved shall by a deed under the hand and seal of the Governor, be settled and confirmed as Master of the said school, but if the Governor shall neglect to nominate according to the time pre-fixed, or shall choose such as are not qualified suitably to these statutes, that then it shall be lawful for the Visitors (after notice first given to the Governor, and no redress within three months after such notice) to elect and present ... any other person, whom in their consciences they shall judge to be well qualified for the place, and also that upon fail of issue male on the body of the said James, Duke of Ormond, the Provost, Fellows, and Scholars of Trinity College, Dublin, and their successors, shall from thenceforth for ever afterwards be Patrons and Governors of said school.

3dly. That the Master shall constantly inhabit and reside at the house belonging to said school, and in person attend the duties of his place, which are to instruct the scholars in religion, virtue & learning in the Latin, Greek and Hebrew languages, as also in oratory, and poetry according to the best method which he and the Visitors shall judge most effectual to promote knowledge and learning, and that being in health, he shall never be absent for above thirty schooldays in one whole year, which shall begin on the twenty fifth of March; nor above a fortnight at any one time, unless upon emergencies the Visitors shall give him leave, being first satisfied that his place shall be well and sufficiently discharged in his absence.

4thly. That there shall always be an usher belonging to said school to be nomin-ated, chosen, and removed by the said Master, who shall have his diet lodging and maintenance in the school house at his allowance, a single man, well skilled in gram-mar learning of good credit for parts and manners, a Batchelor of Arts at least in one [of] the universities of England or Ireland, and he shall constantly attend and assist in the duties of the said school, in such a manner and method, as the Master shall appoint.

5thly. That neither master nor usher shall take upon them any other charge office or employment, which the Visitors shall judge inconsistent with, or prejudicial to the due managery and improvement of the said school, but shall constantly attend and discharge their respective duties, and never be both of them out of the school, at school times.

6thly. That the scholars to be admitted into the said school shall be cleanly and decently habited, and such as shall first have read their accidence, and are fit to enter upon grammar learning, and shall submit to the order, method and correction of the said school.

7thly. That the children of all such as are and continue to be in the service of the Duke of Ormond, shall at all times be admitted to the privileges and benefits of the said school *gratis*.

8thly. That if any well disposed person shall out of charity pay for the tabling of such ingenious and orderly Lads, as shall by the Visitors be recommended to the Master, as fit objects of charity, he shall admit and as long as they shall continue modest and diligent teach them *gratis*.

9thly. That if his Grace the Duke or other pious benefactors shall hereafter make any grants or allowance for the maintenance of any number of scholars at the said school, and afterwards if they prove fit at Trinity College Dublin, the Master shall then be expressly obliged to teach those under the name of Ormond Scholars according to his best skill and industry *gratis*.

10thly. That it shall be lawful for the Master to demand and receive of all other Scholars, according to the rates and usages of the most remarkable school in Dublin, both for entrance and schooling, those children excepted whose parents are, or at the time of their birth were inhabitants of the City of Kilkenny, or in the liberties thereof, shall pay but half so much.

11thly. That if the Master knows any of the scholars to be under any infectious or offensive disease or distemper, or that any infectious disease be in the house where they table, he shall, for the security of the rest discharge such from school till the danger be over.

12thly. That every stubborn and refractory lad, who shall refuse to submit to the orders and correction of the said school, shall by the said Master, be dismissed forthwith from said school, not to be readmitted without due submission to exemplary punishment, and upon his second offence of the said kind, to be discharged and expelled for ever, and in this number are reckoned such as shall offer to shut out the Master or Usher: but the Master shall give them leave to break up eight days before Christmas and three before Easter and Whitsuntide.

13thly. That the Master shall make diligent enquiry after such as shall break, cut or deface or any ways abuse the desks, forms, walls or windows of the school or any parts of the house or trees in the meadow and shall always inflict open and exemplary punishment on all such offenders.

14thly. That from the beginning of March to the middle of September the scholars shall be and continue in School, from six o'clock in the morning till eleven and all the rest of the year from seven or as soon as the gates of the city are open, and in the afternoon from one to five, the afternoons of Thursdays and Saturdays excepted which shall always be allowed for recreation; and that the Master shall grant no play day, except to such as shall pay down ten shillings into the Master's hands, to be by him immediately disposed of, to the most indigent and deserving lads of his school.

15thly. That the Master shall take special care of the scholars of his own family, to intrust [*sic*] them by his own good example at all times as well as by occasional directions, and shall have the prayers of the Church of England & Ireland read to them both morning and evening in some convenient place of the house, and in the school, the prayers seen and approved of by the Lord Bishop of Ossory shall be constantly and duly used, in the same manner and form as they are at the date of these presents.

16thly. That from the beginning of March till the middle of September, all the scholars shall be in the school upon Sundays by eight, to be instructed in the Church Catechism, and afterwards shall attend the Master and Usher to church, in a comely and decent manner, and from the middle of September till March they shall stay in school till half an hour past eleven upon Saturdays, that they may be taught the said Catechism.

17thly. That Edward Hinton, Master of the said school, and the Master for the time being, shall inhabit, possess and enjoy to his own proper use and emolument the school house, with the courts, outhouses and garden, thereunto belonging, as also the meadow adjoining, commonly called the Pigeon House Meadow, provided the scholars be allowed at leisure times, to take their recreation therein, and that the trees in the said meadow be carefully preserved and improved.

18thly. That the Master shall provide a large register, wherein the names, qualities and ages of all such children as shall from time to time be admitted into the said school shall be registered and entered, as also the time of their departure, what class they were in and to what place and employment they go, likewise a catalogue of all such goods, standards, or utensils as do or shall belong to the said house, school, outhouses, gardens and meadow.

19thly. That the Master shall receive for his salary the sum of one hundred and forty pounds per annum of good and lawful money of and in England, by even and equal portions, one moiety of it at the twenty fifth of March, and the other September the twenty ninth, or within a fortnight after either of those feasts, to be paid constantly in the school house without any defalcation out of the tithes settled by the said Duke for payment thereof, except his Grace or his heirs shall settle some particular lands for the payment of the said salary and which shall be of a full value to discharge it yearly, and upon the Master's death or removal his salary *pro rata* shall become due to him to be paid to that very day.

20thly. That the Master shall keep and maintain the school house, school and outhouses in constant, good and sufficient repair, nor shall it be lawful to make any alterations therein without the approbation of the Visitors.

21stly. That Thomas, Lord Bishop of Ossory, Narcissus, Lord Bishop of Leighlin and Ferns, and Robert Huntington, Provost of Trinity College in Dublin, while they live in this Kingdom, and the Bishops of Ossory, Leighlin and Ferns, and the Provost of the College for the time being, be nominated and appointed Visitors of the said school, and that they or the majority of them (For 'tis the greater number of them still which is meant by the Visitors) shall yearly at or upon the last Thursday in July yearly, or oftener if they shall see occasion, publicly visit the said school between the hours of eight and twelve in the morning, where and when they shall first cause the statutes to be read audibly and distinctly by one of the scholars, and afterwards proceed to examine the proficiency of the Scholars, and enquire after any breach of statutes, and after the behaviour of the Master, the sufficiency and manners of the Usher, the authors that are read, the methods, usages, and customs of the school, and if they shall judge any alterations or amendments requisite, in any of these they shall express it to the Master, who by virtue of these statutes is readily to comply with their advice, for the better improvement of the said school, and when there shall be Foundation Scholars, they shall by the Visitors be chosen according to their merit, for the university.

22ndly. That on the said visitation day after dinner, which the Master is to provide soberly and decently, and towards it shall have freely given him a fat buck yearly, out of his Grace's next park, the Visitors then present, shall take a view of the school, house and outhouses, the garden, meadow and trees therein, and if they find occasion, shall specify in writing all those repairs and amendments with the manner and the time when they judge them expedient to he made, and if the Master shall be negligent herein, the Visitors shall signify the same to the Governor of the said School, who forthwith shall order these things to be done by able workmen, and that they be paid out of the salary next due to the Master.

23rdly. That if it appear to the Visitors that the Usher is insufficient or scandalous, and so much be signified to the Master, under their hands and seals, if the Master shall refuse to remove the said Usher, and choose another statutably qualified, or if the Master shall neglect such alterations or amendations as the visitors shall have judged fit to be made, either in the manners of himself or his Usher, the authors to be read, or the method, customs, and management of the said school, or if the Master shall forbear to discharge himself or his Usher from such offices or employments as the Visitors have judged inconsistent with, or prejudicial to the due management of the said school, or shall alter the house without their consent, the Visitors shall under their hands and seals admonish the Master a second time of his said neglect, and if for the space of three months after such second admonition, the Master shall be convicted either by notoriety of fact, or the testimony of two (at the least) credible witnesses, of such obstinate neglect, upon information, thereof by the visitors, under their hands & seals, given to the Patron or Governor, he shall expel and remove the said Master from all duties and benefits of the said school, school house, etc., and shall nominate and choose another in his stead, according to the qualifications above specified.

24thly. That if any doubt or objection shall happen concerning the time, purport, intent and meaning of these Statutes, or anything in them contained, such interpretation as the Visitors shall agree in and signify under their hands and seals, shall he binding and decisive to all persons concerned.

LASTLY. In testimony that all and singular the above written statutes, orders and constitutions are ratified, established and confirmed to com-mence and be in force from the twenty fifth day of March, in the year of our Lord one thousand six hundred and eighty five, the said James, Duke of Ormond, the Founder of the said school, has this present eighteenth day of March in the year of our Lord one thousand six hundred and eighty four hereto set his hand and seal at his Majesty's Castle of Dublin.

Ormond

Signed, sealed and delivered in the presence of
Robert Huntington
James Power
William Robinson

APPENDIX B

Visitors of Kilkenny College

Bishops of Ferns and Leighlin
1666 Richard Boyle
1683 Narcissus Marsh
1691 Bartholomew Vigors
1722 Josiah Hart
1727 John Hoadly
1730 Arthur Price
1734 Edward Synge
1740 George Stone
1743 William Cottrell
1744 Robert Downes
1752 John Garnet
1758 William Carmichael
1758 Thomas Salmon
1759 Richard Robinson
1761 Charles Jackson
1765 Edward Young
1772 Joseph Dean Bourke
1782 Walter Cope
1787 William Preston
1789 Euseby Cleaver
1809 Percy Jocelyn
1820 Robert Ponsonby Tottenham Loftus
1822 Thomas Elrington

Bishops of Ossory
1672 John Parry
1677 Benjamin Parry
1678 Michael Ward
1679 Thomas Otway
1693 John Hartstonge*
1714 Sir Thomas Vesey
1731 Edward Tenison
1735 Charles Este
1740 Anthony Dopping

1743   Michael Cox*
1754   Edward Maurice
1756   Richard Pococke
1765   Charles Dodgson
1775   William Newcombe
1779   John Hotham
1782   The Hon William Beresford*
1795   Thomas Lewis O'Beirne
1799   Hugh Hamilton
1806   John Kearney
1813   Robert Fowler
Ossory and Ferns from 1835
1842   James Thomas O'Brien
1875   Robert Samuel Gregg
1878   William Pakenham Walsh

Provosts of Trinity College
1661   Thomas Seele
1674   Michael Ward
1679   Narcissus Marsh
1683   Robert Huntington
1692   St George Ashe
1695   George Browne
1699   Peter Browne
1710   Benjamin Pratt
1717   Richard Baldwin*
1758   Francis Andrews
1774   John Hely-Hutchinson
1795   Richard Murray
1799   John Kearney
1806   George Hall
1811   Thomas Elrington
1820   Samuel Kyle
1831   Bartholomew Lloyd
1837   Franc Sadleir
1851   Richard MacDonnell
1867   Humphrey Lloyd
1881   John Hewitt Jellett*

* past pupil of Kilkenny College

APPENDIX C

Headmasters and Headmistresses

Headmasters of Kilkenny College
The Revd Edward Jones, D.D., 1667-1679
The Revd Henry Ryder, D.D., 1679-1683
The Revd Edward Hinton, D.D., 1684-1702
The Revd William Andrews, LL.D., 1702-1713
The Revd Edward Lewis, M.A., 1713-1742
The Revd Thomas Hewetson, LL.D., 1743-1773
The Revd Richard Pack, LL.D., 1773-1781* ✚
The Revd John Ellison, D.D., 1781-1793
The Revd Anthony Pack, LL.D., 1793-1810*
The Revd Andrew O'Callaghan, M.A., 1810-1820
The Revd William Baillie, LL.D., 1820-1842
The Revd John Browne, LL.D., 1842-1864
The Revd John H. Martin, LL.D., 1864-1874
James M. Weir, M.A., 1874-1890 ✚
T. Brian MacDermot, LL.D., 1891-1893
The Revd George W. Baile, LL.B., 1894-1900
Thomas W. Pettipice, B.A., 1901-1903
William A. Shekleton, 1903-1907 ✚
The Revd John M. Harden, LL.D., D.D., 1907-1914
The Revd Edward G. Seale, M.A., 1914-1917
Carrodus G. Shankey, M.A., 1917-1952
Gilbert Colton, B.A., 1952-1979
Samuel McClure, M.A., 1979-1996
The Revd R. John E. F. B. Black, M.A., 1996-2005
Philip B. Gray, B.A., 2005-

Headmasters of Pococke School
Edward Graham 1781-1788
Andrew Neelands, 1789-1806‡
James McKowen, 1807-1816‡
The Revd Robert Shaw, 1816-1816 (interim)
John Armstrong, 1816-1818‡
Thomas R. Burrows, 1818-1829

James Pounds, 1829-1840
Richard Jessop, 1840-1841
Alexander P. Hanlon, 1841-1843
John Turner, 1843-1853
John L. Booth, 1853-1857‡
William H. Engledow, 1857-1859
John B. Browne, 1859-1903

Headmistresses of Celbridge School
—

Mary Taylor, -1789
Katherine Holt, 1789-
—

Bridget Boyle, 1810-1850 ✚
John Boyle, 1810-1852 ✚
Mary McKenny 1850-1851 ✚
Anne Boyle 1851-1859
Sarah L. Crawford, 1859-1864 ✚
Anne Crawford, 1864-1867 (interim headmistress)
Eliza Crawford, 1864-1867 (interim headmistress)
Anne E. Crawford, 1867-1894
Bessie St George, 1894-1895 (matron)
Augusta L'Estrange, 1895-1897
Annie McCullagh, 1898-1909
Georgina E. Osborne, M.A., 1909 ✚ (died before taking up office)
Emma McClelland, M.A., 1909-1919
Dora Cox, M.A., 1920-1920 (interim headmistress)
Emma McClelland, M.A., 1920-1942
Anna H. O'Connor, 1942-1967*
Mary Taylor, 1967-1969
Freda D. Yates, 1970-1973*

* – past pupil of the school
‡ – dismissed
✚ – died in office

APPENDIX D

Past Pupils who died in the two World Wars

A lack of pupil registers makes it impossible to compile a full list for the First World War. Some names are recorded on the war memorial in St Canice's Cathedral. Experience suggests that the list for the Second World War is also incomplete.

First World War

Kilkenny College
R. C. Baile (1915)
T. H. Bor (1916)
T. A. Burgess (1916)
A. Corrigan (1917)
K. Elmes (1918)
T. E. England (1918)
R. A. Frizell (1917)
J. D. Gloster (1918)
R. T. Jeffares (1917)
C. D. Newland (1920)
J. H. Tallis (1918)

The Pococke School
W. M. Howe (1918)
H. G. Mulholland (1916)
R. V. Murphy (1918)

Second World War

Kilkenny College
C. H. Anderson (1944)
J. W. Blennerhassett (1942)
J. I. Burne (1944)
W. F. Harris (1944)
W. J. W. Kingston (1942)
J. C. McEvett (1943)
A. H. McFall (1942)
J. G. McFall (1941)

J. G. A. Maguire (1942)
I. T. Paulin (1943)
R. T. Philp (1941)
F. S. White (1940)

Select Bibliography

MANUSCRIPT SOURCES

Abbreviations used in the endnotes are given after the full title.

The Bodleian Library, Oxford (Bodl.)
Carte papers (Carte 1-279)
Draft of proposal for education in Ireland introduced in the Irish House of Commons by Thomas Orde-Powlett (Top. Ireland d. 2-3)

Hampshire Record Office
Will of Isaac Milles of Highclere, 1720 (1720B/54)

Kilkenny College (KCK)
Minute Book of the local committee of Kilkenny College, 1903-1967
Board minutes 1989-2005
Past pupil recollections, including:
Mark Wilson, 'My early schooldays', 1915, typescript copy by his son, 1996
Edgar Roe, interview, 26 January 2007
Victor Griffin, interview, 4 March 2007
George Benn, interview, 8 March 2007
Ken Stanley, interview, 12 June 2007

In addition to those mentioned in the text, MSS recollections of Celbridge past pupils: Rebecca Wilkie (Mrs Power) (1925-31), Joan P. Cochrane (1928-32), May Foster (Mrs Newburn) (1922-28), Martha Deacon (Mrs Jones) (1927-33), Kay Thompson (Mrs Hannagen) (1928-30), Jenny Holmes (1930), Betty Cooke (Mrs Shortt) (1932-34), Muriel Mitchell (Mrs Patterson) (1937-43). Heather Lewis (Mrs Meldrum) (1952-56), Norma Roberts (Mrs Murphy) (1950-55)

Manuscript letters, including:
The Revd Robert Fishbourne to George Annesley Owen, 29 August 1877

National Archives [of England]
Thomas Hussey, Bishop of Waterford and Lismore, a pastoral letter to the catholic clergy of the united dioceses of Waterford and Lismore, 1794 (Home Office 100/69/206-13)

National Archives of Ireland (NA)
Extracts from letters of Alderman William Colles, 1742-1768 (Prim Collection, File 87)

National Library of Ireland (NLI)
Survey of a house in St Johnstown, 31 November 1666 (11,053/5/ii)
Quane Papers

Public Records Office of Northern Ireland
Ledger of schools expenditure of the Incorporated Society, 1896-1911 (D/3480/50D/1)

Representative Church Body Library: (RCB)
Combined Registers, parish of Mayne, diocese of Meath, 1808-1983 (P.0420.01)
Records of the Incorporated Society (IS):
Board Minute Book, 1894-1913 (151/1/1)

Trinity College Dublin: (TCD)
Records of the Incorporated Society (IS):
Board and committee minutes and papers, letter books and pupil returns, etc
Celbridge Charity School cash book 1785-95 (5610)

PRINTED SOURCES

Official Publications

Calendar of the patent and close rolls of chancery in Ireland, Elizabeth, 19 year to end of reign (Cal. pat. rolls Ire., Hen. VIII- Eliz.) ed. James Morrin (Dublin, 1861)
Census of Ireland, 1901, 1911
Scheme No. 210, approved under the Educational Endowments (Ireland) Act, 1885, 48 and 49 Vic., c.78
First report of the commissioners of Irish education inquiry (First report of educational commissioners, 1825) H.C. 1825 (400)
The parliamentary register, or history of the proceedings and debates of the house of commons of Ireland [1781-97] (Parl. reg. Ire.) 17 vols (Dublin, 1782-1801)
Report of the commissioners of the Board of Education in Ireland (Commissioners of Irish education inquiry, 1791) included in *Evidence taken before his majesty's commissioners of inquiry into the state of the endowed schools in Ireland* [2236-111] H.C. 1857-8
Reports of the commissioners of the Board of Education in Ireland. (Commissioners of the Board of Education) *Third report: The Protestant charter schools,* H.C.1809; (*Twelfth report: Classical Schools,* H.C. 1812; *Thirteenth report: English schools of private foundation,* H.C. 1812
Report of the commissioners appointed to inquire into the endowments, funds and actual condition of all schools endowed for the purpose of education in Ireland (Kildare commission) [C2336] H.C.1857-8
Report of Commission to inquire into Endowments, Funds and Condition of Schools endowed for Education in Ireland, 1881 (Rosse commission) (c 2831)
Schools: Funds and Revenues of Schools in Ireland (London, 1821)

Publications of the Incorporated Society

An Abstract of the Proceedings of the Incorporated Society ... from the opening of His Majesty's royal charter on 6 February 1733 to 25 March 1737 (Dublin, 1737)
Annual reports, 1894-1940
Annual reports of the Committee of Fifteen to the General Board of the Incorporated Society (Report of the Committee of Fifteen)

Newspapers, Church Magazines, School Magazines, etc.

The Celbridgite (Celbridge)
Church of Ireland Gazette (Belfast)
The Constitution (Cork)
Cork County Eagle and Munster Advertiser (Skibbereen)

Daily Express (Dublin)
Finn's Leinster Journal (Kilkenny)
Freeman's Journal (Dublin)
The Gentleman's Magazine (London)
The Irish Times (Dublin)
Kilkenny College Magazine (Kilkenny)
Kilkenny Moderator (Kilkenny)
Mountjoy School Magazine (Dublin)
The Nationalist (Clonmel)
Saunders' Newsletter (Dublin)
School Magazine of the Incorporated Society (Dublin)

Dictionaries, Directories, etc.

Alumni Oxonienses, ed. Joseph Foster (Oxford, 1891)
Ardfert and Aghadoe Clergy and Parishes, ed. James B. Leslie (Dublin, 1940)
Athenae Cantabrigienses, eds. Charles Henry Cooper and Thompson Cooper (Cambridge, 1858)
A Biographical Dictionary of Architects in Ireland, 1600-1720, ed. Rolf Loeber (London, 1981)
Biographical Dictionary of Civil Engineers in Great Britain and Ireland, eds. M. M. Chimes et al. (London, 2008)
Clerical and Parochial Records of Cork, Cloyne and Ross, ed. William Mazière Brady (Dublin, 1863)
Clergy of Dublin and Glendalough, ed. Ronnie Wallace (Dublin, 2001)
Concise Dictionary of British Literary Biography, eds. Matthew J. Bruccoli, and Richard Layman (London, 1992)
Dictionary of Canadian Biography, ed. Marc La Terreur (Toronto, 1972)
Dictionary of Irish Artists, ed. Theo Snoddy (Dublin, 1996)
A Dictionary of Irish Artists, ed. W.G. Strickland (Dublin, 1913)
The Irish Education Directory (Dublin, 1882-88)
Kilkenny City and County Guide and Directory (Dublin, 1884)
Ossory Clergy and Parishes, ed. James B. Leslie, (Enniskillen, 1933)
Oxford Dictionary of National Biography (ODNB), eds. H. C. G. Matthew and Brian Harrison (revised edition, Oxford, 2004)
A Topographical Dictionary of Ireland, ed. Samuel Lewis (London, 1837)

SECONDARY SOURCES

Alcock, Nathaniel, *A Treatise on Cholera* (London, 1849)
Anonymous ['An ex-officer of the Royal Irish Constabulary'], *Leaves from my note-book; being a collection of tales, all positive facts portraying Irish life and character* (London, 1879)
Arnold, Bruce, *Swift: an illustrated life* (Dublin, 1999)
Barker, G. F. R., *Memoir of Richard Busby, D.D. (1606-1695), with some account of Westminster School* (London, 1895)
Barnard, Toby, *A New Anatomy of Ireland: the Irish Protestants, 1649-1770* (London, 2003)

— *Irish Protestant ascents and descents, 1641-1770* (Dublin, 2004)

Barnard, Toby and Fenlon, Jane (eds.), *The Dukes of Ormonde, 1610-1745* (Woodbridge, 2000)

Barnard, Toby and Neely, William G. (eds.), *The Clergy of the Church of Ireland, 1000-2000* (Dublin, 2006)

Bennett, George, *The History of Bandon* (Cork, 1869)

Berkeley, George M., *Literary relics* (London, 1789)

Bor, Eleanor, *Adventures of a Botanist's Wife* (London, 1952)

Bowden, Charles Topham, *A tour through Ireland* (Dublin, 1791)

Boylan, Lena, *Castletown and its owners* (Dublin, 1978)

Bradley, John, *Kilkenny, Irish Historic Towns Atlas, x,* (Dublin, 2000)

Browne, John, 'Kilkenny College' in *Transactions of the Kilkenny Archaeological Society*, i, part 2 (1850), pp 221-29

Bryan, Winifred, *Collegiate School Celbridge: a history* (Celbridge, 1971)

Burns, J. F., *Shop Window to the World* (Dublin, 1964)

Burtchaell, G. D., 'Kilkenny Grammar School, now called the College, and its masters' in *Kilkenny Moderator*, 25 June 1904, p. 8

Byrne, Thomas, 'Nathaniel Hooke (1664-1738) and the French embassy to Saxony, 1711-12' in Thomas O'Connor and Mary Ann Lyons (eds.), *Irish Communities in Early Modern Europe* (Dublin, 2006), pp 409-429

Carrigan, William, *The History and Antiquities of the Diocese of Ossory* (Dublin, 1905)

Carte, Thomas, *An History of the Life of James, Duke of Ormond* (London, 1736)

Cathcart, Rex, *An Help for School Boys: the choir and grammar schools* (Dublin, 1991)

Coleman, Michael C., '"The children are used wretchedly": pupil responses to the Irish charter schools in the early nineteenth century' in *History of Education*, xxx, no. 4 (2001), pp 339-57

Corcoran, Timothy, *State Policy in Irish Education, A.D. 1536 to 1816* (Dublin, 1916)

Dagg, Thomas S. C., *Hockey in Ireland* (Tralee, 1944)

Darby, Graham, *King Edward VI School, 1553-2003: an illustrated history* (Southampton, 2004)

de Breffny, Brian, 'Christopher Hewetson' in *Irish Arts Review*, iii, no. 3 (Autumn 1986), pp 52-75

de Búrca, Marcus, *Michael Cusack and the GAA* (Dublin, 1989)

Dickson, David, 'Inland city: reflections on eighteenth century Kilkenny' in William Nolan and Kevin Whelan (eds.), *Kilkenny: History and Society* (Dublin, 1990), pp 333-44

Dobbs, W. E., *Notes on the History of Kilkenny College, 1538-1938* (Kilkenny, 1938)

Dodds, Eric R., *Missing Persons: an autobiography* (Oxford, 1977)

Duncan, Tom, *et al.*, *The 1608 Royal Schools* (Armagh, 2007)

Dunlop, G. D., *Pages from the History of Highclere, Hampshire* (Oxford, 1940)

Ehrenpreis, Irvin, *Swift: the man, his works, and the age* (London, 1983)

Elrington, S. N. and Carr, W. P., *Authentic Report of the Most Important and Interesting Trial of Mathew vs. Harty and Stokes* (Dublin, 1852)

Empey, Adrian, 'From Rags to Riches: Piers Butler, 8th Earl of Ormond, 1515-39' in *Journal of the Butler Society*, ii, no. 3 (1984), pp 299-314

Fancutt, Walter, *With Strange Surprise* (London, 1974)

Fennelly, Teddy, *Thomas Prior – his life, times and legacy* (Portlaoise, 2001)

FitzGerald, Brian, *Lady Louisa Conolly, 1743-1821: an Anglo-Irish biography* (London, 1950)

Foster, Roy, *Modern Ireland 1600-1972* (London, 1998)

Fraser, Annie M., 'The old Clonmel schools' in *The Nationalist*, 20 April 1963

Glassford, James, *Notes of Three Tours in Ireland in 1824 and 1826* (Bristol, 1832)

Graves, James, *The History, Architecture and Antiquities of the Cathedral Church of St Canice, Kilkenny* (Dublin, 1857)

Hamilton, Pádraig, 'The Revd Doctor John Browne (1798-1870): Master of the Bandon Endowed School, 1826-1842 and afterwards Head of Kilkenny College', part 1, in *Bandon Historical Journal*, issue 19 (2003), pp 9-19

Harris, Walter, *The History and Antiquities of the City of Dublin* (Dublin, 1766)

Hartin, James, 'Richard Pococke, Bishop of Ossory' in *Journal of the Butler Society*, ii, no.3 (1984), pp 339-45

Hegarty, Maureen, 'Dr Richard Pococke' in *Old Kilkenny Review*, xv (1963), pp 48-54

Hely-Hutchinson, John, *An Account of some regulations made in Trinity College Dublin since the appointment of the present provost* (Dublin, 1775)

Historical Manuscripts Commission, *Calendar of the Manuscripts of the Marquis of Ormonde, K.P., preserved at Kilkenny Castle (Ormonde MSS)*, 11 vols (new series, iii, vi-vii

Hone, M. and Rossi, Mario M., *Bishop Berkeley: his life, writings and philosophy* (London, 1931)

Jeffares, A. Norman and Kamm, Anthony, *An Irish Childhood* (London, 1987)

Jones, Valerie, *A Gaelic Experiment: the preparatory system, 1926-1961 and Coláiste Moibhí* (Dublin, 2006)

King, William, *The state of the Protestants of Ireland under the late King James's government* (London, 1691)

Kingsmill Moore, Henry, *The Work of the Incorporated Society for Promoting Protestant Schools in Ireland* (Dundalk, 1938)

Lennon, Colm, 'Pedagogy and reform: the influence of Peter White on Irish scholarship in the Renaissance' in Thomas Herron and Michael Potterton (eds.), *Ireland in the Renaissance, c. 1540-1660* (Dublin, 2007), pp 43-51

Leonard, John, *A University for Kilkenny: plans for a royal college in the seventeenth century* (Dún Laoghaire, 1994)

Luce, A.A., 'Some unpublished Berkeley letters with some new Berkeleiana' in *Proceedings of the Royal Irish Academy*, xli, C (1933), pp 141-61

Luce, J. V., *Trinity College Dublin, The First 400 Years* (Dublin, 1992)

Lydon, James, *The Making of Ireland* (London, 1998)

Lynch, Kathleen M. 'Congreve's Irish Friend, Joseph Keally' in *Proceedings of the Modern Language Association*, liii, no. 4 (Dec. 1938), pp 1076-87

McAdoo, H.R., *No New Church* (Dublin, 1945)

Macalister, R. A. S., 'The Charter and Statutes of Kilkenny College' in *Journal of the Royal Society of Antiquaries of Ireland (JRSAI)*, xl, no.1 (March 1910), pp 32-37

Macaulay, T. Babington, *The Modern British Essayists* (Philadelphia, 1882)

McCarthy, Muriel, *All Graduates and Gentlemen: Marsh's Library* (Dublin, 1980)

Macdonnell, John Cotter, *The Life and Correspondence of William Connor Magee, Archbishop of York* (2 vols, London, 1896)

McVeigh, John (ed.), *Richard Pococke's Irish Tours* (Dublin, 1995)

Madden, Dodgson H., *Some Passages in the Early History of Classical Learning in Ireland* (Dublin, 1908)

Madden, Samuel, *Memoir of the life of the late Rev Peter Roe* (Dublin, 1842)

Maher, John, 'Francis Place in Drogheda, Kilkenny and Waterford, etc.' in *JRSAI*, lxiv, no.1 (1934), pp 41-53

Maxwell, William Hamilton, *Life, Military and Civil, of the Duke of Wellington* (London, 1852)

Mercier, Vivian, 'The Old School Tie, No. 3: Portora Royal School, Enniskillen' in *The Bell*, xi, no. 6 (March 1946), pp 1081-90

[Milles], *An Account of the Life and Conversation of the Reverend and Worthy Mr Isaac Milles* (London, 1721)

Milne, Kenneth, 'A Church of Ireland view [on the future of post-primary education], in *Studies*, lvii (Autumn 1968), pp 261-69

— *The Irish Charter Schools, 1730-1830* (Dublin, 1997)

Mulcahy, M. (ed.), *Calendar of Kinsale Documents* (Kinsale, 1994)

Murray, Patrick Joseph, *The Life of John Banim* (London, 1857)

Neely, William G., *Kilkenny: an urban history, 1391-1843* (Belfast, 1989)

O'Callaghan, Andrew, *Thoughts on the tendencies of Bible Societies as affecting the Established Church and Christianity itself as a reasonable service* (Dublin, 1816)

O'Connor, Anne V. and Parkes, Susan M., *Gladly Learn and Gladly Teach: A History of Alexandra College and School, Dublin, 1866-1966* (Dublin, 1966)

Ó Fearghail, Fearghas, *St Kieran's College, Kilkenny, 1782-1982* (Kilkenny, 1982)

Parker, Robert, *Memoirs of the Most Remarkable Military Transactions from the year 1683 to 1718* (Dublin, 1746)

Parkes, Susan M., *Kildare Place: the history of the Church of Ireland Training College, 1811-1969* (Dublin, 1984)

Plowden, Francis, *An Historical Review of the State of Ireland* (Philadelphia, 1805)

Pococke, Richard, *A Sermon preached at Christ Church, Dublin on 27 June 1762 before the Incorporated Society* (Dublin, 1762)

Potterton, Homan, *Rathcormick: A Childhood Revisited* (Dublin, 2001)

— *Potterton People and Places: three centuries of an Irish family* (Drogheda, 2006)

Quane, Michael, 'Pococke School, Kilkenny' in *JRSAI*, lxxx, part 1 (1950), pp 36-72

— 'City of Dublin Free School' in *JRSAI*, xc (1960), pp 163-89

— 'Celbridge Collegiate School' in *Journal of the Kildare Archaeological Society*, xiv (1969), pp 397-414

Randles, Eileen, *Post-primary Education in Ireland, 1957-1970* (Dublin, 1975)

Ruddock, Norman, *The Rambling Rector* (Dublin, 2005)

Russell, C. F., *A History of King Edward VI School, Southampton* (Crosby, 1940)

Seaver, George, *John Allen Fitzgerald Gregg, Archbishop* (London, 1963)

Shaw, G. Bernard, *Collected Letters, Volume 3: 1911-1925*, ed. Dan H. Lawrence (London, 1985)

Stanford, W. B., *A recognised church* (Dublin, 1944)

— *Ireland and the Classical Tradition* (2nd ed, Dublin, 1984)

Stanihurst, Richard, 'The Description of Ireland' in *Holinshed's Irish Chronicle: the historie of Irelande from the first inhabitation thereof unto the year 1509*, ed. Liam Miller and Eileen Power [based on the 1577 edition] (Dublin, 1979)

Stokes, George T. (ed.), *Pococke's Tour in Ireland in 1752* (Dublin, 1891)

Stoney, R. A., *Some old annals of the Stoney family* (London, 1879)

Tempest McCrea, C., *Dundalk Grammar School: the first 250 years* (1739-1989) (Dundalk, 1989)

Tighe, William, *Statistical observations relative to the County of Kilkenny* (Dublin, 1802)

Tillyard, Stella, *Aristocrats: Caroline, Emily, Louisa and Sarah Lennox, 1740-1832* (London, 1995)

Voltaire, *Letters concerning the English nation* (new ed., London, 1778)

Wallace, Ronnie, *Faithful to our Trust* (Dublin, 2004)

Walsh, Pat, 'Linen Weaving in Kilkenny in 18th Century' in *Old Kilkenny Review*, xxiv, (1972), pp 56-57

West, Trevor, *Midleton College, 1696-1996* (Midleton, 1996)

Whelan, Irene, *The Bible War in Ireland: the 'Second Reformation' and the Polarisation of Protestant Catholic Relations, 1800-1840* (Dublin, 2005)

Whitehead, Clive, *Colonial Education: the British Indian and Colonial Education Service, 1858-1983* (London, 2003)

Whiteside, Lesley, *A History of The King's Hospital* (2nd ed., Dublin, 1985)

— *George Otto Simms, a biography* (Gerrards Cross, 1990)

Wigham, Maurice, *Newtown School, Waterford 1798-1998: A History* (Waterford, 1998)

Williams, Harold, ed., *The Correspondence of Jonathan Swift* (Oxford, 1963)

Thesis (unpublished)

Tannam, Gerard J. 'The Later History of the Charter Schools', M.A. thesis, UCD, 1954

Notes

Introduction

1. Founded as the Incorporated Society for Promoting English Schools in Ireland
2. The name came simply from the royal charter.
3. Foster to Sir Robert Peel, 21 Oct. 1824 (BL, Peel papers, Add. MSS 40, 370, f. 114), quoted by Kenneth Milne, *The Irish Charter Schools, 1730-1830* (Dublin, 1997), p. 269
4. Milne, op. cit., p. 310
5. The Educational Endowments Act, 1885 (48 and 49 Vict., c. 78)

1. Origins

1. 'An Humble Address to Both Houses of Parliament' (1725), one of *The Drapier's Letters*, quoted in Irvin Ehrenpreis, *Swift: the man, his works, and the age* (London, 1983), iii, p. 307
2. Walter Harris, *The History and Antiquities of the City of Dublin* (Dublin, 1766), appendix III, i
3. Adrian Empey, 'From Rags to Riches: Piers Butler, 8th Earl of Ormond, 1515-39', in *Journal of the Butler Society*, ii, 3 (1984), pp 299-300
4. William Carrigan, *The History and Antiquities of the Diocese of Ossory* (Dublin, 1905), i, p. 258
5. Charles Henry Cooper and Thompson Cooper, *Athenae Cantabrigienses* (Cambridge, 1858), i, p. 445. James B. Leslie, *Ossory Clergy and Parishes* (Enniskillen, 1933), p. 58, claims that he graduated from All Souls' College, Oxford in 1543, following which he was rector of Clonmore, Co Louth.
6. He died in October 1581 and there is a memorial to him in the cathedral. James Graves, *The History, Architecture and Antiquities of the Cathedral Church of St Canice, Kilkenny* (Dublin, 1857), p. 289
7. James Lydon, *The Making of Ireland* (London, 1998), p. 141
8. Richard Stanihurst, 'The Description of Ireland' in *Holinshed's Irish Chronicle: the historie of Irelande from the first inhabitation thereof unto the year 1509*, ed. Liam Miller and Eileen Power (Dublin, 1979), pp 59-60
9. W. B. Stanford, *Ireland and the Classical Tradition*, pp 20-21. Stanford drew on the curriculum described in Charles Hoole's *New Discovery of the Old Art of Teaching Schoole* (1660) and John Brinsley's *Ludus Literarius* (1627). He mentioned other schools which were successfully teaching classics: that of John Flahy in Waterford and that of Alexander Lynch in Galway. Both flourished at the beginning of the 17th century.
10. James Morrin (ed.), *Cal. pat. rolls Ire., Hen. VIII- Eliz.* (Dublin, 1861), i, p. 494
11. While Carrigan (op. cit., i, p. 259) suggested that White returned to his educational duties in Kilkenny, it seems more likely that he was teaching privately in his native Waterford. Others have claimed that he was forced to flee Ireland. Either way, when he died or departed Kilkenny, it appears probable that the school fell into terminal decline.
12. Colm Lennon, 'Peter White' in *ODNB*, lviii, p. 612
13. Dodgson H. Madden, *Some Passages in the Early History of Classical Learning in Ireland* (Dublin, 1908), p. 81. This is an English translation of the Latin text in Richard Stanihurst, *De Rebus in Hibernia Gestis* (Antwerp, 1584), p. 25.
14. Kildare commission report, p. 6
15. Cited in Carrigan, op. cit., i, p. 259. 'Backwardness' is a euphemistic way of explaining that they were Roman Catholic. Their parents, therefore, did not want to send them to the diocesan school, which by definition taught the faith according to the established church (Church of Ireland).

16. David Edwards, *The Ormond Lordship in County Kilkenny, 1515-1642* (Dublin, 2003), p. 292

17. See Mr Wyttar's account and receipt for monies due to the free school of the Diocese of Ossory, 23 July 1634 (NLI MS 11,064/7). See also Ormond's correspondence with the Rt Revd Jonas Wheeler (NA, Graves Papers, M. 594).

18. Deputations for counties Carlow and Kilkenny, 1641 (TCD, MS 812, ff 202v and 213r)

19. Rex Cathcart, *An Help for School Boys* (Dublin, 1991), pp 7, 9

20. The schools for counties Armagh, Donegal, Fermanagh and Tyrone were originally located in rural settings but were moved to town sites for better security and improved status. Three of the remaining counties of Ulster (Antrim, Down and Monaghan) had not been part of the official plantation and were not included in the scheme.

21. His will was dated 1742 and he died the following year.

22. 'Laws and directions given by Erasmus Smith under his hand and seal for the better government and ordering of the public schools late by him founded and erected', copy in Guildhall Library, London (MS 13,823, p. 18)

23. Ronnie Wallace, *Faithful to our Trust* (Dublin, 2004), p. 46

24. Lesley Whiteside, *A History of The King's Hospital* (2nd ed., Dublin, 1985), pp 16, 20, 216. Freeman status, which was typically granted to tradesmen, gave citizenship of the city. It included commercial and political rights.

25. The Duke of Ormond was one of the original trustees. See Annie M. Fraser, 'The old Clonmel schools' in *The Nationalist*, 20 April 1963.

26. Kildare commission report, p. 116. Elsewhere, in 1686 John Preston granted lands to finance schools at Navan and Ballyroan. A year later Dr Jeremiah Hall founded two charity schools in Limerick, one for boys and one for girls.

27. It came to be known as Joiner's Folly.

28. In 1678 Ormond gave £100 per annum for the duration of his lord lieutenancy to aid the construction of school buildings.

29. Thomas Carte, *An History of the Life of James, Duke of Ormond* (London, 1736), ii, p. 340

2. New beginnings, 1666-1683

1. Although the Irish parliament granted him £30,000 to compensate for the sums he had spent in royal service, it is believed that he was still at a loss. There is some suggestion that the foundation of the school was delayed by legal obstacles to the recovery of his lands.

2. Thomas Carte, *An History of the Life of James, Duke of Ormond* (London, 1736) ii, 510

3. This licence was issued in 1662, in his capacity as Lord Lieutenant.

4. Michael Quane, 'City of Dublin Free School' in *JRSAI*, xc (1960), pp 163-89

5. The 1659 census gave the population of the city and liberties of Kilkenny as 1,722, almost a quarter of which was described as English as opposed to Irish.

6. Survey of a house in St Johnstown, 31 Nov. 1666 (NLI, MS 11,053/5/ii). It was built by Seix and Ormond's tenant was Badge. A similar survey of a different house is mentioned in a letter from John Morton to Ormond, 20 Dec. 1665. (Ormonde MSS, new series, iii, 200). Morton gave estimates for three different ways of repairing the house but nothing came of it.

7. An usher was an assistant teacher, usually without a university education.

8. Rolf Loeber, *A Biographical Dictionary of Architects in Ireland, 1600-1720* (London, 1981), p. 78. Dunmore House, Co. Kilkenny was the duchess's house.

9. Ormond to Edward Butler, 13 Apr.1668 (Bodl., MS Carte 145, f. 323)

10. Ormond to George Mathew, 25 Aug. 1668 (MS Carte 49, f. 604)

11. Ormond to Sir Robert Southwell, 20 Mar. 1679 (MS Carte 70, f. 484)

12. Ormond to the Earl of Ossory (his son), 31 Oct. 1668 (MS Carte 48, f. 301)

13. Ormond to Southwell, 20 Mar. 1679 (MS Carte 70, f. 483)

14. G. D. Burtchaell, letter to editor, *Kilkenny Moderator*, 2 Nov. 1887, p. 4

15. It is among a small number of schoolbooks in the collection of Archbishop Narcissus Marsh. See Muriel McCarthy, *All Graduates and Gentlemen: Marsh's Library* (Dublin, 1980), p. 208.

16. See, for examples, two relatively recent biographies: Bruce Arnold, *Swift: an illustrated life* (Dublin, 1999); Victoria Glendinning, *Jonathan Swift* (London, 1998).

17. Swift to Charles Ford, 12 Nov. 1708, quoted in A. Norman Jeffares & Anthony Kamm, *An Irish Childhood* (London, 1987), p. 29

18. Harold Williams (ed.), *The Correspondence of Jonathan Swift* (Oxford, 1963), i, p. 109

19. Ibid., iii, p. 313

20. Physic is an old term for medicine and should not be confused with today's term physics.

21. *The Drapier's Letters* (1724-5) put an end to the 'Wood's half-pence' affair. The 1720 pamphlet was *Irish Manufacture*.

22. It was first published in London in 1726.

23. Baldwin's attendance at Kilkenny College has been doubted by some but it is confirmed by the school register and the Trinity Entrance Book. See J.V. Luce, *Trinity College Dublin, The First 400 Years* (Dublin, 1992), pp 43-5.

24. R. B. McDowell and D. A. Webb, *Trinity College Dublin, 1592-1952: an academic history* (Cambridge, 1982), p. 38

25. Thomas Byrne, 'Nathaniel Hooke (1664-1738) and the French embassy to Saxony, 1711-12' in Thomas O'Connor and Mary Ann Lyons (eds.), *Irish Communities in Early Modern Europe* (Dublin, 2006), pp 409-29

26. Robert Parker, *Memoirs of the Most Remarkable Military Transactions from the year 1683 to 1718* (Dublin, 1746), pp 2-3

27. Cathcart, *An Help for School Boys*, p. 8

28. *Ormonde MSS*, new series vii, p. 11. Other boys, among them John Doucett and Edward Wolfe, were appointed straight from school to serve either the duke or the duchess. Under the statutes of Kilkenny College, drawn up in 1685, sons of those in the duke's service were entitled to a free education in the college.

29. James Clarke to the Earl of Arran, abstract of letter, 5 June 1684 in *Ormonde MSS*, new series, vii, p. 241. See also pp 444, 452. Giles Clarke is listed in Joseph Foster, *Alumni Oxonienses* (Oxford, 1891), i, p. 280.

30. Removed as Lord Lieutenant in 1669 and the subject of an assassination attempt in 1670, he was restored to the position in 1677 and held it until 1685, three years before his death.

31. Duchess of Ormond to the Earl of Arran, 16 Dec. 1682 in *Ormonde MSS*, new series, vi, p. 495

32. Duchess of Ormond to Earl of Arran, 6 Jan. 1683, ibid., p. 507

33. Ecclesiastical records detail several appointments while Ryder was in Kilkenny. These would have supplemented his income as master. After a short time as bishop, he died in January 1696.

34. G. F. R. Barker, *Memoir of Richard Busby, D.D. (1606-1695), with some account of Westminster School* (London, 1895)

3. Survival, 1683-1702

1. Printed in 1684 in *The Apophthegms or remarkable sayings*, of which there is a copy in the British Library.

2. A very strange letter of 27 Aug. 1689 from Hinton to Huntington is extant (TCD MUN/P/1/556). Although its true import is obscure, it indicates a friendship between them.

3. Statutes of Kilkenny College, 18 Mar. 1685 (TCD, MUN/P/1/2365). See Appendix A.

4. Mary A. Fleming, *Witney Grammar School, 1660-1960* (Witney, 1960), pp 5-15. Even the

title was similar to Witney's 'statutes, constitutions, orders and directions'.

5. See Thomas Carte, *An History of the Life of James, Duke of Ormond* (London, 1736), ii, app., pp 127-132.

6. See Whiteside, *The King's Hospital*, pp 88-9, 96-7.

7. For a vivid account of a rebellion in the Royal School, Armagh in the 1820s, see W. S. Trench, *Realities of Irish Life* (London, 1968), pp 1-35. On other similar incidents in Armagh, see Tom Duncan *et al.*, *The 1608 Royal Schools* (Armagh, 2007), p. 44.

8. See John Maher, 'Francis Place in Drogheda, Kilkenny and Waterford, etc.' in *JRSAI*, LXIV, 1 (1934), p 48

9. Thomas Otway to James Clarke, 18 Aug. 1686, *Ormonde MSS*, new series, vii, p. 444. 'Humorous' is one of the many words which have changed in meaning over time. In this instance, it means 'in a happy frame of mind'. Hinton was also praised by William Moreton, Bishop of Kildare, in a letter to Ormond in September 1688. MSS of Reginald Cholmondeley, *Royal Commission on Historical Manuscripts, 5th report,* (London, 1876), p. 345

10. Ormond to Thomas Otway, 20 Nov. 1686, *Ormonde MSS*, new series, vii, p. 475

11. William King, *The state of the Protestants of Ireland under the late King James's government* (London, 1691), p. 184. King was intimately involved in the events of the time. Appointed Dean of St Patrick's Cathedral in 1688, he was imprisoned by James II. After the Williamite victory, he became Bishop of Derry. 'Attainder' was the legal term used on conviction for treason.

12. The school and its endowments were confiscated by the Dublin parliament of 1688.

13. For the Latin original text of the charter and an English translation, see *Archivium Hibernicum*, xliii (1988), pp 66-76.

14. John Leonard, *A University for Kilkenny: plans for a royal college in the seventeenth century* (Dún Laoghaire, 1994), p. 42

15. The proposals about Kilkenny school (TCD, MUN/P/1/563)

16. Toby Barnard and William G. Neely (eds.), *The Clergy of the Church of Ireland, 1000-2000* (Dublin, 2006), p. 94.

17. Ibid., p. 95. James Butler, second Duke, was the son of the first Duke's eldest son, Thomas Butler, Earl of Ossory, who died in 1680.

18. Toby Caulfeild to Kean O'Hara, 26 Sept. 1703 (NLI, MS 20,388/131)

19. Bartholomew Vigors to Robert Huntington, 26 Feb.1692 (TCD, MUN/P/1/564)

20. They corresponded with each other for many years; most of Berkeley's letters were kept by Prior but are now 'lost to sight'. A. A. Luce, 'Some unpublished Berkeley letters with some new Berkeleiana' in *Proceedings of the Royal Irish Academy*, xli (1933), c, pp 141-42

21. Joseph M. Hone and Mario M. Rossi, *Bishop Berkeley: his life, writings and philosophy* (London, 1931), pp 13-14

22. Roy Foster, *Modern Ireland 1600-1972* (London, 1998), p. 178

23. See chapter 17.

24. Letter to Viscount Percival, 26 Mar. 1743, cited in A.A. Luce, op. cit., p. 149

25. See Kathleen M. Lynch, 'Congreve's Irish Friend, Joseph Keally' in *Proceedings of the Modern Language Association*, liii, no. 4 (Dec. 1938), pp 1076-87. At a less exalted level, another of Hinton's pupils later ran a rival school in Kilkenny. From a local family, James Doggarell successfully prepared many local boys for matriculation to university.

26. These lines come from *The Mourning Bride*. His other comedies include *The Way of the World* and *The Double Dealer*. His earliest known composition was an elegy on the death of Hinton's magpie. George Farquhar, another dramatist of the time, has been named as a past pupil of Kilkenny College, although there is no conclusive documentary evidence that he was.

27. Voltaire, *Letters concerning the English nation* (new ed., London, 1778), p. 159

28. T. Babington Macaulay, 'Comic dramatists of the Restoration' in *The Modern British Essayists* (Philadelphia, 1882), i, p. 449

29. Congreve, *Love for Love*, Act 5, Scene 1

30. Peter Holland, 'William Congreve' in *Concise Dictionary of British Literary Biography*, p. 68

31. Congreve to Keally, 28 Sept. 1707 in George M. Berkeley, *Literary relics* (London, 1789), p. 353. See also letter of 20 May 1704, p. 336.

4. In high reputation, 1702-1781

1. A list of Ormond's payments in 1710 included salaries not only of the master and usher at Kilkenny but also of the masters at the diocesan schools of Cashel and Ossory. Instructions to Robert Fitzgerald Esq., commissioner for managing my estate, directing the application of my rents from Michaelmas 1710 and other purposes (NLI., MS 2545 – not paginated).

2. David Dickson, 'Inland city: reflections on eighteenth century Kilkenny' in William Nolan and Kevin Whelan (eds.), *Kilkenny: History and Society* (Dublin, 1990), p. 340

3. Toby Barnard, *A New Anatomy of Ireland: the Irish Protestants, 1649-1770* (London, 2003), p. xvii

4. Edward Tenison, Bishop of Ossory, reported that six out of the 30 pupils were being taught Latin at Aghaviller and that the master at Aghavoe was teaching 'the first rudiments' of Latin. Typescript copy of *The state of the Diocese of Ossory... collected from my parochial visitation A.D. 1731* (RCB, MS D/11/1/7/4, pp 21, 35)

5. Andrews was probably the son of John Andrews, of Bishop's Connings, Wiltshire. After he left Kilkenny College, he spent the rest of his life in Ireland (d. 1736). Some sources refer to Lewis as 'Edmund'. Both names were often written in abbreviated form as 'Ed.', which often led to confusion. A Londoner, he graduated from Oxford in 1709 and had just completed his M.A. in 1713. It is uncertain whether Lewis, who died in June 1743, remained in office after 1742. (James B. Leslie, *Ossory Clergy*, p. 115)

6. Published posthumously in 1766. Other works included an edition of *The Whole Works of Sir James Ware Concerning Ireland*, 3 vols (Dublin, 1739-46) and a *History of the Life and Reign of William Henry, Prince of Orange* (Dublin, 1749).

7. Cox was Archbishop of Cashel from 1754 to 1779.

8. See Barnard, *Irish Protestant Ascents and Descents, 1641-1770* (Dublin, 2004), p. 332 and M. Mulcahy (ed.), *Calendar of Kinsale Documents* (Kinsale, 1994), iii, p. 54. Markham's son William, who was educated at Westminster School, became headmaster of his *alma mater* and, while Bishop of Chester, was tutor to the Prince of Wales. He was Archbishop of York from 1776 to 1807.

9. Brian de Breffny, 'Christopher Hewetson' in *Irish Arts Review*, vol. 3, no. 3 (Autumn 1986), pp. 52-75

10. William Colles to the Revd John Perry, n.d. (NA, Prim Collection, file 87, p. 20). While he considered the college 'sufficient for the Latin', he saw the need for a local school 'that would teach to read and write English well, teach arithmetic, geometry, some branches of the mathematics and bookkeeping'. (Colles to the Revd Mervyn Archdall, 16 Feb. 1756 [NA, Prim Collection, file 87, p. 65])

11. Fearghas Ó Fearghail, *St Kieran's College, Kilkenny, 1782-1982* (Kilkenny, 1982), p. 25

12. See Duncan, *The 1608 Royal Schools*, pp 89-90.

13. John Browne, 'Kilkenny College' in *Transactions of the Kilkenny Archaeological Society*, i, part ii (1850), p. 224

14. William Mazière Brady, *Clerical and Parochial Records of Cork, Cloyne and Ross* (Dublin, 1863), ii, p. 266. Hewetson died in February 1782.

15. John Hely-Hutchinson, *An Account of some regulations made in Trinity College Dublin since the appointment of the present provost* (Dublin, 1775), pp 2-3

16. Commissioners of Irish education inquiry, 1791, in H.C. 1857-8, ii, 362

5. Turning its back, 1781-1820

1. He graduated from Trinity College in 1764.

2. The King's Hospital, with a royal charter, was rebuilding its premises at the time and failed to get a grant either from the king or parliament.

3. William Tighe, *Statistical observations relative to the County of Kilkenny* (Kilkenny, 1802), p. 527. The house had formerly been owned by the Marquis de St Ruth, a French Jacobite general, who was killed at the Battle of Aughrim. The house was reportedly used by Kilkenny College between 1782 and 1784.

4. *Finn's Leinster Journal*, 6 Feb. 1782, p. 2

5. Ibid. See W. G. Strickland, *A Dictionary of Irish Artists* (Dublin, 1913) ii, p. 490. Brought to Ireland by Lord Charlemont, Simon Vierpyl's reputation was built on his work at the Casino for Lord Charlemont.

6. Commissioners of Irish education inquiry, 1791, ii, 362. William Tighe, *Statistical observations relative to the County of Kilkenny*. Kilkenny, 1802, p. 508. See also *Finn's Leinster Journal*, 6 Feb. 1782, p. 2.

7. Parliamentary Debates, 27 Mar. 1787, *Parl. reg. Ire.*, vii, pp 421-22

8. *Parl. reg. Ire.*, vii, pp 486-96

9. Orde's autograph notes on the scheme are in the Bodleian Library (MSS Top. Ireland d. 2-3).

10. 28 Geo III, c.15, *An act to enable the lord lieutenant....to appoint commissioners for enquiring into the several funds and revenues granted by public or private donations for the purposed of education in this kingdom*

11. Commissioners of Irish education inquiry, 1791, ii, p. 362. Extra tuition in French, dancing, fencing and writing was mentioned in Ellison's advertisement in *Finn's Leinster Journal*, 6 Feb. 1782, p. 2.

12. Commissioners of Irish education inquiry, 1791, ii, pp 347-50

13. William Hamilton Maxwell, *Life, Military and Civil, of the Duke of Wellington* (London, 1852), p. 338. On Ponsonby at Waterloo, see Henry Harris, 'The Irish at Waterloo' in *The Irish Times*, 17 June 1978, p. 6. None of the Ponsonby brothers is recorded in the college register but Richard's education at Kilkenny is confirmed by the records of Trinity College, Dublin.

14. He remained there until his death on 26 February 1809.

15. He graduated from Trinity College in 1778.

16. Commissioners of the Board of Education, twelfth report, p. 4

17. 46 Geo III, c.122.

18. Commissioners of the Board of Education, twelfth report, p. 4

19. Course of education at Kilkenny College, 11 May 1809 (NLI, MS 17,946/8)

20. Stirabout was oat porridge; gruel was a watery equivalent.

21. Whiteside, *A History of The King's Hospital*, pp 76-7

22. Pack remained in the diocese till his death on 3 March 1842.

23. Commissioners of the Board of Education, twelfth report, p. 4

24. P. J. Murray, *The Life of John Banim* (London, 1857), p. 30

25. The Revd Robert Fishbourne to George Annesley Owen, 29 Aug. 1877 (KCK)

26. John Banim, *Tales, by the O'Hara Family* (London, 1825), ii, p. 139

27. Ibid., p. 141

28. Ibid., p. 142

29. *Leaves from my note-book* (London, 1879), pp 57-58, 126-7

30. *The Gentleman's Magazine and Historical Review*, xiv (new series), Jan.-June 1863, p. 249

31. Marc La Terreur (ed.), *Dictionary of Canadian Biography* (Toronto, 1972), x, pp 205-210

32. *Leaves from my note-book*. p. 56. The account continues: 'He unadvisedly published pamphlets against the Bible Society and, in the course of twelve months after, his school dwindled down to half that number; he consequently resigned.' See Andrew O'Callaghan, *Thoughts on*

the tendencies of Bible Societies as affecting the Established Church and Christianity itself as a reasonable service (Dublin, 1816), pp 5-17, in which he expressed concern that Bible distribution might produce 'less fruit than expected, [or] fruit in abundance but of a poisonous quality' and questioned the wisdom of producing scripture texts for mass circulation that did not contain any note or comment. Richard Owen, his counterpart in Midleton College, also opposed the work of the Bible Society. See Trevor West, *Midleton College, 1696-1996* (Midleton, 1996), p. 16.

33. Francis Despard [presumably to the Board of Education], 26 Nov. 1816 (NLI, MS 17,946/3). Despard stated that O'Callaghan's former ushers had, 'by express agreement', been allowed to give private tuition both within the college and externally.

34 William Baillie, memo to William Walker, Board of Education, 12 Feb. 1824 (NLI, MS 17,946/4). It is hard to believe the claim that there were as many as 150 pupils later in O'Callaghan's time (*Leaves from my note-book*, p. 56).

6. Under examination, 1820-1864

1. *Schools: Funds and Revenues of Schools in Ireland* (London, 1821), pp 4-6
2. James Glassford, *Notes of Three Tours in Ireland in 1824 and 1826* (Bristol, 1832), p. 196
3. The silver medal was probably introduced in 1822, as it is not mentioned in the report of the examination results in 1821.
4. John Cotter Macdonnell, *The Life and Correspondence of William Connor Magee, Archbishop of York* (London, 1896), i, p. 3
5. Another notable past pupil, W. H. S. Monck, was said to be a 'chess player of considerable fame' (*The Irish Times*, 26 June 1915, p. 6).
6. All these quotations on Magee come from Macdonnell, *William Connor Magee*, i, pp 3-5. Magee's powers as an orator were obvious in the House of Lords, his speech in opposition to the disestablishment of the Church of Ireland being widely considered as ' the finest speech ever delivered by any living man in either house of parliament' (J.C. Macdonnell, revised Ian Machin, 'William Connor Magee, 1821-1891' in *ODNB*, xxxvi, p. 112)
7. Nathaniel Alcock, *A Treatise on Cholera* (London, 1849), pp 3, 19-21. Cholera had struck Ireland in 1832, the year in which Alcock graduated as a doctor, and he was involved in the treatment of cholera sufferers in his practice in Kilkenny in 1833.
8. This medal in honour of George Berkeley was established as the highest award for classics students at Trinity College.
9. Ron Cox, 'Samuel Downing, MRIA (1811-1882)' in M. M. Chimes, R.C. Cox *et al.* (eds.), *Biographical Dictionary of Civil Engineers in Great Britain and Ireland*, ii, 1830-1890 (London, 2008), p. 253
10. S. N. Elrington and W. P. Carr, *Authentic Report of the Most Important and Interesting Trial of Mathew vs. Harty and Stokes* (Dublin, 1852), p. 35
11. Ibid., p. 23
12. Bernard Shaw, *Collected Letters, iii: 1911-1925,* ed. Dan H. Lawrence (London, 1985), pp 366-7
13. He died there on 1 September 1859.
14. Pádraig Hamilton, 'The Revd Doctor John Browne (1798-1870)', part I, in *Bandon Historical Journal,* issue 19 (2003), p. 11. John Browne was succeeded in Bandon by his brother, Stephen.
15. *The Constitution*, 21 July 1842
16, Kildare commission, i, p. 6ff
17. We know very little about Browne's teaching staff but it is probable that many stayed a short time. Thomas H. Maule may have been typical. He taught classics and Hebrew in the

early 1860s before going to England and then Scotland, where he was headmaster of a small school.

18. Kildare commission, iii, pp 149-50

19. G. D. Burtchaell, 'Kilkenny Grammar School, now called the College, and its masters' in *Kilkenny Moderator*, 25 June 1904, p. 8. Burtchaell was a past pupil. One of those fellows was Benjamin Williamson who was 'held in the highest respect' at Trinity and was said to have 'filled the trying post of junior dean with much success' (*The Irish Times*, 5 Jan. 1916, p. 5).

20. Walter Fancutt, *With Strange Surprise* (London, 1974), pp 11-12

21. George H. Lyster was giving evidence in a court case involving his school friend, George Burnham Swifte (*The Irish Times*, 4 Nov. 1905, p. 9). The carved wooden propeller and a small wheel survive in the museum at Rothe House, Kilkenny.

22. *Kilkenny Moderator*, 26 Aug. 1857, p. 2

23. He remained there till his death in 1870.

7. Decline, 1864-1890

1. Census 1871, part I, vol 1, Prov. Leinster, lxvii table xxxi, 42. There were 28 boarders and 9 day pupils, all members of the Church of Ireland.

2. John Browne had experienced a similar outbreak at Bandon, resulting in a halving of the number of boarders. See Kildare commission, xxii, part 2.

3. On 9 September 1879 John Hornidge died. The death notice in *The Daily Express* of 12 September was specific: 'Hornidge – Sept. 9, at Kilkenny College, of scarlatina, John Graham Hornidge, aged 16 years, only surviving son of Thomas Hornidge, Esq., Parsonstown, deeply regretted.'

4. In 1881 Martin was said to be teaching in Belfast (Rosse commission, p. 461, evid. no. 4108-9). He was later appointed rector of Rasharkin, Co Antrim, where he remained till his death in January 1901. As a student in Trinity, he won the Vice Chancellor's Prize for English verse in 1857 and 1858. Two of his poems appeared in *Lyra Hibernica Sacra*, a collection of Irish sacred poetry published in 1878.

5. Advertisement in *The Irish Times*, 25 Apr. 1864, p. 2

6. Matches were regularly reported in *The Irish Times*.

7. According to a testimonial by the Revd Charles Ward, rector of Kilmurry, 12 Aug. 1872, Weir had run the school since about 1861 and his ability was 'proved by the success of many of his former pupils at Dublin University and the provincial colleges'. Another testimonial by William Lane Joynt, mayor elect of Limerick, said his 'qualifications as a classical, scientific, metaphysical and literary teacher are first rate' (KCK). Weir advertised the sale of the school as a going concern in *The Irish Times*, 15 July 1874, p.8. In the advertisement he claimed that his school 'has been for the last 15 years the most successful in the south of Ireland'.

8. James B. Leslie, *Ardfert and Aghadoe Clergy and Parishes* (Dublin, 1940), p. 78

9. Homan Potterton, *Potterton People and Places* (Drogheda, 2006), p. 39

10. Advertisement in *The Irish Times*, 1 Sept. 1875, p. 7

11. Marcus de Búrca, *Michael Cusack and the GAA* (Dublin, 1989), pp 31-32

12. *The Irish Times*, 24 Sept. 1875, p.2. It is possible that he submitted the piece himself.

13. Rosse commission, p. 245

14. Copy of report of Lord A. Butler and Dr J. P. Mahaffy, 13 Apr.1880 (TCD, MUN/P/1/2385(1))

15. Provost Humphrey Lloyd to Bishop William Pakenham Walsh, 3 July 1880 (TCD, MUN/P/1/2385(2))

16. Weir to T. H. Fleming, Educational Commissioners, 17 Mar. 1884 (NLI, MS 17,946/13). Prior to the epidemic, Weir had three boarders from Westmeath, three from the King's

County, four from the Queen's County, one from Co. Tipperary but only one from Co. Kilkenny (Rosse commission, p. 461, evid. no. 14128).

17. Weir to Walsh, 10 July 1880 (TCD, MUN/P/1/2385 (3))

18. 'Intermediate' was defined as the stage of education between primary and professional or higher studies.

19. The commission had no authority over schools which were provided for the sole benefit of one religious denomination and were operated under the exclusive control of persons of that denomination. When the commission produced a draft scheme, there was time for petitions and appeals before it went to the Lord Lieutenant for approval. Schemes could later be altered under the Commissioners for Charitable Donations and Bequests.

20. One of the three pupils was Reginald Rogers. As he entered in 1886, his education was obviously interrupted by events within the school. He was later a fellow of Trinity College and wrote a history of ethics.

21. Reported in *Kilkenny Moderator*, 2 Nov. 1887, p. 3

22. Brownrigg's claim was not far-fetched. It was agreed that the endowments in the Ulster royal schools would be split between Church of Ireland schools and Roman Catholic schools.

23. Creighton had 37 pupils (Educational Endowments (Ireland) Commissioners: annual report, 1887-88, pp 258-9) See also an advertisement for Creighton's school in the *Daily Express*, 7 Jan. 1893, p. 8.

24. Weir's claim that he was selected from a number of candidates is substantiated by the Trinity College board register, 1871-77 (TCD, MUN/V/5/13). On 11 April 1874, the testimonial of candidates were considered and the Revd Walter Lindesay and Weir were chosen for reconsideration the following Monday. On 13 April Lindesay was elected but he turned down the job and Weir was then appointed.

25. Educational Endowments (Ireland) Act, 1885, Draft Scheme No. 46 (Dublin, 1888) (TCD, MUN/P/1/2429a(1))

26. Preference was to be given to graduates in arts or science of an Irish university or of an English university if no Irish candidate was found suitable.

27. Not more than 1 each year

28. Not more than 2 a year

29. Weir to Fleming, 31 Mar. 1888 (NLI, MS 17946/10)

30. He wrote several articles on Kilkenny College. See, for example, G. D. Burtchaell, 'Kilkenny Grammar School, now called the College, and its masters' in *Kilkenny Moderator*, 25 June 1904, p. 8. See also *Kilkenny Moderator*, 2 Nov. 1887, p. 4, on his own experience of school. Another brother, David, was a well-regarded civil engineer. While at Trinity, he was a successful rower, winning a cup at the Henley Regatta of 1881.

31. Born in Limerick in 1862, he was the son of the Revd David Wilson, a Presbyterian minister.

8. New schemes, 1890-1907

1. His doctorate was an LL.D. It is likely that he was also headmaster at Prior School, Lifford in the early months of 1889. He was the author of several history textbooks. See also Duncan, *The 1608 Royal Schools*, p. 257.

2. *Irish Ecclesiastical Gazette*, 26 Feb. 1892 (xxxiv), p. 182

3. Ibid., 6 May 1892 (xxxiv), p. 381. 'Woolwich' refers to the Royal Military Academy at Woolwich.

4. MacDermot, Report to the Board on the state of the house and out-offices, 28 June 1892 (KCK)

5. *Kilkenny Moderator*, 11 Oct. 1893, p. 2

6. Kilkenny College advertisement in *The Irish Times*, 11 Apr. 1896, p. 7

7. Kilkenny College advertisement in *The Irish Times*, 14 Aug. 1896, p. 1

8. Chris Glennon (ed.), *90 years of the Irish Hockey Union*, (Naas, n.d.), p. 134

9. Copy of the governors' report, 6 Dec. 1898 in *The Irish Times*, 21 Aug. 1899, p. 8

10. *Kilkenny Moderator*, 31 Mar. 1894, p. 3

11. 'Recovering possession of Kilkenny College', case in King's Bench, reported in *The Irish Times,* 9 Feb. 1901, pp 21-22

12. The unpublished lists of clergy of the Diocese of Leighlin (RCB, MS 61/2/12/1) state that he was principal of Derry Cathedral Boys' School for ten years. He had been a student at the Church of Ireland Training College from 1885 to 1886. See Susan Parkes, *Kildare Place* (Dublin, 1984), p. 80.

13. The figures come from the 1901 Census of Ireland.

14. François Gouin set out his 'series' or 'direct method' in *L'art d'enseigner et d'étudier les langues* [The Art of Learning and Studying Foreign Languages] (Paris, 1880).

15. *Church of Ireland Gazette*, 11 Apr. 1902 (xliv), p. 296

16. *Kilkenny Moderator*, 29 Mar. 1903, p. 3

17. The Incorporated Society annual report for 1902 held that 'it is plainly in the interests of church education in the south of Ireland not to maintain in the neighbourhood of Kilkenny two schools when, by joining them together, we can have one strong and well-equipped school, giving a sound literary and commercial education for moderate fees' (p. 16).

18. This required a formal Amending Scheme (No. 210), 13 May 1903.

19. An early example can be seen in 1911, when the eldest son of Constable C. Huggard of Cork won a scholarship to Kilkenny College and his sister won one to Celbridge. (Reported in *The Irish Times*, 15 July 1911, p. 20.)

20. *Kilkenny Moderator*, 4 May 1904, p. 3

21. *An Economic History of Ireland* (Dublin, 1920); *A History of Northern Ireland* (Belfast, 1928)

22. His publications included *Manual of Indian Forest Botany* (London, 1953). His wife wrote an interesting account of his work in India: Eleanor Bor, *Adventures of a Botanist's Wife* (London, 1952).

23. H. Kingsmill Moore, *The Work of the Incorporated Society for Promoting Protestant Schools in Ireland* (Dundalk, 1938), p. 47

9. A golden era, 1907-1917

1. His published works include *The Ethiopic Didascalia, a translation* (London, 1920), *An introduction to Ethiopic Literature*, (London, 1926) and a *Dictionary of the Vulgate New Testament*, (London, 1921). He was also involved with editions of *The Book of Armagh* and *The Book of Moling*.

2. Mark Wilson, 'My early schooldays', Sept. 1915 , typescript copy by his son, 1996 (KCK)

3. He held the post from 1948 to 1956 and received a knighthood.

4. Even with poor coaching, there was some talent. Mark Wilson, for example, went on to captain Wanderers (1920-21) and earned interprovincial caps for Leinster.

5. His first prospectus proclaimed that he held an M.A., was a Prize and Honoursman in Modern History from Trinity, was a Morgan Jellett Prizeman, a registered teacher under the Intermediate Board and a recognised teacher of experimental science, with the Department of Agriculture and Technical Instruction. See C. Tempest McCrea, *Dundalk Grammar School: the first 250 years (1739-1989)* (Dundalk, 1989), p. 27.

6. Harrison then became resident engineer and director of a post-war scheme in Tanganyika to produce groundnut oil for Britain.

7. John G. Frayne and Halley Wolfe, *Elements of Sound Recording*, (New York and London,

1949). He received many awards for his work. See appreciation in *Journal Audio Eng. Soc.*, ixl, nos. 1 and 2, Jan./Feb. 1991, p. 103.

8. His current pupils accompanied their farewell gift with a hand-written, decorated address (KCK).

9. Headmaster's speech at annual prize day, 28 Mar. 1917, reported in *Kilkenny Moderator*, 31 Mar. 1917, p. 3

10. *Kilkenny Moderator*, 29 Sept. 1917, p. 5

11. C. G. Shankey, speech, reported in *Kilkenny Moderator*, 22 Dec. 1917, p.5. A farewell concert was held, at which the boys sang *The College by the Nore* ('the school song'), composed by Seale and set to music by Mrs Seale (KCK).

12. This and the following quotations are from Eric R. Dodds, *Missing Persons: an autobiography* (Oxford, 1977), p. 69.

13. Cited in David Phillips, 'War-time planning for the "Re-education" of Germany: Professor E.R. Dodds and the German universities' in *Oxford Review of Education*, xii, no. 2 (1986), p. 195

14. Dodds was Regius Professor of Greek at Oxford University from 1936 to 1960.

15. A report, including the full text of his letter and a photograph of John Salter, appeared in *Cork County Eagle and Munster Advertiser*, 19 Aug. 1916, p. 4.

16. See appendix for a list of those killed during the war. No roll of honour was finally produced, although Seale had it up to date in March 1917. At that stage he had recorded 106 servicemen, of whom 8 had died, 8 were wounded, 3 were prisoners of war and 2 had been awarded the Military Cross. (Headmaster's speech at annual prize day, 28 Mar. 1917, reported in *Kilkenny Moderator*, 31 Mar. 1917, p. 3)

17. Vivian Mercier, 'The Old School Tie, no. 3: Portora Royal School, Enniskillen' in *The Bell*, xi, no. 6 (Mar. 1946), p. 1087

10. A new state, 1917-1952

1. He graduated from Trinity College in 1910 with a B.A. in engineering.

2. Headmaster's speech at annual prize day, 28 Mar. 1917, in *Kilkenny Moderator*, 31 Mar. 1917, p. 3

3. Shankey recalled this for George Seaver's *John Allen Fitzgerald Gregg, Archbishop* (Dublin, 1963), p. 95.

4. Two Kilkenny College forerunners were John Francis Smithwick, Nationalist MP for Kilkenny, 1880-85 and Thomas P. Gill, Nationalist MP for South Louth, 1885-92.

5. Responsibility was formerly divided between a number of boards.

6. *Report for the school year 1924-5* (Dublin, 1926), p. 51. See also The Intermediate Education (Amendment) Act, 1924.

7. There were exemptions, for pupils whose early education had been outside the state.

8. One of the problems was that, although Trinity established a B.Sc. degree, it was only a pass course, which did not interest the best students.

9. In addition to Edward Coursey, appointed headmaster of Galway Grammar School in 1932, two men went to the Prior Endowed School, Lifford, as headmaster: Gerald V. Kinch in 1919 and Francis T. Byron (also a past pupil) in 1929. T. H. Blackburn, senior assistant master and housemaster, was appointed headmaster of Sligo Grammar School in 1928 and A. L. Horner, made redundant in 1941 because of the Emergency, became headmaster of St Patrick's Cathedral Grammar School. Other losses included senior English teacher and rugby coach, J. Cornish and J. W. Goulden, both of whom went to The High School, Dublin.

10. Department memo, Feb. 1928, (NA, Department of Education Papers, ED Central Registry, Box 409, 19137, 27/2/28)

11. IS report for 1936 (15 Jan. 1937), p. 7

12. This and subsequent recollections of Edgar Roe (1930-34) are from an interview, 26 Jan. 2007.

13. C. G. Shankey, 'Experimental Science in Irish Secondary Schools', paper read to the Irish Schoolmasters' Association, reported in *The Irish Times*, 2 Nov. 1931, p. 8

14. The Revd W. M. Abernethy to Sam McClure, 11 Feb. 1985 (KCK)

15. Al Williams, interview, Nov. 2008

16. These recollections are from the autobiography of Victor Griffin (1936-40), *Mark of Protest* (Dublin, 1993) pp 37-43. He was also interviewed on 4 Mar. 2007.

17. George Benn, interview, 8 Mar. 2007(KCK)

18. It was D. E. Phair.

19. Wilson, see chapter 9.

20. Roe, op.cit.

21. Match account in *The Irish Times*, 15 Mar. 1932, p. 11

22. See Thomas S. C. Dagg, *Hockey in Ireland* (Tralee, 1944), p. 194.

23. For a list of their publications, see Wallace, *Dublin Clergy*, p. 712.

24. J. F. Burns, *Shop Window to the World* (Dublin, 1964), pp 113-14

25. Stanley's younger brother, Alan is the author of *I Met Murder on the Way* (Carlow, 2005), the inspiration for a successful documentary on the notorious killings of two Protestant brothers at Coolacrease in 1921.

26. Ian King, interview, Nov. 2008

27. *The Irish Times*, 4 Apr. 1963, p. 9

28. Norman Ruddock, *The Rambling Rector* (Dublin, 2005), p. 30

11. Into co-education, 1952-1979

1. Colton had previously taught at Foyle College in Derry.

2. 'A Gentleman of the Old School: Mr Gilbert Colton – an appreciation' compiled by Kilkenny College on his death in October 2005 (KCK)

3. David Clarke (1955-59), interview, 26 May 2008

4. Freda Yates, interview, 8 Mar. 2007 (KCK)

5. K. J. Stanley (1949-53), interview, 12 June 2007 (KCK)

6. Ibid.

7. W. B. Stanford, *A recognised Church* (Dublin, 1944), p. 11

8. H.R. McAdoo, *No New Church* (Dublin, 1945), pp 31-2

9. Prospectus, n.d. (KCK)

10. Ken Stanley, as one of two junior masters, was initially paid £150 per annum, 'all found'. Colton, with the support of C. G. Shankey at the Incorporated Society, persuaded the Society to raise his salary to a princely £250.

11. Homan Potterton, *Rathcormick, A Childhood Revisited* (Dublin, 2001), pp 273-4

12. This and the following quotations are from W. R. Grey, 'Morning and Evening: two studies of life in the old "KCK", an unpublished memoir, 1957, p. 4, (copy, KCK). Grey recalls that, when he accepted the job, Colton warned him: 'You'll be buried alive here!'

13. Report of the Advisory Committee on Secondary Education in the Republic of Ireland, in *Journal of the second session of the thirty-second General Synod* (Dublin, 1965), pp 140-61

14. The cut-off point for a pupil's need to board was 15 miles from the nearest suitable school.

15. *Investment in Education, Report of the Survey team appointed by the Minister for Education in October 1962* (Pr. 8311)

16. Kenneth Milne, 'A Church of Ireland view [on the future of post-primary education], in *Studies* lvii (Autumn 1968), p. 265

17. Wilson's Hospital, in Co. Westmeath, developed in the same way, taking over Preston School, Navan, in 1969 and becoming co-educational, although it was to be many years until it acquired modern facilities.

18. Pressure from parents played a part in securing the new arrangement.

12. Into a new millennium, 1979-2005

1. Whereas the majority of pupils came from families with no historic connection to Kilkenny College, more than a quarter of those surveyed in 2007-8 had either a parent or grandparent in Kilkenny College or Celbridge.

2. McClure, Presentation to a conference of primary teachers, 15 May 1996 (KCK). In 1995-6 there were 227 boarder boys, 193 boarder girls, 157 day boys and 96 day girls.

3. When John Wilson, the Minister for Education, met McClure on 16 January 1980, he guaranteed a grant to build a 275-pupil school at the 25-acre site on the Castlecomer Road. The number was revised to 350 but, by the time of the official opening in October 1986, there were 465 pupils and McClure was pressing the Department for an extension.

4. In all, £750,000 was raised.

5. McClure, Memo on signing of contract for sale of John Street, 23 Feb. 1987 (KCK)

6. G. S. Magahy, 'Protestant Secondary Schools' in *Search*, xi, no.1 (Spring 1988), pp 35-41. Magahy was in a good position to know the situation for, in retirement, he acted formally or informally as an advisor to many of the Protestant schools. His influence was important in McClure's decision to develop Kilkenny College as a diocesan school. The Board also sought the advice of Canon Philip Day, rector of Portlaoise and former warden of Wilson's Hospital.

7. For a more detailed account, see L. Whiteside, *George Otto Simms, a biography* (Gerrards Cross, 1990), pp 82-4, 98-9, 147-8. In a pioneering scheme, Bishops Noel Willoughby and Brendan Commiskey oversaw joint pastoral care for such marriages in the diocese of Ferns.

8. 'Future policy', a paper written by McClure and Magahy, for the Board, 21 Mar. 1987 (KCK)

9. They were designed for pupils who merit but are not entitled to an Incorporated Society scholarship.

10. There were 19 subjects in 1995-6.

11. McClure, Presentation to primary teachers, 15 May 1996 (KCK)

12. In a major departure, he asked Herbie Sharman to compile the timetable.

13. The music department was enhanced with a deputy head of department and part-time staff in addition to David Milne. A first-year choir, chamber choir and orchestra were introduced.

14. This French phrase is the heraldic motto of the college's founding family, the Butlers.

15. The vast majority of boarders and 72 per cent of all pupils were in receipt of a grant from the SEC. This meant that Kilkenny College was by far the largest recipient of grants in proportion to its numbers.

16. Interview, 18 Mar. 2008 (KCK)

17. The decision was made by the Leinster branch of the Irish Rugby Football Union.

18. Interview, 18 Mar. 2008

19. Ultimate authority still rests with the board of directors, which has a majority on the school management board.

13. Foundation

1. Pococke was one of the original members in 1750 of the Dublin Society for Promoting Husbandry and Other Useful Arts in Ireland, which was the forerunner of the Royal Dublin Society, and 'continued for many years as an active and useful member of this Society'. M. Quane, 'Pococke School, Kilkenny', in *JRSAI*, lxxx, part 1 (1950), p. 39

2. Whereas Wallace (*Clergy of Dublin and Glendalough*, p. 977) gives the year of his birth as 1705, C. F. Russell, in *A History of King Edward VI School, Southampton* (Crosby, 1940), p. 204, provides a specific date of birth of 19 November 1704 and presumably that is more accurate.

3. Isaac Milles, son of Thomas Milles, of Carrington's Farm, Cockfield, Suffolk, was at St Edmundsbury Free School from 1649 for about seven years and then went to St John's College, Cambridge.

4. *An Account of the Life and Conversation of the Reverend and Worthy Mr Isaac Milles* (London, 1721), pp 76- 78

5. Russell, op. cit., p. 203. Thomas Herbert, 8th Earl of Pembroke acquired Highclere through his marriage.

6. The earliest minute book of Mercer's School has been lost since 1967 but much of it was transcribed by Michael Quane (NLI, MS 16,937, pp 14-58).

7. R. Pococke, *A Sermon preached at Christ Church, Dublin on 27 June 1762 before the Incorporated Society* (Dublin, 1762), p. 4

8. Ibid., p. 11

9. J. McVeigh (ed.), *Richard Pococke's Irish Tours* (Dublin, 1995), p. 100

10. Cambric is a lightweight, closely-woven white linen fabric.

11. J. McVeigh, op.cit., p. 30

12. Ibid., p. 107

13. He reportedly made large personal contributions and personally supervised the workmen, sometimes from as early as 4 a.m. (C. F. Russell, op.cit., p. 208)

14. See NA, Prim Collection, File 87, p. 49, on Pococke's relationship with Archdall and the Colles family.

15. The first will was dated 10 July 1763; the second on 24 March 1765. He died on 15 September 1765 and was buried at Ardbraccan. George Stoney's diary gives an account of Pococke's death, which may have been from mushroom poisoning. R. A. Stoney (compil.), *Some old Annals of the Stoney Family* (London, 1879), p. 13

16. Kingsmill Moore, *The Incorporated Society*, p. 20

17. The will and its codicil are printed in Commissioners of the Board of Education, appendix to third report, pp 31-32.

14. The factory school

1. TCD, MS 5248, 12 June 1805, p. 266. 'The school was endowed by the Corporation of Kilkenny with 20 acres of very good land and an annuity of £30 per annum.' Extracts from a letter, Alderman William Colles to the Revd John Perry, 15 Nov. 1743 (NA, Prim Collection, File 87, p. 3)

2. Committee Minutes, 12 June 1782 (TCD, MS 5237, pp 246-7)

3. Board Minutes, 4 Mar. 1778 (TCD, MS 5226, p. 96)

4. Ibid., 1 Apr. 1778, p. 98. The contractor was to be Thomas Keravan.

5. Committee Minutes, 9 and 16 May 1781 (TCD, MS 5237, pp 54-6)

6. Board Minutes, 7 Nov. 1781 (TCD, MS 5226, p. 203)

7. Committee Minutes, 13 June 1781 (TCD, MS 5237, p. 65)

8. Board Minutes, 24 May 1788 (TCD, MS 5226, p. 429)

9. Committee Minutes, 14 Jan.1789 (TCD, MS 5239, p. 487)

10. Board Minutes, 1 June 1791 (TCD, MS 5227, pp 22-3)

11. *Saunders' News-letter*, 7 June 1799

12. *Parl. reg. Ire.,* xv (1795) referred to 'a linen and cotton factory at Lintown' (p. 47).

13. *Finn's Leinster Journal,* 7 Aug. 1799, p. 4

14. William Tighe, *Statistical observations relative to the County of Kilkenny* (Dublin, 1802), p. 530

15. Committee Minutes, 20 Nov. 1805 (TCD, MS 5248, p. 363). Whereas the Kilkenny College boys attended St John's Church, the Pococke boys went to St Mary's Church.

16. Ibid., 12 June 1805, p. 264

17. Board Minutes, 2 Nov. 1803 (TCD, MS 5228, p. 21). The educational commission com-

mented that Pounds 'was bred at the Kilkenny Charter School' (*Commissioners of the Board of Education, appendix to third report*, p. 83). In 1788 the Kilkenny local committee granted a certificate in favour of William Pounds and Ann, his wife, and the Committee of Fifteen ordered that he be entered on the list of candidate masters for charter schools (Committee Minutes, 9 July 1788 (TCD, MS 5239, p. 383). Perhaps James was William's son.

18. Committee Minutes, 20 Nov. 1805 and 29 Jan. 1806 (TCD, MS 5248, pp 363, 423)

19. Committee Minutes, 10 Sept. 1806 (TCD, MS 5249, p. 266)

20. Board Minutes, 7 May 1806 (TCD, MS 5228, pp 134-5) refer to 'the report of the Committee of Fifteen on the conduct of Mr Andrew Neelands … and their recommendations to dismiss him and also the memorial of said Andrew Neelands acknowledging his offence, together with the report of the local committee thereon'. The Committee Minutes refer to a verbal report from the catechist, the Revd Peter Roe, but no further details are given.

21. Nicholas Hallaron was dismissed as master of Farra School in 1807 (ibid., 4 Mar. 1807, p. 183). Neelands's appointment to the House of Industry was reported in *The Moderator*, 17 Sept. 1814, p. 3. He died shortly afterwards.

22. *Commissioners of the Board of Education, appendix 8 to third report*, pp 82-3. See also Committee Minutes, 24 Aug. 1808 (TCD, MS 5251, p. 217).

23. Elias Thackeray, *General Report of the Charter Schools in Ireland visited in …1817*, ii (TCD, MS 5592, p. 315)

24. Thackeray, *Report*, 1818 (TCD, MS 5593a, p.128)

25. Reports of the Revd William Lee, 1819, 1820 (TCD, MS 5594, p. 53)

26. Board Minutes, 3 Feb. 1819 (TCD, MS 5229, p. 380). The factory at Lintown was converted into a residence around 1821 (see *Kilkenny Moderator*, 27 Feb. 1821) and was retained by the Society as part of the Pococke Estate. In 1841, the 'old and very extensive' buildings were seen to 'require an expenditure of money every year to keep them in the state of tolerable repair they are in at present.' (Report of Mr Pidgeon, 30 Nov. 1841 (TCD, MS 5694/174).

27. For a description of the facilities at the charter school, see *Commissioners of the Board of Education, appendix to third report*, p. 82.

28. Glassford, *Three Tours in Ireland*, pp 202-3. Burrowes may have been a Kilkenny man, a brother of John Burrowes, who entered Trinity College in 1822. Roe was curate of St Mark's, Kilkenny. His diary is quoted in Samuel Madden, *Memoir of the life of the late Rev Peter Roe* (Dublin, 1842), pp 129-30.

29. Thackeray, *Report*, 1817, ii (TCD, MS 5592, p. 320)

30. Reply to commissioner's question 23256, Kildare commission, ii, evidence, p. 235

31. Opinion of Francis Blackburne, presented to the annual general meeting of the Incorporated Society, 6 Feb. 1839 (TCD, MS 5777/4/1)

32. Daniel Murray, Archbishop of Dublin, in *Freeman's Journal*, 15 Aug. 1848; Thomas Hussey, Bishop of Waterford and Lismore, a pastoral letter to the Catholic clergy of the united dioceses of Waterford and Lismore, 1794 (NA (Kew), H.O. 100/69/206-13)

33. Board Minutes, 5 Aug. 1840 (TCD, 5265, p. 14). Those five might have been all that remained when the others had been apprenticed.

34. Proceedings of the local committee of Brownstown Factory, 23 Mar. 1840 (TCD, MS 5777/4/2). He had been employed by the Society for nearly 40 years.

35. Memorial of James Pounds, 30 June 1842, Board and Committee Papers (TCD, MS5695/68)

36. Board Minutes, 5 Aug. 1840, (TCD, 5265, p. 14)

15. New identity, 1840-1859

1. Plan of Brownstown Factory by William Farrell and Son, 7 Oct. 1840 (TCD, MS 5694/74)
2. Board Minutes, 6 Jan. 1841 (TCD, MS 5265, p. 31)
3. Gerard J. Tannam, 'The Later History of the Charter Schools' (M.A. thesis, UCD, 1954, pp 59-61)
4. Minutes of the local committee, 7 June 1842 (TCD, MS 5777/4/5)
5. Alexander Hanlon to the Revd Richard Ardill (IS), 4 July 1842 (TCD, MS 5695/113)
6. Minutes of Local Committee, 27 Oct. 1842 (TCD, MS 5695/299); Board and Committee Papers, (TCD, MS 5695/405, 444, 446)
7. J. T. O'Brien, to IS, 31 Jan. 1843 (TCD, MS 5695/381); Board Minutes, 1 Feb. 1843 (TCD, MS 5231, p. 220)
8. Hanlon was ordained a few years later and served as a priest in the Church of Ireland from 1846 to 1878.
9. John Turner to Ardill, 10 Jan. 1844 (TCD, MS 5777/4/8)
10. Committee Minutes, 7 July 1847 (TCD, MS 5265, p. 309)
11. The Revd Vernon Drapes, catechist of the Pococke School, to the Revd Richard Ardill (IS), 10 Aug. 1848 (TCD, MS 5701/151)
12. TCD, MS 5706/145
13. Kildare commission, xxii, part iv, p. 150
14. Foundation pupils to IS, 12 Oct. 1857, (TCD, MS 5777/4/13)
15. Pococke Institution, 20 Oct. 1857, particulars of evidence as to certain charges brought by the pupils in the institution against the master (TCD, MS 5777/4/14)
16. Ardill, report to IS on the Pococke Institution, adopted 3 Nov. 1857 (TCD, MS 5709/239)
17. John Booth to Ardill, 2 Nov. 1857 (TCD, MS 5709/238)
18. Ardill, op.cit. (TCD, MS 5709/239)
19. Booth to Ardill, 10 Nov. 1857 (TCD, MS 5709/24)
20. Kildare commission, ii, p. 238. Ardill suggested that the Society resolution that any pupil who ran away from school would not be re-admitted deterred pupils from running away.
21. Kildare commission, ii, p. 246
22. The Revd John W. Stubbs to Ardill, 6 Nov. 1857 (TCD, MS 5709/21)
23. W. H. Engledow to IS, 25 Mar. 1859 (TCD, MS 5711/74)

16. Furthering the boys, 1859-1903

1. Kildare commission, evidence, ii, p. 67, question 20,598
2. He was certainly educated in an Incorporated Society school.
3. Samuel Hawkes to the Revd J.W. Hackett (IS), 2 Apr. 1859 (TCD, MS 5711/141)
4. Clive Whitehead, Colonial Education: the British Indian and Colonial Education Service, 1858-1983 (London, 2003), pp 26-27
5. The will was dated 17 Sept. 1845 and the endowment included property in Co Kilkenny.
6. The Revd E. W. Butler to Hackett, 14 June 1872 (TCD, MS 5777/4/27)
7. In 1898 there were two scholarships available for candidates from counties Kilkenny, Carlow, Queen's Co and Waterford; two for Limerick, Clare and Tipperary; and one each for Wexford, Cork and Kerry. Pupil returns record that 'Different schools sent forward year after year candidates as long as they were successful but after a few entire failures ceased altogether to send'. (TCD, MS 5787/14/11)
8. The Kerry Home Industrial School for Boys and the Home Industrial School for Boys, Marble Hill, Blackrock, Cork
9. The Irish Times, 30 Aug. 1902, p. 6
10. Rosse commission, pp 273, 265

11. *Kilkenny Moderator*, 9 June 1882, p. 3

12. George Henry Barrett, *Kilkenny City and County Guide and Directory* (Dublin, 1884), p. 50

13. *Kilkenny Moderator*, 2 Nov. 1887, p. 4

14. John Browne to Hackett, 16 Nov. 1880 (TCD, MS 5777/4/58). The teacher's name was Gordon.

15. This department was an official body which functioned from 1853 to 1899, promoting education in science, technology and design in Britain and Ireland.

16. Board and Committee Papers (TCD, MS 5742/214)

17. Their inspection of 20 Dec. 1898 is in Board and Committee Papers (TCD, MS 5742/291).

18. Board Minutes, 21 Mar. 1901 (RCB, MS 151/1/1, p. 196)

19. Educational Endowments (Ireland) Act, 1885, Scheme No. 210, 26 July 1894, p. 22. The Society was permitted to 'take assignments or transfers … of all or any property … belonging to or held in trust for any school … under the exclusive management of any member or members of the [Church of Ireland]' and to 'provide for the administration by the governors of such property and for the union or amalgamation of the governing body of any such school.' The amalgamation was formalised in an amending scheme of 13 May 1903.

20. Report of sub-committee appointed on 1 Dec. 1898 (TCD, MS 5742/291). Browne submitted a list of nearly 40 improvements: 'Works executed by master of Pococke School at his own cost' (TCD, MS 5742/222).

21. *Kilkenny College Magazine*, Trinity 1923, pp 7-9. The article is marked 'to be continued', the writer promising to expand on 'the humours and delights of Pococke life in our next issue,' but there is no copy of the relevant issue in the college archives. A 'wight' was an unspecified, unfortunate person.

22. Browne's son, Nassau, who appears to have been a Pococke pupil, taught art at Kilkenny College under Baile. He had a distinguished career in art. See Theo Snoddy, *Dictionary of Irish Artists: 20th Century* (Dublin, 1996), p. 57.

23. Browne to IS, 5 Oct. 1898 (TCD, MS 5742/71)

24. *Kilkenny Moderator*, 30 Sept. 1903, p. 3

17. Foundation and early years

1. Her father was Sir Albert Conyngham, lieutenant general of the Irish Ordnance; her brother was Henry Conyngham of Mount Charles, Co Donegal, later of Slane.

2. See J. G. Simms, *The Williamite Confiscation in Ireland, 1690-1703* (London, 1956), pp 125-7, 150. Conolly had lands in counties Derry, Donegal, Dublin, Fermanagh, Leitrim, Kildare, Meath, Queen's County (Laois) and Westmeath.

3. He bought the Castletown estate (c.1,730 acres) in 1709.

4. Patrick Walsh, Castletown, Co Kildare, Dublin, 2007, p. 5. Berkeley, while acknowledging that he had been consulted, wrote that 'the plan is chiefly of Mr Conolly's invention'. George Berkeley to John Percival, 29 July 1722, in A. A. Luce and T. E. Jessop, *The Works of George Berkeley* (Edinburgh, 1948-57) iii, p.123

5. Lena Boylan, *Castletown and its owners* (Dublin, 1978), p. 30. See also Edward McParland, *Public Architecture in Ireland, 1680-1760* (New Haven, 2001), p. 172.

6. Will of William Conolly, 18 Oct. 1729 (NLI)

7. McParland, op. cit.

8. *An Abstract of the Proceedings of the Incorporated Society … from the opening of His Majesty's royal charter on 6 February 1733 to 25 March 1737* (Dublin, 1737), pp 41-2

9. Brian FitzGerald, *Lady Louisa Conolly, 1743-1821: an Anglo-Irish biography* (London, 1950), p. 107

10. Charles Topham Bowden, *A tour through Ireland* (Dublin, 1791), p. 69. For more on her reputation, see Stella Tillyard, *Aristocrats* (London, 1995), pp 223-4.

11. Commission of Irish education inquiry, 1791, ii, p. 377

12. Cash book, 1785-95 (TCD, MS 5610). Wolfe, a local landowner, gave £200 in 1780.

13. Elias Thackeray, *Report of the Charter Schools*, 1817, pp 8-9

14. It is possible that she was in office before November 1783. She left the school in June 1787 but returned in August of that year. The accounts make it clear that she had left her position and was not on vacation.

15. Brenda Collins, of the Irish Linen Centre in Lisburn, advises that pencilling was the application of a pencilled design for use by an embroiderer. The girls who were taught pencilling may also have been taught embroidery, or their pencilled work may have been sold or passed on to others to embroider. The 1789 accounts included wages for an unnamed pencilling mistress; two years later Elizabeth Martin was paid as pencilling teacher.

16. Lena Boylan, *Castletown*, p. 60

17. Commissioners of the Board of Education, thirteenth report, p. 9

18. Committee Minutes, 15 Feb. 1809 (TCD, MS 5251, p. 396)

19. Board Minutes, 27 Dec. 1809 (TCD, MS 5228, p. 314)

20. Committee Minutes, 20 Dec. 1809 (TCD, MS 5252, p. 304)

21. This and the two following quotations are from the Report of the Committee of Fifteen (Dublin, 1812), pp 7-8. The committee declared in December 1812 that £2,630-10-8 had been spent and that it had been necessary to make expensive repairs to the perimeter wall. Committee Minutes, 30 Dec. 1812 (TCD, MS 5254, p. 400)

22. One source suggests there were as few as 27 girls in the school at the time of the takeover (Commissioners of the Board of Education, third report, p. 297). The register of pupils lists almost 100 girls with dates of admission prior to the takeover but it is conceivable that those dates referred to admission to other Society schools.

23. Copy of conveyance of the Charity School of Celbridge, 28 Sept. 1811 (TCD, MS 5792/219)

24. One parish from which Conolly foundationers were selected was Mayne, Co. Westmeath. The extant parish registers for the 19th century provide interesting information on the background of the girls (RCB, P.0420.01/1-3).

18. Stability, 1810-1859

1. Printed in Commissioners of Board of Education, third report, appendix v, p. 51. 'Evil' or 'the king's evil' was a common term for scrofula, a disease with glandular swellings, probably a form of tuberculosis. 'Scald', correctly called tinea, was a highly contagious scalp complaint, often said to be a scrofulous symptom. School authorities were inclined to get rid of any pupil who developed an unspecified skin disorder, fearing that it might be contagious and serious.

2. The Society rule that such a register be kept was not always as well obeyed.

3. Commissioners of Board of Education, third report, appendix v, p. 51

4. Ibid., thirteenth report, p. 10

5. Report of deputation, 7 June 1850, in Board Minutes, 6 Nov. 1850 (TCD, MS 5232, p. 80). The catechist, the Revd Samuel Greer, reported on 7 August 1848, 'I have this day found the great majority of the children employed in the healthy occupation of hay-making' (TCD, MS 5701/147).

6. *Rules for the government of the Protestant Charter Schools and Nurseries*, (Dublin, 1809)

7. Two certainly died of tuberculosis, while the other twelve are said to have died of 'a decline'. This generally indicated tuberculosis.

8. See correspondence, Aug.-Sept. 1826, in Celbridge School orders book (TCD, MS 5612).

9. Commissioners of Board of Education, third report, appendix v, p. 43

10. Milne, *Charter Schools*, p. 328

11. This and the following excerpts come from First report of educational commissioners, 1825, appendixes 54, 74, 123.

12. Local committee annual reports, in Celbridge orders book (TCD, MS 5612). As the Society abandoned any idea of conversion, the last Roman Catholic girl was admitted in 1853.

13. Committee Minutes, 29 Feb. 1832 (TCD, MS 5263, p. 116) and 7 Oct. 1835 (TCD, MS 5264). There is a list of girls who emigrated in 1835 (TCD, MS 5787/19/4).

14. Mary Macdonald to IS, 2 Apr. 1842 (TCD, MS 5694/231)

15. Committee Minutes, 7 Mar. 1838 (TCD, MS 5264)

16. Local committee annual report, 1842 (TCD, MS 5695/475)

17. Board Minutes, 13 Jan. 1841 (TCD, MS 5231, p. 134)

18. Richard Ardill to John Boyle, 24 Dec. 1846, in Letter Book, 1840-7 (TCD, MS 5288, p. 332)

19. Board Minutes, 6 Nov. 1850 (TCD, MS 5232, p. 79)

20. As early as 1812, Boyle had nominated Mary McKenny as assistant usher at Celbridge but the appointment was deemed contrary to the general rules of the Society. In the same year she was approved as a candidate usher by the Society's examining committee. Committee Minutes, 25 Dec. 1812 (TCD, MS 5254, pp 368-70)

21. Committee Minutes, 5 May 1852 (TCD, MS 5266, p. 168)

22. Catechist's report, 13 Sept. 1853 (TCD, MS 5706/262). For a report of a subsequent visit by the girls to the Dublin International Exhibition of 1865, see *The Irish Times*, 22 Sept. 1865, p. 2.

23. Kildare commission, ii, p. 238

24. Committee Minutes, 3 June 1857 (TCD, MS 5267, p. 169)

25. Kildare commission, iii, p. 128

26. The Revd J.W. Hackett to Thomas Conolly, 26 Mar. 1859, Letter Book 1857-89 (TCD, MS 5294, p. 32)

27. Hackett to Miss Boyle, 5 Aug. 1858, ibid., p. 13

28. Hackett to Miss Boyle, 5 Oct. 1858, ibid., p. 17

29. Kildare commission, iii, p. 241

19. Gradual change, 1859-1909

1. Committee Minutes, 6 Feb. 1861 (TCD, MS 5268, p. 24)

2. This cannot be established at present. The archives of the Adelaide Hospital (TCD, MS 11270) are not currently available to researchers. The death certificate of Sarah Crawford gives 'obstruction of the bowels' as the cause of death.

3. Eliza Crawford to the Revd J. W. Hackett, Feb. 1867 (TCD, MS 5776/70)

4. Committee Minutes, 11 July 1894 (TCD, MS 5272, p. 102)

5. Ibid. (27 Sept. 1894), p. 116

6. Bessie St George to IS, 4 Dec. 1894, in Committee Minutes, 9 Jan. 1895 (ibid., p. 145). Callisthenics are gymnastic exercises to achieve bodily strength and grace of movement.

7. Ibid. (7 Feb. 1895), p. 151

8. Minutes of local committee, 1 Apr. 1896, pp 185-6 (KCK)

9. Ibid. (4 Oct. 1895), p. 180

10. Kingsmill Moore, *The Incorporated Society*, p. 35

11. Committee Minutes, 10 Oct. 1895, op. cit., p. 201. Her subsequent letter of resignation on 1 Nov. 1895 was written from Loughgilly Rectory, Co Armagh.

12. Ibid., 7 Nov. 1895, p. 213

13. Ibid., p. 214

14. Committee Minutes, 29 Jan. 1873 (TCD, MS 5269, p. 252)

15. The other shortlisted candidates were Annie McCullagh, who later became headmistress, and Frances Smith, headmistress of Mercer's School, Castleknock, 1897-1930.

16. Committee Minutes, 5 Dec. 1895, op.cit., p. 231

17. Ibid. (14 Oct. 1897), p. 415

18. Kingsmill Moore, *The Incorporated Society*, p. 36

19. Miss Osborne, from Belfast, was described as 'an admirable teacher, uniting to intellectual ability … the power to arouse interest … and to maintain good discipline' (*School Magazine of the Incorporated Society*, i, no. 2, June 1909, pp 12-13). She was aged 31 when she died.

20. Rosse Commission, p. 155, evid. no. 4537

21. Ibid., p. 265

22. This was further extended to Coolock, Kilternan, Malahide and Swords parishes in 1873.

23. Report by Henry J Dix & Sons, 24 Oct. 1889, quoted in Board Minutes, 6 Nov. 1889 (TCD, MS 5234, pp 393-4)

24. Mrs Conolly's Scheme for Education and Maintenance of the Conolly Nominees, 2 November 1897 (TCD, MS 5776/276)

25. H. Vere White, Statement on the Conolly Foundation, 21 Oct. 1901 (TCD, MS 5776/284)

26. Board minutes, 19 Oct. 1899 (RCB, MS 151/1/1, p. 163)

27. Susan M. Parkes, *Kildare Place: the history of the Church of Ireland Training College, 1811-1969* (Dublin, 1984), p. 95

28. *Report of Inspection of Endowed Schools for 1895/6* (printed for the Incorporated Society)

29. All passed with two honours.

30. Annie McCullagh to the Revd Robert Miller (IS), 20 Jan. 1909, in Board Minutes, 21 Jan. 1909 (RCB, MS 151/1/1, p. 335)

31. Cited by Michael Quane, 'Celbridge Collegiate School' in *Journal of the County Kildare Archaeological Society*, xiv (1969), p. 408

20. Academic progress, 1909-1942

1. She was an honours graduate of the Royal University. According to *The Celbridgite*, 1964-5, she had been teaching at Rochelle School, Cork.

2. A. H. O'Connor, 'Echoes of the Past' in *The Celbridgite*, 1971-2

3. The average pass rate in the Intermediate Board examinations rose from 78.6 per cent for the ten years beginning with 1912 to 88.5 per cent for the ten years from 1915, although the comparison is compromised by the fact that the number of entrants had halved by 1924. Irish independence led to a new examination system of Leaving and Intermediate certificates. It took most schools some years to adjust to the new system but in the 1930s Celbridge achieved an average pass rate of 84 per cent and an honours rate of 55 per cent.

4. *Irish Independent*, cutting, n.d. The papers had different ways of calculating the places and the *Freeman's Journal* placed Celbridge 5th, after the St Louis Convent, Monaghan. A large part of the scoring derived from five exhibitions, including Amy Simmons's two first class exhibitions in modern literature and maths at middle level. Overall, she was placed 2nd in her group in the former and 3rd in the latter.

5. Examination successes were recorded in a hand-written book.

6. Not only did Anna O'Connor become first scholar (non-foundation) in modern languages but, during her undergraduate career, won a premium in Irish and made herself extremely proficient in the subject.

7. Obituary in *The Irish Times*, 3 Aug. 1964, p. 7.

8. IS report for 1919 (17 May 1920), p. 5

9. On the introduction of hockey, see Dorothy Fulcher's recollections of her schooldays (1916-1920) (KCK). It is not quite clear who made up the Celbridge Collegiate School team that

won the Leinster junior title in 1914 but it was probably dominated by members of staff, as Misses Batwell and Cox were mentioned as players (*The Irish Times*, 16 Jan. 1914, p. 8 and 12 Mar. 1914, p. 4).

10. Parkes, *Kildare Place*, p. 151, citing Department of Education Report, 1925-6, p. 22

11. Valerie Jones, *A Gaelic Experiment, the Preparatory System 1926-1961 and Coláiste Móibhí* (Dublin, 2006), p.178

12. Florence Huddie came 2nd in the Free State in the Intermediate Certificate in 1925, took 1st place in Latin and in history and geography and won an exhibition. Two years later she took 1st place in French in the Leaving Certificate.

13. Kingsmill Moore, *The Incorporated Society*, p. 36

14. Anna O'Connor, op.cit.

15. Kingsmill Moore, op.cit., p. 35

16. Anna O'Connor, op.cit.

17. Abigail Nuzum (Mrs Kerr), recollections, 27 Aug. 2007

18. Hilda Carter (Mrs Thompson), interview, 24 Jan. 2007

19. Lilian Grace Sheirson died in 1924 of TB.

20. Hilda Carter, op.cit.

21. Cricket was apparently introduced by Miss Lucie Lynd (sister of the poet, Robert) and Celbridge was for a long time the only girls' school in Ireland playing the sport. When Gladys Ruddock arrived as a sports enthusiast in 1949, she was used to playing cricket with her brothers and would not countenance under-arm bowling!

22. 'Teachers in General', *Celbridge Jingles Grave and Gay* (KCK)

23. Anna O'Connor, op.cit.

24. Ibid.

25. *The Celbridgite*, i, no.17, May 1916. The magazine was originally numbered but the system was later abandoned. For the most part, it was not paginated.

26. *The Irish Times*, 19 May 1923, p. 3

27. Hilda Carter, op.cit.

28. Hester Walsh (Mrs Hannan) in *The Celbridgite*, 1970-1, p. 19. Black jack was a laxative.

29. Recollections of Eunice Lochner (Mrs McKiernan), written by her niece, Anna Felton, to Violet Shattock, 1 Sept. 1997

30. Recollections of Freda Lochner (Mrs Buckley), written by her daughter, Anna Felton, to Violet Shattock, 1 Sept. 1997

31. On her retirement, the Association raised funds to have her portrait painted. It is now in Kilkenny College.

32. H. Kingsmill Moore, op. cit., p. 39

33. Freda Yates, interview, 18 Jan. 2007

34. In addition to those quoted, we have drawn on recollections of and material belonging to Grace Tapley, Rebecca Wilkie (Mrs Power), Joan P. Cochrane, May Foster (Mrs Newburn), Martha Deacon (Mrs Jones), Kay Thompson (Mrs Hannagen), Jenny Holmes, Betty Cooke (Mrs Shortt) and Muriel Mitchell (Mrs Patterson).

21. Towards amalgamation, 1942-1972

1. Freda Yates, interview, 18 Jan. 2007. She was a pupil 1938-44, and teacher 1949-51; 1954-91.

2. Valerie Giles, recollections, Sept. 2007. This was a feature of Miss O'Connor's later years. While some Celbridge customs were immutable, others came and went.

3. Nuala Carter (Mrs Howe), letter to LW, 2 Feb. 2008. Things had not improved greatly by the 1960s, when girls remember seeing stew being scooped off the kitchen floor, where it had fallen, and put back in serving dishes. Kitchen maids were paid badly and had little training.

4 'Position of Irish in Protestant Secondary Schools,' 9 June 1950 (UCD, Mulcahy Papers,

P7/C/152), quoted in Valerie Jones, *A Gaelic Experiment*, pp 247-8

5. Sheila Deacon (Mrs Milne), interview, 12 Apr. 2008.

6. Other girls took up the bursary, did not fulfil the contract and had to pay back the bursary.

7. Gladys Ruddock, (pupil,1949-55; teacher 1960-69), recollections, Sept. 2007

8. Rector of Rathdrum, 2007-8, she was appointed to Killeshin in 2008.

9. Nuala Carter, op.cit.

10. Gladys Ruddock, op.cit.

11. Aileen Drewery (Mrs Prole), recollections, 22 Aug. 2007

12. Irene Colton (Mrs Gilsenan), 'Memories of the class of 1963-69', 8 Jan. 2008

13. Abigail Nuzum, recollections, 27 Aug. 2007

14. Helen Coe (Mrs Graham), letter to parents, 11 Sept. 1960. It is rare to trace such an item, written carefully in girlish handwriting and kept for nearly 50 years.

15. Valerie Giles, op.cit.

16. Gladys Ruddock, op.cit.

17. She has been principal of St Andrew's National School, Malahide.

18. Miss Yates had applied for the job on the previous occasion. Interviews were formidable occasions, for the panel, numbering about 30, sat all around the applicant.

19. Rosemary Dunne (Mrs Raughter), tribute, 1997. This recollection reflects those of Freda Yates and June Stuart. Heather Lewis (Mrs Meldrum) recalls Miss Walsh telling her (after she had left school) that, on arrival in Celbridge in 1957, it was so ordered that she felt as though she had stepped back into Dickensian times (interview, 13 Nov. 2007).

20. *The Celbridgite*, 1972-3

21. The other was Masonic Girls' School.

22. G. S. Magahy, in conversation with LW, Aug. 2007

23. *The Celbridgite*, 1972-3

General index

Thematic index